Two week
loan

Please return on or before the last
date stamped below.
Charges are made for late return.

		WITHDRAWN

The Hidden Alcoholic in General Practice

A Method of Detection using a Questionnaire

The Hidden Alcoholic in General Practice

A Method of Detection using a Questionnaire

RODNEY H. WILKINS, M.D., M.R.C.G.P., D.C.H., D.Obst.R.C.O.G.

General Practitioner, Manchester University Teaching Practice, Formerly Lecturer in General Practice, University of Manchester.

Clinical Assistant, Alcoholism Treatment Unit, Manchester University Department of Psychiatry, Springfield Hospital and Clinical Assistant in Psychiatry, Prestwich Hospital, Manchester.

Elek Science
London

First published in 1974 by
Paul Elek (Scientific Books) Ltd
54-58 Caledonian Road, London, N1 9RN

DEDICATION

I dedicate this book to
my darling wife Adele,
our children Johnathan and Shulamit
and to our unborn baby who hopefully
will arrive just in time to greet
the publication of this book.

A Pilgrim Song

Happy is everyone who reveres the Lord,
Who walks in His ways.
When you eat the toil of your hands,
You shall be happy and at ease.
Your wife shall be like a fruitful vine
In the interior of your house;
Your children like olive plants
Around your table.
Behold, thus indeed shall the man be blessed
Who reveres the Lord.
May the Lord bless you from Zion
And may you see the welfare of Jerusalem
All the days of your life,
And may you live to see your children's children.
Peace be upon Israel.

Psalm 128.

Printed in Great Britain by
Unwin Brothers Limited,
The Gresham Press,
Old Woking, Surrey.

Acknowledgements

'He who learns from his fellow, a single chapter, a single
rule, a single verse, a single expression, or even a single
letter, ought to pay him honour'. Ethics of the Fathers: 6, 3.

This book is based on research carried out for an M.D. Thesis
submitted to the University of Manchester in 1972. I welcome
the opportunity to acknowledge my gratitude to many colleagues
in the University, not only for their practical guidance, but above
all, for their constant encouragement.

Professor P. S. Byrne, Department of General Practice, allowed
me time to undertake this research, and provided secretarial and
financial assistance. His inspiration and interest was a constant
stimulus. Professor N. Kessel, Department of Psychiatry,
originally suggested this field of study and gave me the opportunity to learn about the alcoholic in the outpatient clinic. He
was always available to offer helpful advice. Professor A.
Smith, Department of Community Medicine, gave much needed
constructive criticism, and allowed me extensive use of the
facilities of his Department at all times.

Dr C. S. Mellor, formerly Senior Lecturer, Department of
Psychiatry, and now Associate Professor, Memorial University
of Newfoundland, Canada, was of considerable help in the planning
of the study. Dr B. Hore, Consultant Psychiatrist at the University Hospital of South Manchester and Lecturer in Psychiatry,
was a regular source of guidance. Together with his Registrar,
Dr J. Alsafar, he spent many hours in his spare time interviewing patients in a validation study. I remain indebted to Dr
Mellor and Dr Hore who were successively the Consultant-in-
Charge of the Alcoholism Treatment Unit at Springfield Hospital,
Manchester, where they tutored me in the problem of alcoholism.

This study could not have been completed without the invaluable
help of members of the Department of Community Medicine.
Dr J. Leeson, Senior Lecturer, was always willing to offer advice
and comments, often at short notice. She guided me through the
minefields of research methodology with her usual patience.
Mr A. C. Gibbs, Lecturer and Statistician, kindly suggested the
types of statistical analysis required, and painstakingly checked
the results. Mrs A. Fish worked indefatigably coding the
questionnaires and producing the Tables. Her amazing capacity
for hard work and attention to detail shamed me into further
effort.

I am grateful to Dr R. W. J. Ollerenshaw, Director of the Department of Medical Illustration, Manchester Royal Infirmary, for preparing the histograms. Miss C. Hensman, formerly Research Assistant at the Addiction Research Unit, University of London gave me the benefit of her considerable experience in alcoholism research studies.

Mrs E. Ineson, Lecturer in Social Work, Department of General Practice, kindly participated in a validation study by interviewing a sample of patients or their families in their homes.

The review of the literature was dependent on the expert help of the librarians of the Manchester and Leeds Medical Schools, the British Medical Association, Miss M. Hammond, Librarian of the Royal College of General Practitioners, and Mrs F. Pattison, formerly the Medlars Liaison Officer at the Manchester Medical School.

I am obliged to the late Mrs L. M. Thompson who was the Practice Administrator, and her successor, Mrs G. Marks, who together with the other members of the office staff, cheerfully extracted records and typed the preliminary drafts. I was fortunate to have Mrs V. Stirling type the original thesis with her usual care and efficiency under very considerable pressure of time. Mrs S. Burgon willingly stepped into the breach at short notice to type a substantial proportion of the re-edited material for the book. My thanks go the Dr H. W. Acheson, Senior Lecturer in the Department of General Practice, Manchester University, and Dr H. J. Wright, now Senior Lecturer and Head of the Division of General Practice, Department of Community Medicine, Leeds University, who together with Dr Hore and Dr Leeson scrutinised the proofs of the thesis and offered useful comments. The proofs of the book were carefully read by Dr B. Wilkins, my father, and Dr D. Marshall, Senior Registrar in Psychiatry, University Hospital of South Manchester.

The questionnaires were administered during the whole of the survey year by Drs P. S. Byrne, H. W. Ashworth, H. W. Acheson, H. J. Wright and myself, and for part of the time by Drs A. Devine, P. Heywood, I. Zuckerbrodt, C. Harris, and G. Lloyd. To my colleagues, and to the patients of the practice, I record my appreciation for their support, without which the study could not have been carried out.

Contents

APPENDICES

List of Figures

List of Tables

Foreword

by D. L. Davies, D.M.(Oxon)., F.R.C.P., F.R.C.Psych.
*Consultant Psychiatrist, Maudsley Hospital, London and
Medical Director, Alcohol Education Centre, London.*

Hitherto, one of the unsolved mysteries of alcoholism has been the
report from surveys carried out by general practitioners of how few
alcoholics they see, and the generally accepted findings of epidemi-
ologists who stress how many there are.

Various possible explanations for this discrepancy may be advanced. It
is possible that the sufferers go elsewhere, whether or not they are
aware that general practitioners can help them. There is reason to
believe that this does happen, as also that competent doctors under very
favourable conditions tend to fail to diagnose alcoholism for two
reasons. The first of these is that the patient's appearance and social
status does not conform to the popular stereotype of the alcoholic as a
down-and-out vagrant, reeking of drink. The other is that a non-alcoholic satisfactory diagnosis fits the case (e.g. gastritis, peptic ulcer,
fractured rib), and further enquiry seems unnecessary because of the
disarming appearance already mentioned of the patient.

It might be that with increased education of these counts all would come
right, and general practitioners and other medical men would gradually
free themselves from their misleading preconceptions. Unfortunately
this is happening only slowly, and there is need for an alternative and
rapid approach to bridge this information gap.

This is in fact provided here by Dr Rodney Wilkins, who has ingeniously
adapted the idea of being 'at-risk', a concept well accepted in paediatrics, to the alcoholic. He has here set out the use of a simple tool
which will prove enormously helpful to those doctors who wish to
increase their diagnostic skill in this area.

One result already has been that the estimated numbers of alcoholics
existing in a general practice are demonstrably too low. Not only will
the global figures for alcoholics in any area as determined by other
methods of enquiry, seem more credible, but these may have to be
revised upwards with extension of Dr Rodney Wilkins' technique to
other practices.

Another result may be that more demands may arise on general practitioners when alcoholics are less often missed, which in turn of
course may bring along more of sufferers who had previously sought
help elsewhere.

Doctors need not be daunted by this prospect. The missed alcoholic
already consumes so much of his doctor's time—to no avail—that
savings made here may more than compensate for increased demands
elsewhere. Certainly the quality of help and its effectiveness to the
patient will be immeasurably improved.

No longer will general practitioners be able to say—as many have
hitherto—that they have very few alcoholics to deal with. Lest as a
group they might come to reproach themselves for earlier omissions,
it is right to say that the fault has not been theirs, and fitting that the
record has been put straight by an elegant piece of research carried
out by one of their own number in the course of his everyday work.

Summary

For a period of one year, a questionnaire was administered to selected patients attending the general practitioners of a Health Centre in Manchester with the aim of detecting the abnormal drinker, and examining some aspects of his drinking behaviour.

A total of 64 factors, known from previous studies to be associated with alcoholism, were listed on an Alcoholic At Risk Register (AARR). Any patient (aged 15-65 years) who was identified as possessing one of these factors received a Spare Time Activities Questionnaire (STAQ).

Four types of question were asked: quantity-frequency of drinking alcohol, patient's opinion of his own drinking, the problems arising from alcohol abuse, and symptoms of alcohol addiction. The questions related both to the patient, and his immediate family, and were designed to identify three categories of abnormal drinker: the heavy drinker, the problem drinker, and the alcohol addict. The latter two categories were considered to comprise 'the alcoholic'.

A total of 546 questionnaires were analysed, and 28.4% of the patients were classified as present or past alcoholics. The prevalence rate for alcoholics (present and past) was estimated to be 18.2 per 1000 of the practice population aged 15-65 years.

Data relating to the alcoholics was not found to differ markedly from that of previous studies of hospitalised alcoholics.

On the basis of the results, a modified AARR of 45 factors was constructed. The prevalence rate for the alcoholic was at least 25% for any patient identified as possessing one of these factors.

Validation studies of the AARR were carried out firstly by administering questionnaires to patients believed to be 'not at risk'. The proportion of alcoholics was found to be 2.8% which was significantly lower than the proportion in the 'at risk' group ($p < 0.001$). Secondly, general practitioners referring patients to an Alcoholism Treatment Unit were asked if there were any factors *not* on the AAAR which had suggested to them the diagnosis of alcoholism. Only two important ones were mentioned.

The STAQ was validated firstly by the clinical assessment of a sample of the patients by two psychiatrists. All patients classified as alcoholics by the psychiatrists were similarly classified by the STAQ. Secondly, the STAQ was administered to a sample of known hospitalised alcoholics who were all correctly identified by the STAQ.

A reliability study was carried out by re-administering the questionnaire to a sample of patients, and 67% of the alcoholics were reclassified as nonalcoholic on the basis of the responses to the second questionnaire. A family correlation study, in which the responses from different members of the same family were compared, also confirmed the importance of denial by the alcoholic, but found denial by the spouse to be more significant.

It was concluded that general practitioners, by asking questions about alcohol abuse to 'at risk' patients, could detect a considerable proportion of the 'hidden alcoholics'.

PART ONE

Background to the study

'.... I have drunk my wine and my milk.
Eat friends and drink
until you are drunk with love.'

Song of Songs: 5. 1

1 Background to the Study

'Noah, a man of the soil, began the planting of vineyards.
He drank some of the wine, became drunk and lay naked
inside his tent.'

Genesis: 9. 20-21

Over 4 000 years ago, the first recorded act of drunkenness took
place, and indeed the Old Testament contains over 200 references
to alcohol of which some 40 describe its ill-effects.[1] Thus the
problem of alcohol abuse is an old one although this might not
be suspected from the repeated dramatic 'discoveries' of its
dangers in the lay press and even in the general medical press.
When the seeds for this study were being planted five years ago,
little mention of alcoholism was to be found in the mass media,
or in the medical literature likely to be read by general practitioners.

Since then, International Conferences on Alcoholism held in Cardiff, Liverpool, Dublin, London and Manchester have been widely
reported. The Medical Council on Alcoholism was formed in
1967 and the National Council on Alcoholism has expanded its
work of establishing Alcoholism Information Centres. The
Greater Manchester Council on Alcoholism is in its embryo
stage. Recently the Alcohol Education Centre has been set up in
London with a policy of arranging Summer Schools and other
facilities for educating workers in the field.

The government has, in recent years, taken an increasing interest in the subject. Since its recognition in 1962 of alcoholism
as a medical problem deserving attention, three memoranda
have been issued for the guidance of the medical profession[2-4]
and reports have been published on Habitual Drunken Offenders[5]
and the Liquor Licensing Laws in England and Wales[6] and
Scotland.[7] The sum of £2 million has been allocated for alcoholism research over a four year period. Nevertheless much
needs to be done, there still being a dearth of statistical evidence
as to the extent of alcoholism in Great Britain. There is a constant cry for more facts and figures.

Accompanying, and antedating this increasing interest in alcoholism, attitudes have been changing concerning the role and
status of the general practitioner. The Royal College of General
Practitioners has been in the forefront of these developments,

2

analysing his work and making suggestions for the future. The general practitioner of the 1970s, in addition to his other duties, is expected to be an early detector of disease, and to contribute to research.

This study arose out of a desire to relate the increasing emphasis of the role of the general practitioner as a diagnostician of disease in its early stages, to the growing problem of alcoholism in the community.

The *main aims* were:

1. To study the prevalence of the abnormal drinker in general practice in those patients identified as having a condition or risk factor which previous studies have shown to have an association with alcoholism.

2. By virtue of these findings to construct a list of the most commonly associated factors seen in general practice to increase the possibility of recognition of the abnormal drinker.

3. To estimate the prevalence of the abnormal drinker in the practice population.

The *subsidiary aims* were:

1. To analyse some of the characteristics of the abnormal drinker detected in general practice, and compare these findings with those of cases treated in hospital.

2. To illustrate the potentialities of performing research by full time general practitioners who have limited access to research facilities.

These aims were carried out by administering a specially designed questionnaire to patients (aged 15-65 years) consulting in the surgery over a period of one year who were identified as possessing one or more risk factors known to be associated with alcoholism.

As a background to the study, there follow two sections reviewing the current concepts of the definition of the 'alcoholic', and the available statistics on the extent of alcoholism in England and Wales.

1.1   DEFINITIONS OF ALCOHOLISM

'The definitions of alcoholism (and alcoholics) have long been marked by uncertainty, conflict and ambiguity'. [8] When one considers that Jellinek[9] has written 246 pages of detailed analysis of over 100 definitions of alcoholism, it is clear that it is beyond the scope of this chapter to emulate his work. There have been many reviews of this problem[10-18] supporting the conclusion that 'one thing is certain about the topic of alcoholism—the confusion in the minds of medical and nonmedical people alike about the meaning of the term'.[19] It is my intention to dip into the sea of definitions and attempt to extract the main concepts of alcoholism. Further comments are to be found in Chapter 4.

The most difficult problem is that 'different writers use the same words—including some of the fundamental ones, such as "alcoholism"—in different senses'.[12] The literature is full of terms which are used interchangeably by some authorities, but which have distinct meanings according to others, e.g. alcoholic, alcohol addict, chronic alcoholic, nonaddictive alcoholic, habitual symptomatic excessive drinker, problem drinker, abnormal drinker, inebriate, and even preprodromal or incipient problem drinker or alcoholic. There appears to be general agreement that there is one variety of pathological drinking where the individual is physically addicted to alcohol and therefore suffers from a disease which requires medical attention. Such patients are generally accepted as being 'alcoholics' but the conflict arises as to whether other individuals who are not physically addicted, but whose drinking has caused problems for the individual, family, or society, can be included in this term. An examination of the definitions in current usage show that they all have one or more of three components.

Firstly, there is *excessive drinking,* variously defined by different quantitative parameters of quantity or frequency of drinking (*see* Chapter 4). Secondly, there are the *problems* created by drink, which are expressed in different degrees of severity, relating to the effects on personal health, the family, and society. Finally, there is the concept of compulsive, uncontrollable drinking—*loss of control*—of which there are different types.

Some definitions define the 'alcoholic' only in terms of the addictive process, whereas others include the person who has problems from drink. Unfortunately the latter type is termed a 'problem drinker' by some, in contradistinction to the 'alcoholic', but other authorities use this global expression of 'problem drinker' to apply to both types of pathological drinker.[20-22]

There is still more 'ambiguity'. Some workers, although accepting that an 'alcoholic' has loss of control over his drinking, use an operational definition relating only to problems from drink. They assume firstly that the individual must be an 'excessive drinker' to have such problems, and secondly he must have 'loss of control' over his drinking, as otherwise he would have stopped drinking because of the problems it was creating. One of the most widely accepted definitions of alcoholism employs this logic and states that 'alcoholism is a chronic disease manifested by repeated implicative (marked) drinking so as to cause injury to the drinker's health or to his social or economic functioning'.[18] Two other important definitions should be mentioned.

The World Health Organisation originally defined alcoholics in terms of excessive drinking[23] but later redefined alcoholics as 'those excessive drinkers whose dependence on alcohol has attained such a degree that it shows a noticeable mental disturbance or an interference with their bodily and mental health, their interpersonal relations, and their smooth social and economic functioning; or who show the prodromal signs of such development. They therefore require treatment'.[24]

Although this definition has been severely criticised[25-27] and modifications suggested[28,29] it remains the basis of many prevalence studies.

In contrast to this lengthy definition, Jellinek[9] defined as alcoholism 'any use of alcoholic beverages that causes any damage to the individual or society or both'. He then described five main types of pathological drinker, all of whom he considered 'alcoholics', but only two types as being due to 'disease'.

In this Alice in Wonderland situation, there remain two other controversies. Firstly, in prevalence studies, does one include 'recovered' or 'abstaining' alcoholics in a count of 'alcoholics' (*see* Chapter 4)?

Secondly, is there even a need for a universally accepted definition of the 'alcoholic'? Most authorities agree that 'demographic and ecological studies of the pathological aspects of drinking behaviour have been handicapped by the lack of an adequate and well-accepted definition of alcoholism'.[30] In England, a report by the Office of Health Economics[31] concluded that 'this lack of firm definition has been a stumbling block to understanding and progress'. However, Keller[12] opposes this view and has suggested that a 'collection of definitions should be formed in which each term is listed with its variety of meanings as discovered in the literature'.

I have felt obliged to outline some of the problems of definition for two reasons. Firstly, in the review of literature of the At Risk Factors, I have referred to the terms quoted by the authors in their papers. I have not explained the different meanings of the terms used, as my main concern is to illustrate relationships between any form of pathological drinking and certain 'at risk' factors. Secondly, this section forms a background to the conceptual definitions of 'abnormal drinker' that were used in the classifications based on the questionnaire scores (*see* Chapter 5). In general terms, I tend to agree with the view that it is 'an idle pastime to ask whether alcoholism is an illness or not; the main thing is that something should be done for the rehabilitation of the alcoholic'.[32] Edwards[33] in an article addressed to general practitioners, commented that 'drinking is a matter for medical concern when, whatever its quantity, it is causing damage'.

In the discussion of those results where figures are small, I have considered the 'alcoholic' as both the 'problem drinker' and 'alcohol addict' combined, in accordance with the views expressed by the Home Office Report on Habitual Drunken Offenders (1971). This Report considered that 'the dichotomy between the alcohol addict, and the nonaddicted abnormal drinker may not be altogether sound or useful; the drinker who is not yet addicted may be as much in need of help as the person who has become dependent, and helping him may prevent what would otherwise progress to something more serious'.[5]

In conclusion, alcoholism has historically been variously described as a sin, a sign of moral weakness, a disease, or a symptom of an underlying psychopathological condition. Psychiatrists, psychologists, sociologists and workers in other disciplines define alcoholism with reference to their own speciality. Their views also reflect their own personal attitudes, many inexperienced doctors defining the alcoholic in terms of the stereotyped skid-row image that they often have of him.[34—38] Definitions are also influenced by the particular country in which the alcoholic and his physician find themselves.[9] One moral that can be drawn is that until Utopia is attained, every research worker must clearly define the terms he is using to describe the 'alcoholic'.

> 'Peril lurks in definitions, so runs an ancient maxim of law'.[39]

1.2   ALCOHOLISM IN ENGLAND AND WALES

There are no accurate figures for the prevalence of alcoholism, and it will be seen that such figures as are available are believed to underestimate the size of the problem. The earliest references suggesting that alcoholism is a disease are those of Rush, an American surgeon, in 1785[40] and Trotter, a British physician, in 1788.[41] The latter in his Doctoral thesis wrote: 'In medical language, I consider drunkenness, strictly speaking, to be a disease, produced by a remote cause, and giving actions and movements in the living body that disorder the functions of health'. Although the abuse of alcohol has existed in this island to a greater or lesser extent since the Roman conquest[42] it was not until 1962 that the Ministry of Health recognised that alcoholism was a serious problem falling into the sphere of medicine.[43] Despite this pronouncement, there is still today inadequate information concerning how 'serious' is the problem of alcoholism in Great Britain.

There are two ways in which the prevalence of alcoholism in a selected population can be estimated: by examination of indirect indices, and by direct community studies.

1.2.1 Indirect Indices

In many countries statistics are published which, although not direct measures of alcoholism, may have some correlation with the prevalence of alcoholism. [44,45] These figures include:

1. Certified deaths from cirrhosis of the liver.

2. Certified deaths from alcoholism.

3. Hospital admission rates for alcoholism.

4. Offences of drunkenness.

5. Motoring offences relating to alcohol.

6. Alcohol consumption.

The Office of Health Economics (1970)[31] stated: 'In this country, there have not been, in fact, as in America, any estimates of trends in the rate of alcoholism. There are, however, a number of indications which can be used. These are at best tentative and crude, at worst misleading. Nevertheless taken together they may possibly give a broad outline of trends'. Glatt[46] has written that 'whilst an upward trend in one indirect index might have little significance, the matter may be different if all these various indices seem to point in the same direction'. These recent statements echo similar comments made by the World Health Organisation (1952). [24] The available statistics for England and Wales will be considered.

Cirrhosis of the liver death rates

The most important indirect index that has been developed is the formula described by Jellinek.[47] It is based on the total annual death rate from cirrhosis of the liver in a given area, the proportion of such deaths due to alcoholic cirrhosis, the annual death rate from cirrhosis among 'alcoholics with complications', and the ratio of 'all alcoholics' to 'alcoholics with complications'. This formula produced a prevalence rate of 2.78 per 1 000 adults aged 20 years and over for 'alcoholics with complications', and a suggested total of 11 per 1 000 adults aged 20 years and over for all alcoholics in England and Wales in 1948.

The Jellinek formula relies on a number of assumptions and has been severely criticised.[26-28, 48-51] Consequently, the formula has been modified[28,29] and Jellinek[52] himself concluded that 'generally, I would not be in favour of the continued use of my formula, nor of any modification of it, as there are too many fluctuation factors present. Much more to be desired is a new basis, and particularly actual field surveys'. However, Popham[51] has compared the prevalence rates obtained by the Jellinek formula in 16 areas where there have also been field surveys. There was excellent agreement in 8 cases, good agreement in 3 cases and fair or poor agreement in 5 cases. It is generally believed that the Jellinek formula probably *under-estimates* the actual prevalence although there are very few English studies suggesting a rate even approaching that of Jellinek (see Table 1, page 10).

The Registrar General has reported an increase in certified cirrhosis deaths from 1 397 in 1961, to 1 570 in 1971, representing an increase in death rate per million of the population from 30 to 32.[53] Alcoholism was recorded as a contributory factor in less than 10% of the deaths from cirrhosis.[54,57] However, autopsy studies (in Eire) have suggested that the true death rate from cirrhosis may be almost double that calculated from death certificates.[55]

It is noteworthy that in 1972 there were about 5 100 cases of cirrhosis of the liver treated in non-psychiatric hospitals of which 1 220 were recorded as being due to alcohol. Since 1963 cirrhosis of the liver, considered to be due to alcohol, has increased by 164%.[438]

Alcoholism Death Rates

Alcoholism is probably under-reported on death certificates because of its stigma and difficulty of diagnosis. Thus the available statistics are likely to be only a poor indication of the true death rate.[56]

In 1971, there were 90 deaths reported from alcoholism and alcoholic psychosis representing a death rate of 1.62 per million of the population. The corresponding figures for 1961 were

48 deaths and a death rate of 0. 92.[53] A more realistic estimate of the contribution of alcoholism to mortality is a rate calculated by the Registrar General for all deaths directly and indirectly attributed to alcohol. In 1967 there were 216 deaths due to alcoholic psychosis, acute alcoholism, chronic alcoholism, unspecified alcoholism, cirrhosis of the liver with alcoholism, and poisoning with alcohol, and 501 deaths indirectly attributed to alcohol. The corresponding death rates per million of the population were 4. 7 and 10. 3. The combined death rate represented a 35% increase over the previous four year period.[54]

Hospital admission rates for alcoholism

The first admission rate to hospitals for alcoholism and alcoholic psychosis is considered by Walsh and Walsh[45] to be the best indirect index. However, they point out that many cases are not admitted for hospital treatment and the admittance rate depends on availability and use of hospital facilities, and on community tolerance of alcoholism. The definition of 'alcoholism' may vary. The rates usually quoted relate to admissions to psychiatric hospitals or psychiatric units in general hospitals. Glatt[56] has pointed out that only a small proportion of alcoholics are ever admitted to a psychiatric bed; some die without ever receiving psychiatric treatment and many are treated in general hospitals for physical illnesses without their alcoholism being diagnosed or recorded.

In 1972 the first admission rate to Mental Illness Hospitals and Units in England and Wales for patients with a primary or secondary diagnosis of alcoholism or alcoholic psychosis was 6. 5 per 100 000 of the population. This represents a 21. 9% increase in two years. The pre-1970 figures are not directly comparable due to an alteration in the question wording used to obtain the data. Nevertheless it is striking that the increase in the two years from 1970 exceeded that for the five years from 1964 to 1969.[58]

Offences of Drunkenness

The offences of drunkenness refer to simple drunkenness, drunkenness with aggravations, and drunkenness at the same time as another offence, but do not include offences relating to road vehicles. In 1972[60] there were 90 198 convictions being equivalent to 24 convictions per 10 000 of the population aged 14 years and over (46 males: 3 females). The corresponding figures for 1966 were 70 499 convictions and a total conviction rate of 19 per 10 000 of the population aged 14 years and over (37 males: 2 females).

Table 1 Prevalence Studies of Alcoholism in England and Wales

Reference	Source	Area	Prevalence Rate per 1000			Population
			Male	Female	Total	
Parr (1957)	General Practitioners	England	1.7	0.8	1.1	15 and over
Logan and Cushion (1958)	General Practitioners	England and Wales	0.3	0.1	0.2	Total
Watts et al. (1964)	General Practitioners	England and Wales			0.2	Total
Hughes (1966)	Psychiatric Clinics	Cardiff	6.8	1.52		15 and over
Prys Williams and Glatt (1966)	Health Visitors and Probation Officers	Five English towns			5.8*	Total
Shepherd et al. (1966)	General Practitioners	London			2.0†	15 and over
Hawker et al. (1967)	Industry	London	3.54	0.09	1.82	Adults
Moss and Davies (1967)	13 sources	Cambridge-shire	6.2	1.4		15 and over
Hensman et al. (1968)	General Practitioners Clergy	London	5.0 1.00	1.7 0.35	3.4 0.68	20 and over

Reference	Source	Location				Population
Abbott (1970)	1 General Practice	Cardiff	70.0			Adult males
Searle-Jordan (1970)	Visitors to a Health Exhibition	London			50.0	Adults
Gaind (1971)	Hospital patients	London			170.0	Adults
Pollak (1971)	1 General Practice	London	6.0	1.3	3.6	15 and over
Patterson (1972)	General Practitioners	Leicestershire			15.0	Adults
Wilkins (1972)	General Practitioners	Manchester	17.3–28.6	3.5–5.7	11.1–18.2	15–65 years of age
Edwards et al. (1973)	Householders	London	61.3	7.7	31.3	18 and over
Edwards et al. (1973)	16 sources	London	8.6	1.3	4.7	16 and over
Office of Population Censuses and Survey (1974)	General Practitioners	England and Wales	0.9	0.6	0.8†	Total
Wilkins and Hore (1974)	General Practitioners	Manchester			4.7	Total

* Calculation based on figures reported in the reference

† Refers to alcoholism and drug dependence

These figures must be interpreted with considerable caution. All drunkards are not alcoholics, and all alcoholics are not drunkards. Not all publically drunk people are arrested by the police, and not all those arrested are convicted.[56] The statistics quoted refer to the number of convictions annually, but some individuals are convicted more than once in any one year. The Home Office report *Habitual Drunken Offenders*[5] estimated that in 1967 about 40 000 men received 71 000 convictions and that 5 000 of them were convicted three or more times.

Motoring Offences

The convictions for drink-related motor offences refer to those for being unfit to drive through drink or drugs, driving with an undue proportion of alcohol in the blood, in charge of a motor vehicle while unfit through drink or drugs, and being in charge of a motor vehicle with an undue proportion of alcohol in the blood.

In 1972, there were 45 994 convictions, the blood alcohol level being over 80 mg/100 ml in 43 996 cases, and over 150 mg/100 ml in 21 160 cases.[61] A total of 69 718 positive breathalyser tests were reported.[62]

The total number of convictions has doubled in the past four years due in part to the increased vigilance of the police and partly to the introduction of the breathalyser test in October 1967, and the increased number of licensed motor vehicles. The figures refer to convictions, and not to the number of individuals involved. How many of these motorists are alcoholics is not known, but it may be in the region of 25%.[56]

Alcohol consumption

The use of crude or age-corrected *per capita* rates of alcohol consumption are clearly not a valid measure of alcoholism prevalence as the national average consumption does not indicate the proporiton of the population that drink or how many drink how much.[24,63-64] However it has been demonstrated in North America, Finland, and France, that the distribution of drinkers for a given level of average daily volume of consumption closely approximates to a logarithmic normal curve.[65,66] If one knows the average alcohol consumption per drinker, it is possible to estimate the percentage of drinkers at various consumption levels. This technique was used by Schmidt and De Lint[67] who found in Ontario a similar prevalence rate to estimates based on mortality rates of alcoholics, cirrhosis of the liver death rates, and suicides attributable to alcoholism. The authors arbitrarily defined alcoholic drinking as consumption in excess of a daily average of about 15 cl of absolute alcohol which, they

stated, very closely approximates to the range of consumption
typically reported by patients in alcoholism clinics. They have
estimated that the prevalence rate of drinkers who consume in
excess of a daily average of 15 cl of absolute alcohol in England
and Wales is 19.46 per 1 000 of the population aged 15 years and
older.[68]

The Alcohol Industry

Although not indicators of the prevalence of alcoholism, statistics are available illustrating the importance of the alcohol industry to the economy of the country. These figures may partially explain why, until recently, vigorous attempts to detect and
reduce the incidence of alcoholism have been lacking. For example:

1.   It has been calculated that the industry has an invested
     capital of over £1 700 millions representing more than
     4.5% of the Gross National Product.[69]

2.   A total of 90 000 people were employed in the brewing and
     malting industry[70] and there were 130 029 outlets in England
     and Wales for the retail sale or supply of intoxicating liquor
     in 1971.[6]

3.   Customs and Excise figures showed that in 1972-3 in England
     and Wales, 36.7 million bulk barrels of beer, 24.3 million
     proof gallons of spirits, and 62 million gallons of wine were
     consumed. The total alcohol consumption produced £1 073
     millions in taxation, representing 17.5% of the total net
     receipts from all Customs and Excise duties and 6.5% of
     the total revenue from all sources.[71] In the period 1960-
     70 there was a 43% growth in alcohol consumption which
     was considered 'eminently satisfactory' by the author of an
     article in a trade magazine.[72]

4.   The total consumer expenditure on alcohol in 1970 was
     £2 948 millions.[73] It has been estimated that this probably
     represents about £80 per annum for drinkers.[74]

5.   The Family Expenditure Survey in 1972[75] showed that
     69.9% of all households reported some expenditure on
     alcohol. The average weekly household expenditure on
     alcohol in the United Kingdom was £1.65 corresponding to
     4.7% of the total average weekly household expenditure.

6.   The total national advertising bill for alcohol drinks in
     Great Britain is £25-£30 millions per annum.[6]

The miscellany of facts obtained from Government publications
and other sources indicates that there is more information
available on alcohol use and abuse than is often appreciated.

However, they cannot pretend to provide accurate estimates of the prevalence of alcoholism.

As the Ministry of Health in 1968 stated: 'There is a need for studies of the public health pattern designed to enumerate abnormal drinkers in selected populations; not enough studies of this kind are on record. [2] The next section considers the studies that have been reported.

1.2.2   Community Studies

There are two main methods of directly estimating the prevalence of alcoholism:

1.   Questioning 'key informants'—obtaining estimates of prevalence from various agencies (passive case-identification)

2.   Field surveys—personal interviewing of potential alcoholics (active case-identification).

Although most reviews only refer to a handful of prevalence studies, there have in fact been at least 27 in Great Britain and Eire, including the present one. Some of the studies were specifically designed to identify alcoholics whereas others were part of wider psychiatric or general morbidity surveys.

Passive Case Identification

There have been 19 studies which are described according to the type of the survey.

Psychiatric Morbidity Surveys: A review of the literature[76-79] showed that although over 20 psychiatric morbidity surveys have been carried out in Great Britain, in only four of them was a prevalence rate for alcoholism specifically mentioned.

Mayer-Gross (1948)[80] in a rural area in Scotland, obtained information on the mental health of the inhabitants from key sources such as the local mental hospital, welfare officers and the clergy. He reported a prevalence rate for alcoholism of 3.9 per 1 000 of the population.

Primrose (1962)[81] again in rural Scotland, recorded the prevalence of psychological disorder in his general practice of 1 701 people. He found a prevalence rate for chronic alcoholism of 19.4 per 1 000 males of the practice population, and 1.1 per 1 000 females.

Watts *et al.* (1964)[82] obtained estimates of the psychiatric morbidity of 261 general practices in Great Britain in 1961-62, and found that 0.2 per 1 000 of the population were judged to be 'mentally disabled' by alcohol.

Shepherd *et al.* (1966)[83] in a similar study of 46 general practices in London, reported that 2.0 per 1 000 persons aged 15 years and over consulted during the survey year because of alcoholism or drug addition.

In three of these studies[81-83], the original clinical assessment was made by general practitioners, and the results collated from the patients' records.

General Morbidity Surveys: Although a number of general morbidity surveys have been carried out from general practice, in only three of them was alcoholism specifically mentioned.

Two national general morbidity surveys reported figures for alcoholism. Logan and Cushion (1958)[84] analysed the morbidity statistics of all diseases for which patients consulted a random sample of 171 general practitioners throughout England and Wales in 1955-56. During the survey year, 0.2 per 1 000 of the total population consulted because of alcoholism. A similar study of 53 practices was carried out in 1970-71 by the Office of Population Censuses and Surveys. [439] During the survey year, 0.8 per 1 000 of the total population consulted because of alcoholism or drug dependence. A separate consultation rate for alcoholism was not calculated. However, other provisional figures from this study tentatively indicate that the consultation rate for alcoholism was approximately 0.4 per 1 000 of the total population.[58]

Waterston (1965)[436] recorded all the diseases diagnosed in his general practice of 2627 patients in a small town in South West Scotland in 1962. The prevalence rate of alcoholism and alcoholic psychosis was found to be 1.5 per 1 000 of the total population.

Psychiatric Clinics: Hughes[85] investigated the records of alcoholics presenting for treatment at psychiatric clinics in Cardiff. He obtained a prevalence rate of 6.8 per 1 000 males aged 15 years and over, and 1.52 per 1 000 females aged 15 years and over.

Kearney *et al.*[86] examined the records of psychiatric clinics, a social information centre, and a casework service in a Dublin Corporation housing estate in 1966 and 1967. A prevalence rate of 2.6 per 1 000 of the population aged 10 years and over was found.

Alcoholism Prevalence Studies (from General Practice): There have been six specific alcoholism prevalence studies utilising general practitioners as key informants.

Parr (1957)[87] asked 480 single-handed general practitioners who were on the Research Register of the (then) College of

General Practitioners how many alcoholics were known to them. From the 369 useful replies, he calculated an overall prevalence rate of 1.1 per 1000 of the population aged 15 years and over.

Grant and Boyd (1961)[440] asked general practitioners from 14 general practices in one area of Northern Ireland how many alcoholics they knew of, and repeated this study with 18 practices in five of the six counties in Northern Ireland.[88] The combined prevalence rate from the two studies was 1.91 per 1000 adults.

The (then) College of General Practitioners (1963)[89] asked 165 general practitioners in Scotland how many alcoholics they had encountered in the previous year. An overall prevalence rate of 1.52 per 1000 of the population in rural areas, and 0.98 per 1000 in the urban area, was found.

Pollak (1971)[90] examined the morbidity register of his own practice of 6712 patients in London, and obtained a prevalence rate of 6.0 per 1000 of the practice population aged 15 years and over for males, and 1.3 per 1000 for females.

Wilkins and Hore (1974)[91] asked the 192 general practitioners in the Manchester area who had referred at least one patient to the local Alcoholism Treatment Unit how many alcoholics they thought they had in their practices. From 73 useful replies, the following prevalence rates were estimated, per 1000 of the practice population: 3.36 problem drinkers, 1.35 alcohol addicts.

Alcoholism Prevalence Studies (multi-source): There have been five specific alcoholism prevalence studies utilising various sources as key informants.

Prys Williams and Glatt (1966)[92] reported a study, under the auspices of the Joseph Rowntree Social Service Trust, of health visitors and probation officers in five localities in England who were asked how many alcoholics were known to them. Their results suggested that there may be 1.5 per 1000 of the population who are 'obvious chronic alcoholics' and a further 4.3 per 1000 of the population in the 'earlier stages of deterioration'.

Hawker *et al.* (1967)[93] questioned 247 firms about the prevalence of problem drinkers in industry. They found that 1.8 per 1000 of the adult population at risk were judged to be problem drinkers.

Moss and Davies (1967)[94] carried out a very comprehensive study of all the known alcoholics in the county of Cambridgeshire. They obtained figures from 13 sources, including general practitioners, hospitals, clergymen, probation and after care officers, Alcoholics Anonymous, hostel staff, police, and other social and welfare agencies. They calculated an overall prevalence rate, for the three year survey period, of 6.2 per 1000 of the male population

aged 15 years and over, and 1.4 per 1 000 of the female population aged 15 years and over.

Hensman *et al.* (1968)[95] sent questionnaires to all the general
practitioners and clergy in one London borough. The results
from the general practitioners (those from the clergy being much
lower) suggested a prevalence rate of 5.0 per 1 000 males aged
20 years and over and 1.7 per 1 000 females aged 20 and over
who were 'abnormal drinkers'. This was one of only two studies
in Great Britain[22] which have attempted to differentiate alcohol
addicts from non-addicted problem drinkers, and they found an
equal prevalence of these two categories of abnormal drinker.

Edwards *et al.* (1973)[96] reported a prevalence study of alcoholics in the Camberwell district of London utilising 16 different
types of agency similar to the Moss and Davies survey.[94] A
rate of 8.6 males and 1.3 females per 1 000 of the population
aged 16 years and over was found.

Active Case-Identification

In the past three years, six studies have been reported where
individuals have personally been questioned to determine their
drinking status.

Abbott (1970)[97] visited the 411 families known to her in the
course of her work as a health visitor attached to a Cardiff
general practice. Of the 409 completed interviews, conducted in
most cases with the wife, she found that 7% of the males were
'compulsive drinkers'.

Searle-Jordan (1970)[98] questioned a random sample of 232
people (70 male, 162 female) in Hammersmith, London, who
visited a Health Education exhibition relating to alcoholism. In
this highly biased sample, only 1 person (0.4%) admitted to being
a 'heavy drinker', and 1 person (0.4%) to being an 'excessive
drinker'. However, 12 (5%) admitted they could not give up drinking, and 17 (7%) admitted to having driven a car when feeling
'tight' or drunk on more than one occasion.

In 1971 Gaind[99] in a pilot study, adminstered a questionnaire to
107 consecutive admissions to a medical unit in a South London
hospital, and found that 17% of them had a primary or secondary
diagnosis of alcoholism. This is the only hospital study reported
in England, and the incidence of alcoholism appears high. However it compares closely with the average rate obtained from
much larger similar studies in America and Australia.[100-112]

Edwards *et al.*[96] interviewed a random sample of 408 males and
520 females at their homes in a London suburb to obtain infor-

Table 2 Prevalence Studies of Alcoholism in Scotland

Reference	Source	Area	Prevalence Rate per 1000			Population
			Male	Female	Total	
Mayer-Gross (1948)	Multi-source	Rural			3.9	Total
Parr (1957)*	General Practice	Scotland			2.4	15 and over
Primrose (1962)	Multi-source	Rural	19.4	1.1	10.0	Total
College of General Practitioners (1963)	General Practice	Rural Scotland	1.37	0.15	1.52	Total
		Urban Scotland	0.78	0.20	0.98	Total
Watts *et al.*(1964)*	General Practice	Scotland			0.4	Total
Waterston (1965)	General Practice	Semi-rural town			1.5	Total

* These studies were simultaneously carried out in England and Wales (Table 1)

Table 3 Prevalence Studies of Alcoholism in Northern Ireland and Eire.

Reference	Source	Area	Prevalence Rate per 1000			Population
			Male	Female	Total	
Parr (1957)*	General Practitioners	Northern Ireland			0.9	15 and over
Grant and Boyd (1961 and 1962)	General Practitioners	Northern Ireland			1.91	Adults
Kearney *et al.* (1969)	3 sources	Dublin			2.6	10 and over
Blaney and Radford (1973)	Householders	Larne (Northern Ireland)	23.0	0.0	11.0	18 and over

* This study was carried out simultaneously in England and Wales (Table 1) and Scotland (Table 2).

mation about their drinking habits. Although not primarily designed as a prevalence study, 61. 3 per 1 000 males aged 18 years
and over, and 7. 7 per 1 000 females aged 18 years and over, were
classified as 'problem drinkers'.

Patterson (1972)[113] and 11 other general practitioners in Leicester administered 1 200 questionnaires to patients attending
the surgery. Most of the questionnaires were given to the first
two patients in each surgery session. Although the aim of the
survey was to examine drinking patterns, the results indicated
that 15 per 1 000 of the patients interviewed may have a serious
drinking problem.

Blaney and Radford (1973)[114] carried out a household survey in
the town of Larne in Northern Ireland. They utilised the Iowa
scales of Mulford and Miller (see Chapter 4) and interviewed a
random sample of 392 householders. They obtained a prevalence
rate of alcoholism of 11 per 1 000 of the population aged 18 years
and over based on the Iowa Preoccupation Scale criteria.

1.3 DISCUSSION

All the prevalence studies (listed in Tables 1-3 in chronological
order) suffer from some defects. [115] The diagnosis of the 'alcoholic' is made differently by the psychiatrist, the general practitioner, the probation officer or any other agency. Some definitions refer only to the 'alcohol addict', who is physically dependent on alcohol, whereas others include those who have problems from alcohol abuse but are not physically addicted

The majority of the studies are passive case-identification ones
which pick up only the 'known' alcoholic. General practitioners
only have the opportunity of diagnosing those patients who have
consulted them, or may obtain information from members of the
family. As shown in Chapter 2, all alcoholics are not registered
with a general practitioner, and they do not necessarily consult because of a drinking problem. If they seek medical attention for physical symptoms perhaps due to alcohol abuse, the
general practitioner may not make the correct diagnosis.
Most estimates from general practice relied on memory and not
on analysis of a morbidity register or patients' records. Psychiatrists see only the cases referred to the clinics. Health
visitors and clergy know only a limited segment of the population.
Probation officers only come into contact with those who have
broken the law. Industrial personnel officers may detect those
workers who have shown signs of alcoholism on the job.

It is only by direct interview of a sample of the population that an attempt can be made to detect the 'hidden' alcoholic. However, the alcoholic may deny his symptoms to the interviewer, may not visit his general practitioner, or not be at home when a household survey is carried out. Ideally, a total population should be interviewed but this is very expensive.

In comparing the different prevalence rates, it should be noted that the population at risk may vary quite widely—for example, by selected groups being chosen, or one or both sexes, or different age groups. Some studies have produced point prevalence rates, and others period prevalence rates. A further difficulty is the possibility of wide variations in the known and the actual prevalence in different parts of the country.

It is clear that the rates obtained in the active case-identification studies are far higher than those reported in the passive case-identification studies. Although the prevalence of alcoholism in America is believed to be higher than in England, the reported 2-8% prevalence of alcoholism in the major American household surveys[116-119] suggests that the English direct interview studies are probably a better indicator of the extent of the problem than the indirect studies. Nevertheless, the information so far available strongly indicates that there is a major problem of alcohol abuse in Great Britain, and that it is very likely that many patients remain undetected until a late stage.

PART TWO

Review of the literature

'Be careful to drink no wine or strong drink'

Judges: 13. 5

2 The General Practitioner and the Alcoholic

'Wine is an insolent fellow, and strong drink makes an uproar; none addicted to their company grows wise'.

Proverbs: 20.1

'Should alcoholism be the G.P.'s concern' was the title of a paper by one general practitioner[120] who then proceeded to deliver a resounding 'NO' to his question. Because the general practitioner is too busy, 'to add the management of alcoholism to his duties is plainly absurd...the G.P. is not by disposition, character or activity, suited to an interest in alcoholism'. I suspect that this attitude is not a unique one and may partially account for the criticism that has been directed towards the general practitioner in recent years.

Kessel and Walton[121] have stated that 'many patients report that their general practitioners do not seem to have taken their alcoholism seriously'. The Office of Health Economics in their publication 'Alcohol Abuse'[31] pointed out that 'many general practitioners still do not recognise the disease or accept its medical content'. The Medical Council of Alcoholism in its 1970 Annual Report[122] wrote that 'most G.P.s are unable to diagnose and treat the disease because they have not received responsible advice or training'.

In defence of these remarks, the family doctor can take comfort in the views of Glatt[123] who has pointed out that doctors are not trained in medical school to recognise alcoholism in its early stages, that many alcoholics (and their families) never go to doctors, or if they do, they conceal their drinking problem. The alcoholic may be frightened that the doctor will be unsympathetic, and that he might demand his giving up of drink without an alternative way of life being suggested.

The role of the general practitioner in diagnosing and treating the alcoholic is reviewed in the following two Sections.

2.1 DIAGNOSIS

It is widely held that the general practitioner has considerable scope to exercise his abilities as a diagnostician of early disease in the field of alcoholism.

Twenty years ago, Saint *et al.* [124] in Australia pointed out that 'the general practitioner is more likely to come closer to the problem (of alcoholism) than the consultant or hospital physician, for he may have the opportunity of detecting alcoholism in its earliest stages, before addiction is complicated by mental, physical or social disablement, and it should be his duty to broach the subject with his patients'. Five years later, Parr[87] in England, commenting on his prevalence study of alcoholism in general practice, wrote that 'so far as recognition is concerned, the G. P. occupies an extremely favourable point of vantage. It is to the family doctor that the alcoholic has to go when he wants certificates for time off work or treatment for dyspepsia, gastritis, or any other of the physical concomitants of alcoholism. Whether or not the true diagnosis is spotted depends, of course, on whether the physician is on the lookout for it'. Glatt[123] has stated that 'the family doctor who knows the domestic and occupational background of his patient and other family members, may be in a particularly fortunate position for early diagnosis'. Block[125] in America has echoed these sentiments: 'Family doctors are in the best position for case finding in the field of alcoholism. There is no reason why they cannot at least detect the incipient cases as a matter of routine investigation, once the techniques for this case-finding are learned and employed'. Cooney[126] considers that 'Since to date no generally accepted physical or psychological test is at hand to identify the potential alcoholic, the doctor in practice must watch out for the danger signs in his patient's drinking pattern. Only by being *au fait* with the various stages of alcoholism can the family doctor be in a position to arrest the progress of the social drinker through the stage of heavy drinker on to frank alcoholism'. Rathod[127] stated that 'in my opinion the family doctor can do a great deal by both early diagnosis and treatment, and even more in preventing relapse'.

The alcoholic may present in general practice with a variety of medical and social disorders which should alert the family doctor to the possibility of alcoholism as the primary diagnosis.[33,56,128-132] Noting that alcoholism is often a hidden problem, Silversides[133] added that 'it can only be uncovered by the astute doctor who maintains a high degree of suspicion as to its presence'. In Australia, Chegwidden[134] commented that 'we general practitioners should learn to recognise the alcoholics in our practice at an early stage of this progressively downward disease...'. Williams and Long[135] also believe that the general practitioner 'must be able to spot the incipient alcoholic'. Lereboullet[136] from France pointed out that 'the tracing of cases is one of the main roles of the G.P. He should be able to recognise alcoholism even when the patient denies it'.

The past two years has seen an upsurge in articles on the clinical features of alcoholism written specifically for the general practitioner, and in the past four years there have been as many papers published as in the previous twenty years. Those commenting on the detective role of the general practitioner, include Crimm[137] who enjoined his colleagues to 'learn to practise preventive medicine in trying to pick up the alcoholic at an earlier stage in his drinking'. Gardiner[138] asked the general practitioner to 'make a drive for early diagnosis'. Reflecting the importance of alcoholism in Ireland, Kehoe[139] in his Presidential address to the Irish Medical Association on 'The family doctor and his role in the community' devoted a special section to the problems of alcoholism. He made the wry comment that 'anyone who attempts to draw attention to it is looked upon as an oddity'. Owen[140] remarked that 'the chief function of the family doctor in dealing with alcoholism is that of a detective and he must develop a high index of suspicion'. Other papers have been written commenting on the need for early diagnosis, and with the aim of educating the family doctor to be aware of the symptoms and signs of alcoholism.[19,141-147]

In the past, the detection of the alcoholic by the general practitioner has been considered very difficult because of inadequate undergraduate and postgraduate education and the unwillingness of the alcoholic to present for treatment. It is not surprising that Edwards[33] considered that 'in alcoholism, the diagnostic acumen of the family doctor receives one of its greatest challenges'. The general practitioner is now being bombarded with information which, hopefully, will remove one of the barriers to early diagnosis.

2.2   TREATMENT

Although it is generally accepted that the general practitioner has an important *diagnostic* role, opinions differ as to his competence to *treat* alcoholics.

One of my patients, classified as an alcohol addict from the questionnaire, presented with peptic ulcer symptoms. When confronted with the diagnosis, he readily accepted my opinion, and indeed returned the following day so that I could record an interview on audiotape. I asked him why he had not come to me for help and he answered that he did not consider it was my job to treat alcoholics! This case history is reflected in some studies of alcoholics who were asked whether they had sought help from their general practitioner.

One study showed that only 15 out of a group of 48 alcoholics said that they felt the need for help; only 10 actually asked for it, and only 3 went to their general practitioner.[148] Edwards *et al.*[149] questioned 300 clients of Alcoholism Information Centres and found that only 22% believed their general practitioner to be unaware of their drinking problem. However, only 44% had personally sought help from their general practitioner, and a further 30% believed that their wives had consulted the general practitioner for assistance. It is noteworthy that 74% said that, during the previous year, they had attempted to 'fool' a doctor, and had given false reasons for requiring a medical certificate. Edwards *et al.*[150] also interviewed 306 members of Alcoholics Anonymous of whom 80% of the males and 88% of the females thought that the general practitioner knew them to have a drinking problem. The authors pointed out that those alcoholics who attend Alcoholism Information Centres and Alcoholics Anonymous are likely to be highly motivated to seek help. Moss and Davies[94] in their study of alcoholics in the county of Cambridgeshire reported that only 25% had consulted their general practitioner because of their drinking problem, and a further 15% for 'conditions attributable to alcoholism' such as peptic ulcer, etc. A study of 132 drunkenness offenders in London found that only half of those who considered themselves alcoholics had previously consulted a general practitioner for drink-related problems.[437]

We are therefore faced with the situation that, even if the family doctor is willing to undertake treatment, many alcoholics are not equally willing to ask him for help.

Whether the general practitioner undertakes treatment or not, his initial attitude is very important. Hobson[151] commented that 'unless the G.P. can win the confidence of these (alcoholic) patients, he fails'. Williams[152] has pointed out that 'as a rule, the family doctor is the first person to be consulted by an alcoholic needing treatment, and on the outcome of this first consultation, the patient's future may well depend'. Similar comments have been made by others.[153-155]

There have been three important surveys of general practitioners' opinions about the alcoholic and his treatment. Levy[156] reported that 15% of a group of general practitioners in Johannesburg did not consider that alcoholism was a disease. Rathod[157] reviewed the results of 114 questionnaires he received from family doctors in England. A total of 26% of the doctors whose answers could be analysed stated that the 'most appropriate' terms to describe alcoholism were 'moral weakness', 'vice', 'bad habit', or 'weakness of willpower'. A further 21% considered that 'moral weakness' or 'weakness of willpower' were 'moderately appropriate' terms. Only 57% out of 74 doctors felt that the medical profession was best suited to manage alcohol addicts. In America, of a group of almost 7000 general practitioners replying to a questionnaire 26% thought that the chief cause of alcoholism was immorality or lack of will.[158]

There are basically two schools of thought concerning the extent to which the family doctor should involve himself in treatment. Some authorities restrict his role to diagnosis, referral for specialist care, aftercare and support of the family. For example, Churan[159] stated that 'the role of the family physician becomes vital, and the doctor can *begin* (my italics) the process of treatment'. A number of general practitioners[140,160-162] support the view of Lereboullet[136] that 'the actual treatment itself is beyond the general practitioner's scope'.

On the other hand there are those who consider that the general practitioner is competent to undertake the management of the alcoholic to a greater or lesser degree.[163-169] Two papers from South Africa have described the different aspects of treatment the general practitioner should undertake.[170-172] Solomon[172] suggested that 'in most instances it is the general practitioner who should treat the alcoholic patient'. Parry[173] has commented that 'successful treatment is certainly possible in general practice and for many alcoholics, the family doctor is the ideal therapist'.

Whether, and how, we treat our alcoholic patients, it is surely our duty to identify them, and then ensure that they are offered the best possible care.

2.3   RESEARCH

As yet only a handful of general practitioners have personally undertaken quantitative studies relating to the diagnosis or treatment of alcoholism. Over ten years ago Edwards[174] referring to alcoholism, suggested that 'the research needed is again perhaps eminently appropriate for the family doctor'. Pacy wrote in 1968[175] that 'there are magnificent opportunities for research by general practitioners who personally know an entire population'. The challenge has so far not been widely taken up.

There follows a consideration of general practice studies which have calculated prevalence rates of alcoholism, and surveys of the effectiveness of its treatment by general practitioners.

Finally research into the use of psychiatric questionnaires in general practice is described because of its relevance to the present study.

2.3.1   Prevalence Studies

There have been at least 17 prevalence studies in Great Britain and Eire utilising the records of some 1 500 general practitioners but in only seven of them was the work directed by the general practitioners themselves. It has been suggested that the general practitioner is only able to diagnose about one in ten of all alcoholics.[33] Excluding the studies of Abbott,[97] Patterson,[113] and the author, where a deliberate attempt was made to increase the detection rate of alcoholism by giving questionnaires to patients, it can be seen that general practice prevalence rates are far lower than those found from household surveys or multi-source inquiries (*see* Tables 1-3, pages 10-11, 18, 19). Furthermore, Edwards *et al.*[96] who questioned 16 sources to detect the alcoholics in a London borough reported a prevalence rate of 0.7 per 1 000 adults from the inquiries to general practitioners compared with an overall rate of 4.7 per 1 000 adults.

Three of the studies have been selected for further comment because the data obtained was of particular interest.

Because it was the first, and remains the most extensive study of alcoholism in general practice, the work of Parr (1957)[87], a psychiatrist, merits attention. He sent questionnaires to the 480 members of the Research Register of the (then) College of General Practitioners asking them four questions: how many alcoholics were known in each practice; how many sought treatment for their excessive drinking in the previous year; how many patients were referred for specialist treatment for alcoholism; and whether the general practitioner considered the facilities for treating alcoholics locally were adequate, or whether special clinics should be opened.

From the 369 replies suitable for analysis he obtained a prevalence rate of 1.1 alcoholics per 1000 of the population aged 15 years and over. The results showed a higher prevalence in the larger practices than in the smaller ones, and higher in the rural and mixed practices than in the urban practices. It has been suggested that the more intimate knowledge of their patients' lives by country doctors may have enabled them to spot a relatively higher proportion of alcoholics among their patients than the doctors in urban practices.[176] A possible explanation of the higher reported prevalence in the smaller practices was that in large busy practices the general practitioner has less time to diagnose a complaint which does not obviously present to him.[92]

In the year prior to the survey, 0.25 alcoholics per 1000 of the population came for treatment or advice for excessive drinking. Those who were sent for specialist treatment in that year number- ed 0.14 per 1000 of the population. On the question of adequacy of local treatment facilities and the need for special clinics, 25% of all doctors thought that facilities were inadequate and/or special clinics were desirable.

As previously observed, it should be noted that the general prac- titioners were not asked to examine their patients' records, but to rely on memory for their estimate of the number of alcoholics known to them. Such estimates were therefore likely to produce a prevalence rate lower than the actual one. Secondly, the general practitioners were asked to base their figures on the World Health Organisation (1952)[24] definition of the alcoholic (*see* Chapter 1). Hensman *et al.*[95] pointed out (with reference to their study) that general practitioners are unlikely to have sufficient information about their patients to assess accurately whether they are alcohol-dependent in the terms of the World Health Organisation definition. Thus Parr's survey probably underestimated the number of alcohol addicts, and excluded the problem drinkers who are not physically dependent on alcohol. Parr concluded from his study that 'the most important function of the family doctor is in recognition of the alcoholic addict and his recruitment for treatment, rather than necessarily the carrying out of such treatment'.

Pollak (1971)[90], a general practitioner in a South London working class practice, reported the prevalence of alcoholism (based on the 1952 WHO definition[24]) in his own practice. On one day in 1969, analysis of a morbidity index indicated that there were 30 patients who had been diagnosed as being alcoholics. The overall prevalence rate was 3.6 per 1000 of the practice popula- tion aged 15 years and over. The study found that in 80% of cases information on the abnormal drinking was offered to the family doctor by the patients themselves (20%), their relatives (30%), or obtained from various reports gathered from patients' medical records (30%). In only 20% of cases had the diagnosis to rely primarily on the doctor's own findings and probings. Pollak con- cluded that 'the desirability of further surveys in this field is stressed'.

Patterson (1972)[113], a general practitioner in Leicester, together with 11 colleagues comprising six practices, administered 1200 questionnaires to patients attending the surgery. Most of the questionnaires were given to the first two patients in each surgery session. The questionnaire was designed to answer four questions: what proportion of people drink alcohol; how often do they drink; how much do they drink; and in what context do they drink. The questionnaires were handed to the patient who, after completion (before he left the surgery), returned them to the doctor or his secretary. There was a 96% response rate. A total of 498 males and 576 females completed questionnaires suitable for analysis. The results indicated that there were 5. 2% (48 males and 8 females) heavy drinkers, 40. 2% regular drinkers, 44. 8% social drinkers, and 9. 4% nondrinkers. He suggested that 15 per 1 000 of the patients interviewed may have a serious drinking problem based on the answers revealed by the questionnaire.

This study and the one of Hes[177] in Israel (*see* below) are particularly noteworthy because they are the only surveys, similar to the present one, in which a general practitioner administered a questionnaire to some of his patients. It should be noted that Patterson's study was not designed primarily to detect alcoholics but to learn something of the drinking habits of his patients.

The only study of prevalence in General Practice, reported *outside Great Britain,* is that of Hes (1970),[177] a psychiatrist, in Israel. He studied 3 general practices in Jerusalem with a total practice population of 6 000 patients. The general practitioners knew of 6 alcoholics, and the social worker knew of a further 5 alcoholics. The interest in this study is that he administered the Michigan Alcoholism Screening Test (MAST) (*see* Chapter 4) to 111 unselected patients aged 14 years and over, who were waiting to be seen by the general practitioner. This screening test detected a further 4 alcoholics. On the basis of this investigation, the author concluded that the prevalence rate of alcoholism was 3. 6% of the population aged 14 years and over.

The results support the contention that apparently the general practitioners (prior to the administration of the questionnaire) were only aware of the tip of the 'iceberg' of alcoholism if it is assumed that the MAST technique is applicable to a non-American population. This study is particularly interesting because it is the only reported study of a questionnaire being adminstered in general practice as a screening procedure to detect alcoholism.

2. 3. 2   Treatment of Alcoholism

Although there have been a number of papers by general practitioners outlining the principles of treatment there have only been a few describing the results quantitatively.

Dent[178-180] assessed the effect of apomorphine in treatment. He reported a 60-70% 'cure' rate which he defined as remaining teetotal for at least one year, and 'having done this they generally continue happily'.

Moynihan[181] followed up this work and analysed the results of apomorphine treatment by the Dent method with 87 alcoholics over a two year period. The patients came from his own practice and other general practices in the neighbourhood. After one year, he also found that 70% of the patients were abstinent.

Pollak[182] wrote a paper entitled *The Role of the General Practitioner in Support of an Alcoholic Rehabilitation Hostel.* He examined the medical characteristics of 83 residents of a therapeutic community hostel for alcoholics who were registered with him. He suggested that 'local family doctors be encouraged to look after this type of alcoholic'.

The only study reported *outside Great Britain* is apparently that of Bastoe[183] who analysed the results of treatment of 97 alcoholics in a Norwegian general practice. He was able to follow up 63 patients and found that 8 had become total abstainers, and 26 had 'improved'. The time interval was not mentioned.

2.3.3   Psychiatric Questionnaires in General Practice

Most of the psychiatric morbidity studies carried out in general practice have relied on clinical interview by the general practitioner. Varying prevalence rates have been reported because of differences in case-definition and the populations studied and the influence of observer bias.[184,185] Goldberg[79] commented that 'it is clear that while general practice is a rich potential source of information about neurotic illness in the community, there is a pressing need for a research instrument that will assess psychiatric morbidity irrespective of the differing standards of different observers.'

Those general practice studies in which psychiatric questionnaires were used will be briefly outlined. They are relevant to the present study as they involved the administration of a questionnaire to patients in the consulting room.

The Cornell Medical Index (CMI) has been validated in hospital practice as a screening method to differentiate 'normal' from 'neurotic' patients. It has been used in a number of general practice studies.[78,185-189] The overall results indicated that, depending on which cut-off point was adopted, the CMI correctly identified about two-thirds of all patients classified as 'neurotic' by the general practitioner. However, it incorrectly identified about one-quarter of patients classified as 'normal' by the general practitioner. In one of the studies, a psychiatric assessment was also made.[187] The CMI correctly identified 84% of patients classified as 'neurotic' by both the psychiatrist and the general practitioner, compared with 57% of 'neurotic' patients assessed only by the general practitioner.

The General Health Questionnaire (GHQ) designed by Goldberg[79] to detect nonpsychotic psychiatric illness was administered to 553 consecutive attenders at a general practice. A random sample of 200 patients were independently assessed by a psychiatrist. It was found that over 90% of the patients were correctly identified as 'well' or 'ill' by the questionnaire.

The Maudsley Personality Inventory (MPI) was given to 500 general practice patients by Jacob.[190] He reported 'a clear correlation' between the incidence of frank neurotic breakdown as diagnosed clinically by the general practitioner, and a high score on one or more of the parameters of the MPI scale.

Zung's Self-Rating Depression Scale (SDS) was administered by Popoff[191] to 32 patients diagnosed clinically by a psychiatrist as being depressed. The SDS indicated that only 53% were depressed. The author devised a questionnaire, the Index of Depression (ID) which he administered, together with the SDS, to 171 patients selected randomly, who later had psychiatric interviews. Ninety-six of the patients were clinically diagnosed as being depressed. The ID correctly classified 97% of the patients compared with 53% classified by the SDS.

The Beck Depression Inventory (BDI) was administered by Salkind[192] to 50 general practice patients to determine the different scores relating to the different degrees of depression as diagnosed by the general practitioner.

The Health Opinion Survey (HOS) was given by Semmence[193] to 16 patients diagnosed as 'neurotic' by the general practitioner. He reported that only 2 of them were not similarly classified by the questionnaire.

Summary

In all 11 studies reviewed, the questionnaire was self-administered. A 100% response rate was reported in all but one of the studies. In four of the studies, the questionnaire was validated by independent assessment by a psychiatrist, in six by the general practitioner only, and in one study, the questionnaire was not validated in the general practice setting.

Of the seven different types of questionnaire, five of them had previously been extensively tested in hospital practice. Only three of the questionnaires were designed to detect a specific psychiatric disorder i.e. depression. None of the questionnaires were designed to detect alcoholism.

The results suggest that questionnaires have a useful role in the detection of psychiatric morbidity in general practice.

3 The Alcoholic At Risk Register

'Give strong drink to the desperate and wine to the
embittered; such men will drink and forget their poverty
and remember their trouble no longer'.

Proverbs: 31. 6-7

3.1 INTRODUCTION

The concept of 'at risk registers' has been well developed in the
field of Paediatrics; every child who falls into one or more of a
defined group of categories is 'at risk' to have or develop a
particular disease.[194] Alberman and Goldstein[195] have discussed
the importance of the Paediatric at risk register; by substituting
the word 'alcoholic' for 'child', their comment provides a valid
justification for the creation of an Alcoholic At Risk Register.
They write: 'It is now universally accepted that the earliest
possible diagnosis and treatment are essential in order to prevent, or at least to minimise the handicapping effects of a dis-
ability and to make the most of the assets an *alcoholic* possesses'.

An Alcoholic At Risk Register has not previously been described
as such, although the principle behind it has been hinted at.

Glatt[196] pointed out that 'if, however, the patient belongs to such
"alcoholism-prone" occupations or groups, the doctor may be
put on his guard, and may perhaps ask more direct questions'
about alcoholism. Grundy and Day[197] discussed similar 'clues'
to aid the identification of the alcoholic.

The World Health Organisation in 1967[198] called for research to
'determine the high- and low-risk individuals' with reference to
alcoholism and drug dependence. Blane[199] suggested that 'if we
can identify high-risk individuals, then the way is open for early
treatment or for intervention'. Edwards[33] listed a variety of
factors which might suggest the possibility of alcoholism in
those patients so categorised. Keller[200] considered that 'it is
more feasible (than giving school children information) to identify the vulnerable and the endangered high-risk segments of the
general population'. Others have echoed these sentiments.[109,201]

There are various stages in the progression from a social
drinker to an established alcohol addict where one can attempt
to exercise one's skills of diagnosis. My study was concerned
with one type of 'secondary prevention' which has been defined

as 'the application of procedures to stop, or reverse processes that if continued would, on actuarial evidence, lead to alcoholism.[202] It was not the intention to identify those individuals whose abnormal behaviour is believed to herald, in a proportion of cases, the development of problems created by drink, and ultimately alcohol addiction. For example, in the early stages there may be sneaking of drinks, gulping down of drinks, preoccupation with drinking, and guilt feelings.

The present study was primarily concerned with detecting those individuals whose drinking has already caused problems, and who may have become addicts. Ideally, patients should be identified as being 'at risk' when they *first* show signs of any abnormality in their drinking behaviour. Nevertheless it was hoped to detect individuals when there was still a possibility of arresting the disease, many years before irreversible effects have set in.

An Alcoholic At Risk Register (AARR) was developed comprising factors that are known or believed to be associated with a higher prevalence of alcoholism than that found in people possessing none of these factors.

A review of three types of study formed the basis for constructing the list of 'at risk' factors.

Firstly, analysis of known alcoholics has suggested a correlation with certain diseases, occupations, types of social status, etc. Secondly, by interviewing patients in hospital with certain diseases, a significant correlation with alcoholism has been found. Finally, for some of the factors no statistics have been published, but anecdotal evidence suggests they are likely to be significant.

The review of the literature suggesting these factors contain selected representative references as, for most of the categories, the evidence has been well documented, and is widely known and accepted. Most of the references quoted are from recent studies in Great Britain where they are available.

No attempt is made to discuss whether the various factors are causes or effects of alcoholism. The concern is the usefulness of the factors as means of identifying potential alcoholics.

3.2   THE AT RISK FACTORS

The AARR comprises 17 categories within which there are 64 items (*see* Appendix 1, Part IV).

3. 2. 1.   Category 1.   Physical Diseases

Category 1 consists of 11 physical conditions known to be associated with alcoholism, which are detailed below.

Pancreatitis

American studies of patients with acute pancreatitis have suggested that 14-60% are alcoholics.[203-206] The varying prevalance rates may reflect actual differences in different States, and the definition of 'alcoholic' adopted. In Great Britain, although a relationship between alcoholism and pancreatitis is often referred to, the evidence is limited and conflicting. No cases of alcoholism were found in a study of 1000 patients with acute pancreatitis in Leeds.[207] In Bristol, only four alcoholics were identified from 324 patients.[208] However, in Edinburgh 23% of a series of 93 patients were alcoholics or the episode was precipitated by a drinking bout. The proportion rose to 57% in the males under 60 years.[209] In Manchester, 11 alcoholics were found in a group of 54 patients with chronic pancreatitis.[210] In London, heavy drinking was considered a probable aetiological factor in 42% of 107 patients with chronic pancreatitis.[211]

Studies of *known alcoholics* in America have indicated that about half of those who died of acute alcoholism were found to have haemorrhagic pancreatitis at postmortem.[212-213]

Cirrhosis of the Liver

There have been numerous studies confirming a relationship between alcoholism and cirrhosis of the liver. In 1969, Galambos reviewed 111 papers on the subject.[214]

A study of 155 cirrhotics in Birmingham found that one-third of them were heavy drinkers.[215] In Liverpool, almost two-thirds of 67 cirrhotics admitted to being heavy drinkers.[216] In London, 24% of 561 cirrhotics were alcoholics.[217]

Amongst *known alcoholics* in England, about 8% of them develop cirrhosis.[218] This is a lower figure than has been reported from America where prevalence rates of about 40% have been found.[219,220] The prevalence of cirrhosis in a group of 922 known or suspected problem drinkers in a large American firm was estimated as 29 times that of a control group.[221]

Peptic Ulcer

Peptic ulcer has similarly often been reported as being a possible consequence of heavy drinking.

There have been few quantitative studies of the prevalence of alcoholism amongst peptic ulcer patients. Retterstol and Sund[222] in Norway found that the prevalence of alcohol abuse in peptic ulcer patients seen in a psychiatric clinic was three times that of a control group of psychiatric patients without peptic ulcer.

A study of *known alcoholics* in England by Edwards *et al.*[150] of 306 alcoholics attending Alcoholics Anonymous found that 19% had developed peptic ulceration at some time. Other surveys report that 11-22% of alcoholics have a history of gastric ulcer.[182,223,224]

It should be noted that, in the current study, any patient who was clinically diagnosed as having a peptic ulcer, or had a past history of proven peptic ulcer (on barium meal examination), qualified for inclusion in the survey. It is therefore possible that a proportion of these patients might not have had radiographic evidence of a peptic ulcer, and should have been labelled as having gastritis.

Gastritis

Gastritis is often regarded as a frequent consequence of excessive drinking. However, few statistics are available, probably because of the difficulty of making a definitive diagnosis. Palmer[225] found signs of acute gastritis on endoscopic examination in all but four of 34 patients with acute alcoholism. In a review article, he concluded that although excessive drinking could produce *acute* gastritis, there was no substantial evidence confirming a relationship between *chronic* gastritis and alcoholism. Wolff[226] examined the gastric mucosae of 1006 people and found no correlation between alcohol consumption and the development of chronic gastritis. However, Joske *el al.*[227] reported abnormal gastric biopsies in all of 51 chronic alcoholics studied. Ferguson[228] analysed the records of sickness absenteeism amongst office staff in Australia. He found that 30% of heavy drinkers (compared with 3% of other employees) had been absent because of one or more episodes of gastritis.

De Wet Vorster[229] stated that 'patients who present complaining of gastritis may constitute hidden alcoholics who are concealing the true picture'. Edwards[33] suggested that the general practitioner should 'never give an antacid without enquiring into the patient's drinking'. Similar comments can be found in many general articles on alcoholism.[44,230,231]

Despite the difficulty of defining accurately a pathological entity of 'gastritis', many patients seen in general practice are given this diagnosis. There is sufficient anecdotal evidence to warrant its inclusion in the AARR.

Peripheral Neuritis

It has been estimated that peripheral neuritis occurs in 15-20% of alcoholics in Europe.[232] A study of 68 female alcoholics in England by Judge and Glatt[233] showed that 15% of them had evidence of peripheral neuritis. Another study of 49 chronic alcoholics in England by Fennelly et al.[234] found that 65% of them had this condition.

Tuberculosis

Studies of patients with tuberculosis include that of Lewis and Chamberlain[235] who reported that 39% of tuberculosis patients admitted to the Brompton Chest Hospital, London, were 'regular drinkers' compared to approximately 20% of a matched control group. Similar studies in Canada[236], America[237] and Australia[238] have suggested a prevalence rate for alcoholism of 15-22%

Studies of *known alcoholics* in England have reported a history of tuberculosis in about 5% of cases.[150,182] Foreman and Chalke[239] found that about 8% of a group of 243 alcoholics in a Welsh hospital had evidence of healed primary or post-primary tuberculosis on their chest X-ray films.

Congestive heart failure of unknown origin

In 1970, Sanders[240] reviewed over 150 studies of alcoholic cardiomyopathy. In England, Brigden[241] investigated 50 cases of cardiomyopathy and found that 26% had a long history of alcoholism. In America, 65-83% of patients with cardiomyopathy were considered to be heavy drinkers or alcoholics.[242,243]

A study of *known alcoholics* by Hartel .et al.[244] in Helsinki found no definite cases of alcoholic cardiomyopathy amongst 100 male chronic alcoholics. Two alcoholics in a series of 100 cases in New York were found to have cardiomyopathy.[245] In England, Priest et al.[246] reported abnormalities in the electrocardiographs of 40% of a group of 37 alcoholics suggestive of cardiomyopathy.

Epilepsy appearing for the first time at 25 years of age or over

Reports from America[9,247,248] and Australia[231] have suggested that the occurrence of epilepsy for the first time over 25 years of age may be a warning sign of alcoholism. In England, Lees[249] commented that any form of epilepsy may be precipitated by alcohol in those who already have the susceptibility. Epilepsy may also occur for the first time in an alcoholic in relation to acute alcoholism, withdrawal of alcohol from an addict ('rum fits'), delerium tremens, Marchiafa's disease, other forms of cerebral degeneration e.g. alcoholic dementia, hypoglycaemia in acute alcoholism, and brain disease.

A study of *known alcoholics* by Glatt[250] in England showed that 22.7% of 110 male and 10% of 50 female alcoholics admitted to having convulsions in the past. An American survey of 321 chronic alcoholics found that 13% developed epilepsy after more than 2 years of addiction, although they gave no history of neurological disorder or epilepsy prior to their heavy drinking. The average age of onset of seizures was 35 years.[251]

Malnutrition and Obesity

Either malnutrition, due to inadequate diet and absorption, or obesity due to excessive calory intake, are generally recognised to occur in established alcoholics. Most of the evidence is anecdotal, but Joske and Turner[101] examined 78 chronic alcoholics in Australia, and found them all to be under weight and to be living on deficient diets. Olsen[252] has written a review on the importance of malnutrition, but no figures are quoted. Bates[253] and Wilson[231] have both commented on the association of malnutrition and obesity with alcoholism. A major underwriting company in England has included both obesity and malnutrition as possible effects of alcoholism which may lead to an increase in the premium.[254]

The AARR refers to obesity in men only, as female obesity is much more common and less likely to be due to alcoholism.

Haematemesis and Melaena

Haematemesis and melaena were included in the AARR as they may occur in peptic ulcer, bleeding oesophageal varices from cirrhosis of the liver, and in acute vomiting (Mallory-Weiss syndrome).

3.2.2. Category 2. Mental Diseases

Category 2 refers to patients who present with mental disease. Psychological disorder may indicate a drinking problem in either the informant or the spouse.

Anxiety and Depression

Anxiety and depression have often been cited as possible presenting symptoms in the alcoholic. Edwards[33] has pointed out that the alcoholic often comes into the surgery asking for 'something for bad nerves', and others have made similar observations.[44,128] De Wet Vorster[229] and Rathod[44] state that depression may be a presenting symptom.

There have been many American studies of the wife of the
alcoholic showing that she is often mentally disturbed although
there is dispute as to whether her disturbance antedates the
partner's alcoholism or stems from it.[255] Whalan[256] has described four different personality types seen in wives of alcoholics. A study by Kogan *et al.* [257] of 50 wives of alcoholics
showed that although more than half of them were mentally
normal, as a group they exhibited more personality disturbance
than a control group, and in particular tended to have higher
Anxiety Index scores. Similar results have been reported by
other workers.[258,259]

As yet the *husband* of the alcoholic has received little attention.
In England, Flintoff[260] has described three types of husband, all
of whom had personality traits which could accentuate the probability of the break-up of the marriage, and bring the husbands
to the family doctor for treatment of anxiety or depression.

Attempted suicide

American studies of attempted suicide have suggested a varying
incidence of associated alcoholism in 13-50% of cases, and in
successful suicides of 10-30%.[261-264] In Great Britain, the
incidence has varied according to the locality. Surveys in
Edinburgh and Glasgow have shown that 25-45% of males and
8-12% of females who had attempted suicide were alcoholics or
excessive drinkers.[265-268] In Newcastle-upon-Tyne, the incidence of alcoholism in a series of attempted suicides in 1962-64
was 12% males and nil in the females.[269] In 1966-69 the reported
figures were 17% males and 2% females.[270] In Bristol,[271] 1.5%
of a series of successful suicides were known alcoholics, and in
Brighton, the figure was 3%.[272] In Edinburgh, a history of alcohol
abuse was found in 54% of a group of males and 36% of females
who had committed suicide.[267]

Studies of *known alcoholics* confirm the relationship. In America
a review of the literature showed that 11-17% of alcoholics com-
mit suicide.[263,273] In England, Glatt[274] reported that 25.3% of
75 male alcoholics had attempted suicide. Kessel and Gross-
man[275] found that approximately 7% of two series of alcoholics
had committed suicide. This was 75-85 times the expected
figures. Smith-Moorhouse and Lynn[276] reported that 25.9% of
200 alcoholics had attempted suicide. In Edinburgh, Ritson[277]
found that 2.7% of 300 alcoholics had committed suicide.

Other mental disorders

This item was included to identify the 'symptomatic alcoholic'
whose alcoholism was secondary to a severe psychiatric disorder

such as schizophrenia and manic-depressive psychosis, psychiatric illness due to brain disease, or mental subnormality.[121] A review of 137 papers by Freed[278] indicated that the prevalence of alcoholism in manic-depressive patients is 6-10%. A study of 100 male schizophrenic patients in Sweden showed that 35 of them were heavy drinkers.[279] A history of alcohol abuse was found in 17% of male (0.75% of female) schizophrenics, also in Sweden.[280]

A study of *known alcoholics* in Edinburgh revealed that of 83 patients, 4% were psychotic, 17% had a diagnosis of sociopathy, and 41% were considered to have a personality disorder of moderate degree.[281] Another Edinburgh study of 100 alcoholics found that 27% were psychopaths, 2% were psychotic, and the remainder had a psychoneurosis or personality disorder.[282]

3.2.3   Category 3. Symptoms of Alcohol Addiction

Patients presenting with 'the shakes', blackouts, delirium tremens, or other manifestations of alcohol addiction such as alcoholic hallucinosis, fugue states, morbid jealousy, or craving were obvious candidates to receive questionnaires. This category was also utilised for patients with a known past history of such symptoms, or who mentioned them in the course of answering the questionnaire for some other reason.

3.2.4   Category 4. Occupations

The following occupations are often quoted as being associated with a significant prevalence of alcoholism, although there are few statistics available:

Catering trade
Publicans and others working in a pub, or the drink industry
Travelling salesmen
Journalists
Entertainers
Executives
Printing industry
Market porters
Seamen
Miners

Kessell and Walton[121] have pointed out that those whose work brings them into contact with alcohol have the highest rates for alcoholism. The occupations mentioned include publicans and barmen, waiters and others in the catering trade, brewers and distillers, and commercial travellers. Other 'at risk' occupations such as coopers and draymen, and officers in the Armed Forces

were omitted from the AARR because of their very low incidence
in the practice population. Mellor[283] comments that there is
anecdotal evidence that newspaper workers and actors have a
higher prevalence of alcoholism than other occupations. Miners,
market porters, entertainers, and executives are also believed to
be particularly prone to alcoholism. Publicans have a standardised mortality rate for cirrhosis of the liver nine times as high as
the expected rate for all men of comparable age, and barmen five
times the expected rate.[284] There have been a number of studies
suggesting a relationship between merchant seamen and alcoholism.[285,286] Analysis of 2 000 alcoholics referred to the
Merseyside Council on Alcoholism[287] showed that there were
31 working in the catering trade, 44 working in a pub, 18 commercial travellers, 16 Directors and 173 seamen (Liverpool being a
port). There were 266 labourers but this category was not
included in the AARR as it would have made the 'at risk' group
too large.

3.2.5   Category 5.   Work Problems

There can be no doubt that many alcoholics have work problems.
However there is still considerable criticism of Industry for
failing to take up the challenge to detect the alcoholic and offer
rehabilitation programmes.[288,289] What information is available,
comes from studies in hospitals and the community, and not from
Industry itself (unlike the situation in America).

The Wessex Council on Alcoholism[290] reported that of 63
employees seeking advice, 29 believed that their employers were
unaware of their drinking problem. The Merseyside Council on
Alcoholism[291] has stated that only 10% of alcoholics in full time
employment were known by their employer to have a drinking
problem. The Medical Council on Alcoholism[292] has suggested
that alcoholism may cost £250 million *per annum* to Industry and
the economy. Between June 1970 and June 1971, the number of
days of certified incapacity attributed to alcoholism or alcoholic
psychosis and recorded for National Insurance purposes was
about 100 000. This represented some 1 400 spells of incapacity.[293] These figures can only be regarded as the tip of the iceberg, general practitioners being loathe to record Alcoholism on
Insurance certificates.

Three or more jobs in the year preceding consultation

It was felt that the more changes of job made, the greater was
the likelihood of alcoholism being a factor.

Edwards *et al.*[149] questioned 264 male clients of Alcoholism
Information Centres and found that 75% of them admitted to

having at some time lost a job because of their drinking, and 12% of the alcoholics had been sacked more than 5 times because of drinking. Questionnaires were also administered to 306 members of Alcoholics Anonymous of whom 63% of the males and 43% of the females admitted to losing a job because of drinking.[150] Loss of a job through alcoholism was acknowledged by 24% of 423 male alcoholics and 7% of 104 female alcoholics in the Cambridgeshire study of Moss and Davies.[94]

Three or more spells of absence off work in the year preceding consultation for three days or less

Absence from work is a common feature amongst alcoholics. Short spells of absence were considered a more likely indicator of alcoholism than longer ones which could be due to other reasons.

A study of 40 English male alcoholics admitted to hospital showed that the average loss of work per year was 18 days.[294] American studies have reported average losses of 13-24 days annually.[221,295,296] The highest figure recorded is 86 days in one year from a survey of clients of Alcoholism Information Centres by Edwards *et al.*[149] Loss of time was admitted by 43% of male alcoholics and 8% of female alcoholics in the Cambridge-shire study of Moss and Davies.[94] Pell and D'Alonzo[221] analysed absenteeism statistics of 746 alcoholics in a large company in America and found that 32.7% of the alcoholics (15% of 863 controls) had 2 or more absences per year, and 17.6% of the alcoholics (6.1% of the controls) had 3 or more absences per year. These results were statistically significant.

Patient requesting certificate for absence from work for conditions which are possibly not genuine

This item was included to pick up the alcoholic who requests sickness certificates for absence from work often for only a day or two for vague illnesses; the true cause might be a 'hangover' or acute gastritis.

Most of the evidence for this 'at risk' factor is anecdotal. Franco[297] included recurring excuses for absence due to minor illnesses as one of the early signs of a drinking problem. Williams[298] pointed out that absenteeism, especially on Monday mornings, because of 'influenza' and 'gastroenteritis' are 'popular alibis'. Blane[299] has referred to the Monday morning absentee as a high risk individual.

Edwards *et al.*[149] in a study of clients of Alcoholism Information Centres found that 61% of them admitted to Monday morning absenteeism once or twice a month or more, and 27% to once or twice a year or more.

3.2.6   Category 6.   Accidents

The accident rate amongst alcoholics is higher than in the general population. A Scandinavian study compared the hospital records of 180 alcoholics with an equal number of controls over a period of 20 years.[300] 35% of the alcoholics (11% controls) had previously been admitted because of accidents, and 51% (25% controls) had been treated for minor accidents at a clinic. In America, a study of 1 343 alcoholics showed that they were 7 times more likely to become a victim of some type of fatal accident than the nonalcoholics in the same population area.[301] Watson[302] examined a 1 in 3 sample of records of patients attending the Accident Department of a busy London hospital. Alcohol was implicated in 1% of all new attendances.

Accidents at work

No English studies have been reported, but there is considerable evidence from America. Accidents in the public transport industry were found to be 19 times more frequent amongst alcoholic employees than amongst nonalcoholic employees.[303] Questionnaires were administered to 379 workers known to be alcoholics of whom 14% admitted to having had serious or moderately serious accidents at work.[304] A positive breathalyser reading was found in 15.5% of patients admitted to an emergency service hospital because of accidents at work.[305] In another study of 764 alcoholics, their accident rate at work was found to be 3.5 times that of a control group.[221]

Home accidents

American studies suggest that home accidents may sometimes result from heavy drinking. One-third of 94 home accident patients attending a Casualty Department in Boston had blood alcohol levels greater than 50 mg/100 ml.[306] An American Life Assurance company analysed the deaths of 847 policy holders who had died in home accidents in one year. Drinking was associated with the deaths of 15% of the males and 20% of the females.[307] A study of 5 622 patients admitted to an emergency service hospital showed that 22.3% of the home accident cases had a positive breathalyser reading compared to 9% of the non-accident cases.[305]

Road Traffic Accidents

Numerous studies from America suggest that about 50% of

drivers involved in road traffic accidents are alcoholics or intoxicated at the time of the accident.[308-310] One study of pedestrians fatally injured in road traffic accidents showed that 74% of them had been drinking compared with 33% of a control group not involved in an accident.[311] Although less research has been carried out in England, there is confirmation of the importance of alcohol as a cause of accidents. A number of studies have shown that about one-fifth of those involved in fatal road traffic accidents were intoxicated or had consumed alcohol prior to the accident.[312-314] A Government publication[315] reported that in 1971 25% of drivers involved in road traffic accidents had a blood alcohol level greater than 80 mg/100 ml. About 15% of drivers of cars and light vans aged 18-54 years involved in injury accidents between 10 p.m. and 4 a.m., had a positive breathalyser reading.

In America, one study of *known alcoholics* showed that male alcoholic drivers had $2\frac{1}{2}$ times the expected number of road traffic accidents and 9 times the expected number of convictions for drunken driving.[316] In another study, 63% of male alcoholic drivers admitted being responsible for one or more accidents while intoxicated.[317] In Dublin, a group of 100 male alcoholic drivers had a history of twice as many road accidents as a control group.[318] In London, Glatt[319] found that 50% of male and female alcoholic drivers admitted previous court appearances for 'driving under the influence', and only 15% denied ever having driven 'under the influence'. He concluded that 'recurrent impaired and drunken driving seems to be a (more) objective prodromal sign of alcoholism which could be recognised more easily'.

3.2.7   Category 7.   Criminal Offences

There is a wealth of literature stressing the importance of criminal offences as a predictor of alcoholism. Glatt[320] defined the 'alcoholic criminal' as a criminal who apart from other abnormal behavioural aspects, also drinks, and sometimes drinks to excess (and in time may also develop into an alcoholic). This is in contrast to the 'criminal alcoholic' i.e. an alcoholic who, after years of drinking, is driven to behave in a criminal manner as a consequence of his alcoholism. A representative sample of the numerous studies from America and England will be considered.

Offences of drunkenness and motoring offences related to alcohol

These types of criminal offence have often been used as an index of the degree of alcoholism in a population, although not all drunkards are alcoholic, and vice versa (*see* Chapter 1). This section is mainly concerned with offences of drunkenness, as the relationship between alcohol and road traffic accidents has already been considered above.

Studies of *drunken offenders* include that of Gath[321] who interviewed 151 men in London who had been charged with simple drunkenness, being drunk and disorderly, or drunk and indecent, but excluding those who had been charged with motoring or other drink-associated offences. He considered that 26% of them were problem drinkers, and another 50% were alcohol addicts. Interviews with 58 drunkenness offenders in an Edinburgh prison showed that 100% of them had lost control over their drinking, and 80% were chemically dependent on alcohol.[323]

Studies of *known alcoholics* include those by Edwards *et al.* Out of 248 male members of Alcoholics Anonymous, 22% had been imprisoned for drunkenness, and 16% convicted for drunken driving; the corresponding figures for 58 females were 12% and 7%.[150] In another study of 264 male clients of Alcoholism Information Centres, 68% admitted to having been convicted on a drunkenness charge, and 28% for dangerous driving; the corresponding figures for the 36 females were 18% and nil.[149] A study of the alcoholics in Cambridgeshire by Moss and Davies[94] found that 13% of the 423 men and 0.9% of the 104 women had been prosecuted for drunkenness.

Other criminal offences

There have been a number of studies of the incidence of alcohol abuse amongst London prisoners. Gibbens and Silberman[323] interviewed 404 prisoners and ex-prisoners and classified 40% of them as excessive drinkers. Drunken offenders with very short sentences were excluded from the survey. Edwards *et al.*[324] studied a group of 188 males serving sentences for three months or less (short term), and a group of 312 males serving sentences for one year or more (long term). The prevalence of problem drinkers ranged from 60-100% for the short term group and 6-41% for the long term group depending on whether prevalence was defined in terms of a disease entity, statistically abnormal drinking behaviour, or adverse consequences stemming from drink. Interviews with female prisoners have suggested that 13-26% of them have drinking problems.[325,326]

Studies of *known alcoholics* include that of Glatt[319] who found that 20% of male hospitalised alcoholics had been in prison. Smith-Moorhouse and Lynn[276] reported that about 20% of 200 alcoholic outpatients had a history of previous criminal offences.

3.2.8   Category 8.   Family Problems

Alcoholism has been called the 'family disease' because of the
effects it invariably has on the whole family. The tensions
created may have harmful consequences for the marriage, and
for the health of the spouse and the children.

*Children suffering from neglect and children with mental dis-
turbance, including nocturnal enuresis*

Moss and Davies[94] reported that about 25% of the 391 alcoholics
in Cambridgeshire who had been married admitted that their
drinking had ill-effects on the children. They were usually
victims of neglect due to financial difficulties, or fear caused by
frequent parental quarrels, or injury because of physical cruelty.
Glatt[327] has pointed out that 'the all important early detection of
emotional neglect of children is in general a very difficult task,
but its frequency in the case of an alcoholic's family makes
successful treatment of the alcoholic an important prophylactic
measure in regard to the threatened maladjustment of his
children'.

A significant proportion of juvenile delinquents have been found
to have an alcoholic parent.[327,328] In a series of 21 fathers convicted for cruelty with violence to their children, there were 10
heavy drinkers or alcoholics.[329]

Irwin[330] has commented that behaviour disorders in children
may be the presenting symptom of a hidden alcoholic mother.
There is suggestive evidence from a number of studies that
children of alcoholics are particularly prone to anxiety and depression and risk of suicide.[331,332]

Family Disharmony

Disruption of family life is a common effect of alcoholism and
much has been written of the possible psychological consequences
for the wife. It has been suggested that there are seven stages in
the development of the wife's attitude to her husband's drinking
which might ultimately result in the break-up of the marriage.[333]
The anxiety and depression of the wife has already been considered (*see* Category 2), and the likelihood of separation or divorce
will be discussed later (*see* Category 11).

Studies by Glatt[334], Moss and Davies[94] and Ritson and Hassall[282]
have shown that almost two-thirds of married alcoholics admit to
frequent arguments with their spouse about their drinking habits.

If a history of family disharmony was elicited, a questionnaire
was administered to detect a potential drinking problem in either
the informant or a family member or both.

3.2.9   Category 9. Help requested for Treatment

A request for treatment of alcoholism by a suspected alcoholic, a family member, a member of the health team (health visitor, social worker, district nurse, midwife) or any other source, is clearly a very important 'at risk' factor. However, very often both the alcoholic and the family are ashamed and frightened to seek help from the family doctor.

A study of 264 male clients of Alcoholism Information Centres showed that only 44% of them had personally sought help from their family doctor, and 30% believed that their wives had consulted the doctor for assistance.[149] Moss and Davies[94] in their analysis of 527 alcoholics in Cambridgeshire, found that only 25% of them had attended their general practitioner for their alcoholism, and a further 15.5% for a physical or psychiatric condition attributable to alcoholism.

If the alcoholic or his family will not seek help, then the astute health visitor, community nurse or social worker, may detect a potential alcoholic and refer him to the family doctor.[335,336]

3.2.10   Category 10. Smelling of Alcohol

The patient who smells of alcohol at a consultation may have only had one drink on the way home from work before seeing his doctor. However, it was considered possible that he might well be an abnormal drinker.

3.2.11   Category 11. Marital Status.

Some categories of marital status of the patient were included in the At Risk Register because it is well known that the alcoholic may not marry or may be the cause of a broken marriage. Although, contrary to popular supposition, many alcoholics are married and working, alcoholism *is* a feature of *some* broken marriages.

Single male of 40 years and over

This item was selected as a result of the study of known alcoholics in the county of Cambridgeshire by Moss and Davies.[94] They found that there were four times as many male alcoholics as females, and the proportion of single males in the alcoholic population exceeded by 2.4% their counterparts in the county population, but the proportion of single females was about half that expected. Furthermore, the rate among single men rose to a peak in the 45-54 age group and was nearly three times as great as in the 25-34 age group.

Married more than once

Patients known to have been married more than once will
obviously form a very small group, but they were included in the
AARR because Bates[253] in America reported that about one-third
of his series of alcoholics had been married at least twice. As
the number of such patients was considered likely to be very
small, it was considered justified to spend the time administering
questionnaires in the expectation of identifying some alcoholics.

Divorced or Separated

An analysis of 1 434 Philadelphian divorces in the period 1937-50
showed that excessive drinking was a causal factor in 21.2% of
cases. Drunkenness by the husband was also reported in 25% of
over 60 000 cases of desertion and nonsupport.[258] In Australia,
40% of divorces and separations have been stated to be associated
with the problem of alcoholism[337], and 55% of a sample of 254
deserted wives were found to have alcoholic or heavy drinking
husbands.[338] There have been no comparable statistics published
in England.[339]

There have been numerous studies of English *alcoholics* all
showing a significant proportion of divorced and separated
amongst them. Studies of hospitalised alcoholics have indicated an incidence of 15-42% who were divorced or separated.[276,340-342] Moss and Davies[94] in their community study of
524 alcoholics obtained from many different agencies reported
that 6% of them were divorced. Compared to the general population, there were nearly 12 times as many divorces among the
males and more than 6 times as many among the females.
Edwards *et al.*[150] in a study of 306 members of Alcoholics
Anonymous found that 20% were divorced or separated. In another study, Edwards *et al.*[149] reported that 32% of 300 clients of
Alcoholism Information Centres were divorced or separated. The
authors pointed out that the 'true' picture of alcoholism is almost
impossible to obtain as there are likely to be differences between
the type of alcoholic seen at the Information Centre, Alcoholics
Anonymous, or in hospital.

3.2.12   Category 12.   Hostels for Destitutes

Patients living in hostel accommodation for destitutes are a high
'at risk' group. However it should be emphasised that the 'skid-
row' alcoholic who lives in such surroundings is believed to form
a minority of the total alcoholic population. In America, the
incidence has been estimated to be under 10%.[11,337] In England,
the few surveys carried out have produced conflicting results.
Moss and Davies[94] derived 11% of their total of known alcoholics

in Cambridgeshire from hostel sources. However, Edwards
et al. [96] in their 'count' of alcoholics in the Camberwell district
of London found that 32% of them were of 'no fixed abode'.
Tidmarsh[342] reported that 44.5% of alcoholic patients admitted
to a London mental hospital were of 'no fixed abode'. He pointed
out that an abnormally high proportion of vagrants lived in the
catchment area.

There have been a number of studies to determine the prevalence
of alcoholism among the 'homeless' in England. A study of 837
men living in various types of accommodation for the homeless
suggested that 7% were suspected alcoholics.[344] In a sample of
51 male attenders at a soup kitchen in London, 47 were alcoholics.[345] In Edinburgh, a study of 77 men residing in common
lodging houses showed that 7 were definitely alcoholics, and a
further 7 probably alcoholics.[346] The prevalence of alcoholism
in Reception Centres has been estimated as 33-45%.[347,348] In
two Salvation Army hostels in London, 21% admitted to heavy
drinking or symptoms of addiction[349], and in Cambridgeshire 11%
were alcoholics.[94] The prevalence of alcoholism in a Church
Army hostel in Manchester was estimated as being 16%[350] and
in Cambridgeshire was 3%.[94]

The evidence suggests that residents of the three hostels in the
practice area were likely to be a useful source of alcoholics.

3.2.13   Category 13. Known Alcoholic

All known alcoholics i.e. patients who had been diagnosed previously by a psychiatrist, were included in the AARR for the sake
of completeness.

3.2.14   Category 14. Family History

There have been a number of studies from Great Britain and
elsewhere showing that alcoholics have a significant family history of alcoholism, especially amongst the fathers and husbands.
Walton[351] has stated that 'one of the good indicators of pre-
alcoholism, i.e. the state of being at risk of developing alcoholism,
is to have an alcoholic father'.

In Glasgow, 36% of 100 alcoholics admitted to having an alcoholic
relative.[334] There were 16 mothers, 11 fathers, 4 husbands, 3
siblings, and 2 grandparents. In another study, a family history
of alcoholism was reported in 20% of an alcoholic group compared
to 7% of a nonalcoholic control group.[352] Further studies have
suggested a prevalence rate for alcoholism in 45-75% of near
relatives.[157,282,353]

Alcoholics tend to marry alcoholics, have alcoholic parents, and produce children who become alcoholics. This category was therefore considered likely to be a useful indicator of alcoholism in the informant or family.

3.2.15   Category 15.   Relatives of Informant

When a patient had received a questionnaire, the National Health Service records of every member of his family with the same surname (aged 15-65 years of age) registered in the practice were marked. If any of these family members consulted for any reason during the survey year, a questionnaire was administered.

This policy was adopted as, firstly, a proportion of patients were initially interviewed not because they were necessarily alcoholics themselves, but because they were at risk to have an alcoholic spouse, for example, anxiety or depression, separation or divorce. In such cases, questioning of the family member might detect the alcoholic.

Secondly, it was considered very useful to interview as many relatives of suspected alcoholics as possible to correlate the findings from the alcoholic with those of family members. In this way, it was hoped to study the possibility of denial by the alcoholic or his family (*see* Chapter 11).

3.2.16   Category 16.   Relatives of 'At Risk' Patients

Not all patients with 'at risk' factors consulted during the survey year and completed questionnaires. Consequently, near relatives of patients known to have at risk factors received questionnaires if they were seen during the survey year. For example, if a son of a publican consulted for any reason, he was interviewed in the hope of identifying possible alcoholism in his father.

3.2.17   Category 17.   Other Factors

The final category on the AARR allowed the interviewers to administer a questionnaire to anyone they thought might be an alcoholic for reasons not included in the register. For example, the patient might complain of constant fatigue or insomnia.[354] He might have a red face, puffiness of the eyelids, or a hoarse voice. His appearance might be dishevelled, or he might be tatooed.[253]

4   The Spare Time Activities Questionnaire

'Wake up, you drunkards, and lament your fate'

Joel: 1. 5

Questionnaires have previously been used as a tool in alcoholism prevalence studies in two ways.

Firstly, they have been administered to groups of *case finders* e.g. general practitioners, psychiatrists, and community agencies, who complete the questionnaire about known alcoholics under their care. There have been a number of such surveys reported from America,[355-357] Chile[358] Canada[359] and Great Britain (*see* Chapter 1). This type of survey has been criticised.[355,359] Blane[299] has argued that 'a prominent reason for lack of identification is that alcoholism is based on individuals who come to hospitals, clinics, social agencies, Alcoholics Anonymous etc. with problems related to alcohol use. Little attempt has been made to seek out and identify persons with varying gradations of alcohol use who do *not* present themselves for help. '

The second type of questionnaire, which is relevant to the present study, is one administered to the *potential or actual alcoholic*. It is completed either by the interviewer, or by the individual being questioned.

Most of the questionnaires are based on the classical questionnaire on drinking habits and effects developed by Jellinek in 1946.[360] However, they vary considerably in a number of ways, for example:

1.   The average time taken for completion

2.   Whether the questions only ask about drink, or include other topics to disguise the true purpose of the questionnaire

3.   Who fills in the answers—informant or interviewer

4.   How structured or open is the questionnaire

5.   Whether questions are asked about the family of the informant

6.   The actual type of question asked about drinking

1.   The *time factor* is of paramount importance when a questionnaire is being administered in a busy general practice, and this

depends on the number of questions asked, their length and ease of understanding, and the type of response required.

The average time of completion of such direct interview questionnaires has been variously reported to be 3½ hours,[21] 1 hour,[361,362] 40 minutes,[363] and 15-17 minutes.[364]

2. Most of the questionnaires have *only contained questions about drinking,* although the World Health Organisation in 1952 stated that 'for reasons which hardly need to be mentioned, any survey on drinking should be part of a broader survey......
Surveys on means of relaxation, on mode of living etc., may be devised to yield the required information on drinking habits. The principle is to avoid the singling out of drinking as a subject of inquiry'.[24] The report emphasised the difficulty of making drinking the only subject of inquiry, because of the 'natural resistance of ordinary people to truthful disclosure of information about their drinking habits, especially when consumption of alcohol is excessive'. Gordon[365] also favoured an indirect approach and suggested the use of a combined nutritional and alcoholic survey.

The reason for this type of inquiry is the known tendency of the alcoholic to deny his symptoms. The hope is that a disguised questionnaire, which includes questions on drinking embedded amongst others relating to a variety of topics, may improve the validity of the responses. The disadvantage of this disguised approach is the necessity for superfluous questions, thus increasing the length of the questionnaire and diminishing the number of relevant questions.

Perhaps for this reason, and because the problem of alcoholism is widely talked about, most surveys in America have favoured the direct approach of asking questions only about drinking. There have been exceptions where drinking questions were asked as part of a much larger general health survey.[117] The California Drinking Practices Study introduced drinking questions through a series of questions on recreational patterns.[361]

In England, all the direct interview surveys have used an undisguised questionnaire (*see* Chapter 1). On the basis of a pilot study comparing a disguised and an undisguised questionnaire, Edwards *et al.*[366] concluded that there was no advantage in disguising the questionnaire. However, the households questioned in his study had previously taken part in many research studies, and so were perhaps less likely to give false information.[367]

Previous community studies have used reasearch workers who were not previously known to the patient. In the present study, the questionnaire was administered by the patient's own family

doctor or one of his colleagues. I felt that the doctor-patient
relationship would not be enhanced by a direct frontal assault
of a battery of questions only concerned with the emotive subject of drinking. This, coupled with the belief that the patient
was likely to under-report the effects of his drinking—especially
to his own general practitioner—persuaded me to design a
disguised questionnaire, despite its inadequacies.

3.   The *form of administration* of the questionnaire has varied
to some extent. In most cases, the research worker asked the
questions, sometimes with the use of flash cards, and wrote
down the responses. One exception is the California Drinking
Practices Study in which important drinking questions were
self-administered, but in the presence of an interviewer.[361] The
informant, who was handed an answer booklet, recorded his
answers without having to say anything. It was hypothesised
that the informant would be more likely to tell the truth if he
were relieved of the need to *tell* the interviewer what to write.

4.   The questionnaire is usually *structured* and there is little
opportunity for probing by the interviewer.

However, Bailey *et al.*[117] instructed the interviewers to observe
any abnormal drinking behaviour during the interview, and to
note any relevant remarks about drinking made by the informant
which were not a direct response to a specific question. They
reported one man who kept excusing himself every few minutes
to take a drink, and then 'passed out' before the end of the
interview!

Stone *et al.*[362] utilised a relatively open-ended structured interview rather than a question-answer situation, taking the form
of a discussion lasting about an hour. They had previously used
a self-administered 'drinking check list' but found that the
subject who was self-protective, recalcitrant or indecisive did
not complete the questionnaire in the same manner as one who
was cooperative and trusting. They interviewed relatives in
an effort to test the validity of the information and found that the
self-administered check list was unsatisfactory.

5.   In most household surveys, one member of the household
was questioned about himself and the other members of the
household. The other members of the household were not interviewed to check validity.

6.   The general principles of questionnaire design apply in
alcoholism research. However there are also specific problems
to be considered before designing a suitable questionnaire for
administration to the potential alcoholic.

It has been pointed out[16,21,119,368] that different surveys have used different definitions of the alcoholic which may produce very different prevalence rates. For example, alcoholism may be defined in terms of the quantity of alcohol consumed over a certain length of time and the way in which it is drunk; the physical, mental and social consequences of such heavy drinking; the attitudes of the patient towards his drinking, and the presence or absence of symptoms of physical dependence on alcohol.

An important attempt at defining the alcoholic in terms of his *alcohol consumption* was that of Mulford and Miller[363] who utilised a Quantity-Frequency Index (Q-F) based on the work of Strauss and Bacon.[369]

There were five Q-F Index types described, based on the informant's report of the number of drinks (converted to ounces of absolute alcohol) which he ordinarily consumed at one 'sitting', combined with the reported frequency of these sittings during the preceding year.

In England, Edwards *et al.*[366] used the Q-F Index, and Patterson[113] adopted a definition of heavy drinkers based on the same principles.

Knupfer[21] developed a Quantity-Frequency-Variability Index (QFV) which took account of both the individual's usual, and his maximum drinking quantity on any one day.

Cahalan[119] used a 'Volume-Variability' of 'Volume-Maximum' Index which allowed for the spacing or bunching of drinking.

Ewing and Rouse[109] have described an Alcohol Quotient (AQ) defined as 'an arbitrary figure calculated from the blood alcohol percentage probably reached, multiplied by the number of hours of drinking, multiplied by the number of occasions, multiplied by a factor for absorption rate'.

A definition of alcoholism based on alcohol consumption requires the administration of a number of detailed questions. It is open to criticism because of the particular Index used, and the likelihood of the patient underestimating his drinking habits. Bailey *et al.*[370] found that over half of those admitting to drinking problems failed to acknowledge heavy drinking. They concluded that 'the active alcoholic's common pattern of minimising the amount of alcohol he consumes suggests that quantity-frequency questions, which were designed for studies of normal populations, are of limited value in alcoholism surveys'. As time was a critical factor, and the validity of responses suspect, I included only a brief reference to drinking habits in the Spare Time Activities Questionnaire.

A definition which relies on the *problems* resulting from drink
is also not immune from criticism. It might be thought that
eliciting admissions of problems arising from drink in the
sphere of work, health, financial or police trouble would produce
a fairly standard set of definitions. However, it has been pointed
out that the three factors of severity, recency and reversibility
have to be considered. 'At what point in the usual gradual development of alcoholism has the case become severe enough to be
counted?'[368] Clark[16] showed that the prevalence rate obtained
will depend on which cut-off point one arbitrarily decides upon,
and this can vary quite widely. He also discussed the effect of
recency and the dispute whether alcoholism can be considered
reversible or irreversible.

Knupfer[21] considered it important to distinguish between past
and current problems, i.e. 'inactive' and 'active' alcoholism.
She considered 'current problems' to relate to the year preceding the study, and asked questions beginning 'have you *ever*
had problems due to.....' to include past and current problems.
Although most authorities have considered that 'once an alcoholic always an alcoholic', there is now some evidence that
alcoholics may revert to social drinking without any ill-effects
(*see* Chapter 7). Most prevalence studies have coupled current
and past problems from drink as representing one entity.
However, Bailey *et al.*[371] classified their cases into a number of
different categories: actively drinking alcohol addicts, abstaining alcohol addicts, persons with acute situational drinking
problems, alcohol addicts who had succeeded in achieving moderate drinking patterns, and persons with somewhat marginal
drinking difficulties who might or might not be considered as
alcohol addicts by some authorities.

In the present study an attempt was made to separate those
patients who admitted to current problems from those who
admitted only to past problems.

Another difficulty in analysing responses to questions on problems from drink is that no individual will perceive his own
problems, or those of others, in exactly the same way, and
subjective bias is therefore inevitable.

There are perhaps the least problems in defining an alcoholic
in terms of *symptoms of alcohol addiction*. It is generally
accepted that a person admitting to being physically addicted to
alcohol is indeed an 'alcoholic'. Additionally there is general
agreement on what symptoms constitute addiction such as
'loss of control' of which there are two types. Some people
have to drink alcohol every day but are able to regulate their
alcoholic intake. Others, after ingestion of a small amount of

alcohol find themselves compelled to continue drinking increasingly greater quantities until stopped by external or internal factors. After that episode they are able to refrain from drinking for weeks or even months, but within a drinking bout they cannot control their drinking.[372]

A patient addicted to alcohol will experience withdrawal symptoms such as 'the shakes', and delirium tremens, and is likely to drink alcohol in the morning to relieve the withdrawal symptoms. He will suffer from blackouts, and develop gradually increasing tolerance to alcohol until the later stages when tolerance decreases.

Unlike drinking behaviour, and problems from drink, the criteria for *established* alcohol addiction are reasonably clear cut, and one is 'only' left with the difficulty of the denial by the alcoholic of his symptoms.

4.1   EXAMPLES OF QUESTIONNAIRES

Connor[373] has collated 180 questionnaires that have been used in research on drinking behaviour and alcoholism, of which a handful will be mentioned. The source of most of the questionnaires is the study by Jellinek[360] in America who administered a detailed questionnaire on many aspects of drinking behaviour and effects to over 2000 members of Alcoholics Anonymous. This questionnaire was *not* designed to detect alcoholism, but to study its characteristics in established cases.

A number of *psychometric tests* have been developed, with varying success, to differentiate between alcoholics and non-alcoholics. One of the earliest was the Manson Evaluation which assessed certain personality traits by questions relating to habitual feelings, reactions to persons and situations, goals and aspirations, physical states, and emotional trends.[374]

A number of different scales all derived from the Minnesota Multiphasic Personality Inventory have been tested on hospitalised alcoholics e.g. the Hampton,[375] Holmes,[376] Hoyt and Sedlacek,[377] MacAndrew,[378] Rich and Davis[379] and the Rosenberg Composite scale.[380] There is dispute as to which of these scales are best able to discriminate between alcoholics and nonalcoholics.[379,381-383] So far there has been no published report of the use of these psychometric tests to detect alcoholics in the general population.

Among the *check-lists* of questions requiring a yes/no response, there are two relevant to the present study.

The Alcadd Test consists of 60 items relating to reasons for drinking, symptoms of alcohol addiction, attitudes of self and family, drinking behaviour, and emotional attributes.[384] It was administered to 123 alcohol addicts and correctly identified 97% of them, and incorrectly classified as alcoholic only 6% of a group of nonalcoholics. This test has not been used in population surveys.

The Michigan Alcoholism Screening Test (MAST) was devised to 'provide a consistent interviewing instrument that will identify all alcoholic patients—if they respond truthfully'[385] It comprises 25 questions relating to personal opinions on drinking, opinions of family and friends, problems from drink, and symptoms of alcohol addiction. The quantity of alcohol consumed was not mentioned. The questions scored 0-5 points depending on the significance attached to them, and a total score of 5 or over was considered diagnostic of alcoholism. Only 2% false negatives were found in a study of hospitalised alcoholics, and 5% false positives in a control group.[386]

The use of the MAST to identify alcoholics in a general hospital population has been reported from California.[111] It has also been administered to a random sample of general practice patients in Israel.[177] A shortened version of only ten questions (the Brief MAST) was found to discriminate equally well between alcoholics and nonalcoholics as the longer version[387] and has been used to detect alcoholics in a tuberculous population in New Orleans.[388]

Finally, mention must be made of the detailed scales developed by Mulford and Miller in their study of the drinking practices of the adult population of the state of Iowa.[363] They employed a quantity-frequency index to measure the extent of drinking, a Definitions of Alcohol scale consisting of 18 statements defining alcohol in terms of what benefits it bestows on the individual, a Scale of Preoccupation with Alcohol consisting of 12 statements relating to the individual's concern with alcohol, and an index of Problems from drinking in the medical, social, financial and legal spheres.

It was concluded that the Preoccupation Scale was the one most predictive of each of the other three scales. These scales were used by Blaney and Radford[114] in their household survey in Eire.

4.2   SUMMARY

Research workers in community surveys are faced with considerable problems relating to the definition of the 'alcoholic', the parameters for classifying the alcoholic, and the severity and recency of such parameters. A further difficulty is that 'very considerable under-reporting seems inevitable when only personal interviews are used'.[48] Questionnaires rely on information from the informant or a relative in most household studies. It might almost be said that denial of symptoms is diagnostic of the alcoholic (*see* Chapter 10). It is unlikely that the alcoholic will exaggerate his symptoms, but it is possible that the spouse might either overestimate or underestimate the problem. Difficulties in performing reliability and validity studies will be considered later.

PART THREE

The main study

'Their wine is the venom of serpents; the cruel poison of asps; '

Deuteronomy: 32, 33.

5 Patients and Methods

'Do not keep company with drunkards
or those who are greedy for the fleshpots;
for drink and greed will end in poverty, ,
and drunken stupor goes in rags'.

Proverbs, 23: 20-21.

This Chapter describes the practice population with which the
patients 'at risk' were registered, discusses the methods used
in administering the questionnaire, and the classification of the
different categories of abnormal drinker.

5.1 THE PRACTICE POPULATION

Darbishire House Health Centre is situated 2 miles from the
city centre of Manchester, on the periphery of the University
campus. Most of the patients registered at the Health Centre
live in a densely populated urban area. It has been estimated
that about 80% of the patients live in Moss Side, Rusholme and
Longsight where considerable slum clearance and re-housing
is taking place. This area attracts individuals from other cities
who tend not to remain there for any length of time.

Consequently, although the total practice population has remained
fairly stable around the 12 000 mark over the past few years,
the proportion of patients leaving and entering the practice per
annum has been estimated as 22%. This compares with a
national average of 8% of patients leaving a practice (range 3-
18%) and 9% joining a practice in any one year.[84]

The remaining 20% of the practice live in the Fallowfield and
Didsbury area which comprises accommodation of a much
higher standard, and patients living in this area tend to be of
a higher social class.

Certain demographic data relating to the practice is available.

5.1.1 Age-Sex

Figure 1 illustrates the age-sex structures compared with that
for England and Wales.[389]

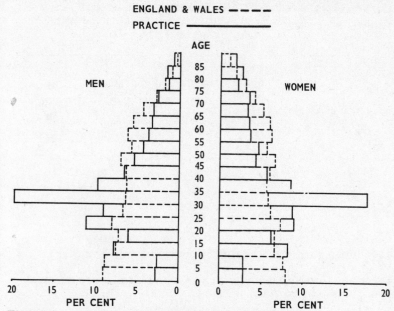

Figure 1.   Age and sex distribution of the population
(England and Wales, and the Practice)

The practice figures are based on an analysis of a 50% sample
of the patients' National Health Service records.

In the practice population, for both males and females, there is
an excess of young adults (ages 20-39), and a deficit of older
people, as compared with the national figures. As mentioned
above, there is a high turnover of patients, and the majority
of them are believed to be in the 20-39 age range.

5.1.2   Social Class

It is not possible to make a direct comparison between the
Social Class structure of the practice population and that of
England and Wales, as a different method of classification was
adopted. The classification of England and Wales covers only
the economically active segment of the population (61.2% in
1971) and comprises 5 Social Classes based on the occupation
of the individuals.

The method used for the practice population incorporated the
above, but also classified dependent relatives and students according to the occupation of the breadwinner in the household.

The percentages obtained from a random sample of 50% of the practice are compared with those for England and Wales[389] using the methods of classification described above.

Social Class	Percentage distribution in practice population	Percentage distribution in England and Wales[389]
I	5. 6%	2. 9%
II	10. 6%	14. 6%
III	42. 9%	49. 1%
IV	14. 9%	22. 3%
V	26. 0%	8. 0%
		(3% not classified)

There are fewer patients in Social Class IV, and more in Social Class V, in the practice population.

5. 1. 3   Marital Status and Ethnic Group

Data relating to the marital status and ethnic groups of the practice have been placed on a computer, but the results are not yet available. All that can be said is that there is believed to be a higher proportion of single, and divorced or separated individuals (who are living in the slum areas) than in the general population. There is also a strong impression that the practice has a higher proportion of patients of Irish and Asian extraction than the general population (*see* Table 53).

5. 2   PRINCIPLES

Patients (aged 15-65 years) who attended the surgery during the survey year and were considered 'at risk' to have a drinking problem were invited to complete a questionnaire by the general practitioner at the end of the consultation. All general practitioners working in the Health Centre during the year (1 July 1970-30 June 1971) participated in the survey.

Questionnaires were also given to those patients where there was evidence that a member of the patient's immediate family, i.e. parents, spouse, children or sibs might have a drinking problem.

When a patient had received a questionnaire, the National Health Service record was marked, and the records of the immediate family who were known to be registered at the Health Centre were also labelled; if any of them attended the surgery during the survey year, they also were invited to complete a questionnaire. It was hoped to correlate the answers from different members of the family to check the validity of the results.

The questionnaire was termed a Spare Time Activities Questionnaire (STAQ) as it contained questions not only relating to the use and effects of alcohol but also to smoking, food and television. The questionnaire was thus disguised in the hope that the informant would not realise that its purpose was to elicit information about drinking problems.

5.3   THE ALCOHOLIC AT RISK REGISTER (AARR)

The Alcoholic At Risk Register (AARR) consisted of 17 groups with a total of 64 factors which the review of literature (Chapter 3) suggested were associated with a significant incidence of alcoholism. The 17 groups were:

1.   Physical diseases associated with alcoholism

2.   Mental disorders

3.   Symptoms of alcohol addiction

4.   Occupations associated with alcoholism

5.   Work problems

6.   Accidents

7.   Criminal offences

8.   Family problems

9.   Help asked for treatment of alcoholism

10. Patient smelling of drink at the consultation

11. Certain categories of marital status

12. Residence in a hostel for destitutes

13. Known alcoholic (confirmed by a psychiatrist)

14. Family history of abnormal drinking

15. Informant's record card indicated a member of the family had already received a questionnaire

16. Informant is known to have a relative with one of the above factors

17. Any other reason, not included in the above groups, considered by the interviewer to be significant

An appointment system is employed in the Health Centre and, for the majority of the consultations, the patient's National Health Service (NHS) Record Card could be examined before the patient was seen by the doctor.

The front of all NHS envelopes should contain certain basic data relevant to the AARR, i.e. marital status, address and occupation, (AARR groups 11, 12, 4). These three groups should therefore be immediately obvious, and all relevant patients seen during the survey year should theoretically have received a questionnaire. It is evident from the results that not all interviewers were equally conscientious and in some cases a questionnaire may not have been administered because of lack of time, forgetfulness, or because for medical reasons it was considered inadvisable to ask the patients the questions.

Theoretically again, all patients presenting *at the time of consultation* with any of the 'at risk' factors should have received questionnaires. However, there was a group of conditions where knowledge of the informant's previous history was required and a complete coverage of all patients was therefore unlikely. In the case of physical diseases, symptoms of alcohol addiction, work problems, family problems, criminal offences and a family history of abnormal drinking, it was decided that a *previous history* of such conditions was an indication for a questionnaire. These categories are so important that even if they were not the presenting reason for a consultation during the survey year, a questionnaire was considered justified. Most of the NHS envelopes contained a Summary Card of previous conditions, and in other cases the general practitioner relied on his previous knowledge of the patient and his family.

It is evident that in groups such as previous criminal offences, patients who had three or more jobs in the year preceding consultation, and factors requiring knowledge of the family, the interviewer might not have all relevant information to hand at the time of the consultation. The prevalence rates for these groups cannot therefore be considered as accurate as the other groups, but nevertheless they indicate trends.

5.4   THE QUESTIONNAIRE

Every patient (aged 15-65 years) attending the surgery during the survey year (but not on home visits) who had at least one 'at risk' factor was asked if he would mind answering a few questions about his spare time activities so that the doctors could learn more about their patients to help them to provide better treatment. It was emphasised that the questionnaire was confidential, and bore no relationship to the reason why that particular patient had visited his doctor.

The interviewer was instructed to draw a line down the front page of the questionnaire of those patients who refused to answer any of the questions, and to draw a line through any specific question which the informant refused to answer. There was only one refusal to answer the questionnaire out of 554 patients who were invited to complete the questionnaire and that was from a male patient who was a paranoid schizophrenic.

The average time of completion of the whole questionnaire was 7 minutes.

A number of variations of the Spare Time Activities Questionnaire (STAQ) were developed before the final version was introduced in the survey (Appendix 1). There were two definitive versions used which differed very slightly. The first version (STAQ 1) was used for the first 22 weeks, and the modified one (STAQ 2) for the remainder of the year. The modifications, and the reasons for them, are discussed in Appendix 2. The description of the questionnaire which follows refers to STAQ 2.

The Questionnaire was divided into four sections:

I.   The Informant

    A.   Informant Profile
    B.   The Questionnaire

II.   The Family

III.   Questions to be answered by the general practitioner

IV.   Alcoholic At Risk Register

I. A   Informant Profile

The first page of the questionnaire contained basic data which was completed partly by the interviewer, and partly by the Practice Administrator, after the informant had answered the questions in Section I. B of the questionnaire.

The basic data comprised the informant's name, date of interview, date of birth, sex, marital status, social status, occupation, ethnic group, residential unit and which general practitioner had administered the questionnaire. It also included an Index Number, which was a different number for each questionnaire, and the patient's Serial Number, which was a unique number previously allocated to each patient registered in the Health Centre.

I. B   The Questionnaire

The questions relating to alcohol were embedded amongst other questions concerning overeating, smoking, unemployment and gambling. Four broad types of question were asked.

The first type were attitude questions relating to the informant and his family's opinion of his drinking, the second type asked about the quantity and frequency of drinking, the third type concerned the problems created by drink, and the fourth type related to symptoms of alcohol addiction. These groups will be considered separately.

Most of the questions were also asked about the immediate family to determine if there was a family history of drinking, and to correlate the answers with those from other members of the family, who might be interviewed on a later occasion.

'Attitude' Questions. The Informant was asked if he thought he drank too much either *now* or in the *past* (Q. 9) or whether anyone in his family thought he drank too much *now* or in the *past* (Q. 10). A similar question was asked in the family section (Q.3).

'Quantity—Frequency' Questions. The informant was asked how often he drank alcohol and was offered the following alternatives: never, only on special occasions, every few weeks, once or twice a week, more than twice a week, every day, or don't know (Q. 4). He was then asked whether he was drinking the 'same, or more, or less, than he used to' (Q. 5).

The final question of the questionnaire inquired how much money he spent on alcohol per week: whether it was none, up to £4, £4-8, or £8 or more (Q.21). If he had admitted to a change in drinking habits, he was asked how much money he used to spend on alcohol (Q. 22).

'Problems from drink' Questions. The informant was asked if he had *ever* had problems with his health (Q. 7), arguments in the family, and criminal offences (Q. 8), serious money problems (Q. 11), and job problems (Q. 12) resulting from drink. Similar questions were asked in the Family Section (Q. 1, 2, 4, 5).

The criminal offences were separated into those directly related to drink, and other offences, and whether there were one, two, or

more offences. The severity of the money problems was not
defined. The job question was phrased: 'Have you ever lost a job
or got into trouble at work, such as arriving late, or being off
work for a few days' because of drinking.

Drinking was included as one of a number of possible causes of
the problems about which questions were being asked.

'Alcohol Addiction' Questions. An attempt was made to identify
the Alcohol Addict by asking the informant if he preferred to
drink alone rather than in company (Q.14), and 'Have you ever
woken up in the morning after some drinking the night before and
found you could not remember a part of the previous evening,
even though you weren't incapable?' (Q.15). This question
ascertained whether the informant had ever experienced an alcoholic blackout ('palimpsest'). Loss of control was considered by
asking whether he had tried to cut down or stop drinking and
whether he had succeeded or not (Q.16), and whether after taking
one or two drinks, he could usually stop drinking (Q.18). The
fifth question in this group asked whether he sometimes had a
drink on waking up in the morning (Q.17).

These five questions were also asked in the family section (Q.6,
7, 8, 9, 10).

Other Questions. The Questionnaire was broadened to disguise
its purpose by also asking about eating habits (Q.1), smoking
cigarettes (Q.2), television viewing (Q.3), drug taking (Q.6) and
how much money was spent on cigarettes (Q.19) and entertainment (Q.20). These questions were not asked in the Family
Section, in the interests of restricting the length of the questionnaire.

II   Family Questionnaire

The informant was invited to answer a similar series of questions about his immediate family, i.e. parents, children, wife or
husband, cohabitant, or any other relative who had assumed the
role of a 'parent' in childhood. If, on questioning, more than one
member of the immediate family was found to have a drinking
problem, the interviewer was instructed to choose only *one*
family member about whom the questions were directed. A
spouse took preference over any other relative, but otherwise the
decision was left to the interviewer.

III   Questions to the general practitioner

This section, and the final section referring to the Alcoholic At
Risk Register were completed by the interviewer at his leisure.

Question 1 asked the name of the member of the family with a drinking problem about whom all the questions had been asked, and which general practitioner, if any, with whom he was registered. The family relationship was also noted.

Question 2 asked for the names and the family relationships of any other relatives who were found to have a drinking problem, but who were not asked the questions.

Questions 3-6 asked the interviewer for his assessment of the drinking status of the informant, and the family member if relevant, at the time of interview and in the past. The interviewer was asked to make a judgement based on his previous knowledge of the patient and his family and the manner in which the questions were answered. These questions were inserted in an attempt to overcome the possible denial of the alcoholic patient who might answer negatively to the questions in a way suggesting to the interviewer that he might be lying.

Before the survey began, the interviewers were given a group of clinical definitions to guide them in their answers.

A *social drinker* was defined as someone who did not drink excessively on a regular basis and had no problems from drinking, or symptoms of alcohol addiction.

A *heavy drinker* was defined as someone whom the interviewer considered was a habitual excessive drinker, but had no problems from drinking, or symptoms of alcohol addiction.

A *problem drinker* was defined as someone who drank to such an extent that he created problems either for himself or for his family, but had no symptoms of alcohol addiction.

An *alcoholic addict* was defined as someone who had the symptoms of alcohol addiction, e.g. shakes, blackouts, loss of control.

The remaining categories were 'not applicable' when the informant was teetotal, or no family member had a drinking problem, and 'don't know' when the interviewer could not make a judgement on the evidence available.

Question 7 asked whether the interviewer knew of any members of the informant's family who had previously received a questionnaire.

IV   Alcoholic At Risk Register

The interviewer was asked to ring the number of any factor which the informant possessed, and in the final category (number 18) the factor which the interviewer initially considered as

the reason for administering the questionnaire. If the NHS
record card indicated that the informant was one of a family
who had already received a questionnaire, then this category
(number 15) took preference over all the other factors as the
initial reason for interview.

5.5   ADMINISTRATION OF THE QUESTIONNAIRE

All but one of the 32 questions were structured, the informant
being verbally presented with a list of alternative answers. The
only open question was the one on drug taking by the informant
(Q.6) where the drugs mentioned by the informant were categorised according to the relevant medical classification.

As the time taken to administer the questionnaire was a crucial
factor in the success of the research, opportunity was provided
for the interviewer to stop the interview at selected points when
questions had been answered in the negative.

In the informant section, the first cut-off point came after only
5 of the 22 questions. If the informant stated he was teetotal and
always had been, the interviewer missed out the succeeding questions, and proceeded with the family section.

The second cut-off point occurred after the informant had been
asked about problems from drinking with his health, family, or the
police, and whether he or his family considered he was a heavy
drinker. If the informant denied any drinking problems, and stated
that both he *and* his family did not consider his drinking heavy,
this section was concluded.

In the family section, there was only one cut-off point—after the
problems from drinking with health, family and police, and the
attitude question.

5.6   MODIFICATION OF THE QUESTIONNAIRE

The main reason that a modified questionnaire (STAQ 2) was
introduced after 22 weeks was the realisation that difficulty was
being experienced in finding time to complete the questionnaires.
It was found very laborious to ask a series of 32 questions which
might all produce negative responses. The results of the first
98 questionnaires (first three weeks) were therefore analysed to
determine whether an extra cut-off point could be introduced to
reduce the number of questions that had to be asked to all patients.

The analysis suggested (*see* Appendix 2) that a cut-off point could
be inserted before the questions on money and job problems

without significantly altering the validity of the results. The small error which might result was considered justifiable in view of the likelihood that the doctors' interviewing rate would otherwise have almost certainly fallen off. The opportunity was taken to make some further slight alteration in the wording of some of the questions (*see* Appendix 2).

5.7   SCORING METHOD

A scoring system was devised on *a priori* grounds in which one or more points were allocated to the answers depending on the significance attached to them. The total score reflected the severity of the abnormal drinking. The general principles of the scoring method are as follows, the detailed instructions being described in Appendix 3.

Two points were awarded for each drinking problem, and for each positive response to an alcohol addiction question with the exception of the questions referring to drinking alone, and succeeding in cutting down in drinking, which scored one point each. More than two points could be scored in the drunken offences question depending on how many offences were committed. All other relevant questions (drinking patterns and attitudes) scored one point.

Two points were scored for each of the following items on the AARR: cirrhosis of the liver, alcoholic addiction symptoms excluding blackouts, publicans and other workers in the drink industry, help asked for by the informant, smelling of drink, living in a hostel for destitutes, and known alcoholic. One point was scored for help asked for by someone other than the informant.

5.7.1   Classification

Social Drinker or Teetotaller—Score of 0 or 1 point.
Heavy Drinker—Score of 2 or more points without criteria below.
Problem Drinker—Score of 2 or more points, which included at least one 2 point problem answer.
Alcohol Addict—6 or more points which included two Alcohol Addiction answers, (including Alcohol Addiction symptoms in AARR).
Present or Past—If informant considered he drank too much in past only, or family thought same, classified as *past* drinker. If present *and* past, classified as present. If informant thought family member drank too much in past only, classified as *past*. If present *and* past, classified as present.

5.8 INSTRUCTIONS TO STAFF

When patients were seen and identified as possessing at least
one 'at risk' factor, the general practitioner asked the patients
if they would mind answering a few questions about their spare
time activities for research purposes. The patients had been
prepared by means of two posters in the waiting room briefly
explaining the research.[390]

The completed questionnaire was placed in the out-tray. A
marker slip was inserted in the National Health Service (NHS)
record envelope to alert the staff. The office staff collected all
questionnaires and marked NHS records daily, and gave them to
the practice administrator. She completed the Patient Profile,
marked the NHS envelope with dark blue tape, and gave each
STAQ an individual Index Number. The Index Number and the
name of the patient was entered into an Index Book. The NHS
records of known immediate family members were marked with
a light blue tape.

Each day I examined the questionnaires for evidence of inadequate information, or apparent errors in completion and discussed
them with the general practitioner concerned. If any details of
the Patient Profile were missing, the general practitioner was
asked to complete it if the patient attended again. At the end of
the survey year, the patients who still had insufficient data collected were written to, enclosing a stamped addressed envelope
requesting the missing information.

During the survey year, batches of STAQs were coded at the
Manchester University Department of Community Medicine. All
coded STAQs were returned to me for checking. The individual
scores were transferred to a scoring Grid for hand sorting and
again were checked. After the final check, the results were
transferred to IBM cards for punching and sorting.

5.9 COOPERATION OF COLLEAGUES

An essential feature of the project was that the doctors partici-
pating were not full time highly trained research workers but
general practitioners with a heavy service load who had to 'fit in'
the research with their everyday work. Most of my colleagues had
some previous research experience but not in the administering
of questionnaires to patients. I therefore considered it essential
to make a special effort to obtain their cooperation and maintain
their enthusiasm.

A campaign of education began 10 weeks before the commencement of the survey. At intervals, selected items of literature [33, 135, 253] and information notes were distributed to each doctor. These handouts, which are reproduced elsewhere [390] outlined the reasons for the study and contained guidance on the methodology. Meetings were held to discuss queries.

During the survey, every week a STAQ Bulletin was circulated detailing the number of questionnaires administered by each doctor, and the number of abnormal drinkers identified. Thus the weekly progress of the study could be observed by the participants who were made aware of their own and their colleagues' contributions.

Examples of case histories were distributed in the early months to illustrate the usefulness of the questionnaire and the at risk register. From time to time, at the fortnightly staff meetings, other cases were discussed to maintain interest.

Finally, the modified questionnaire was introduced to cut down the time of completion in negative cases in the hope of improving the cooperation by all the participants.

6   Results

'New wine and old steal my people's wits'.

Hosea: 4.12

The results appertaining to the informants who were personally interviewed are presented. Most of the characteristics of the family members, and informant data relating to cigarette smoking, drug taking, gambling, and troubles with the police, are considered in detail elsewhere.[390] The methods used in the statistical analysis are described in outline in Appendix 4.

The data from STAQ 1 and STAQ 2 were combined, since an analysis of the proportions of the different categories of informant drinker identified by the two STAQs showed no significant difference (Appendix 5).

The results are tabulated under the following headings:

A.   Totals of categories of drinkers identified

B.   Basic Data—age, sex, social class, marital status, ethnic group, residential unit

C.   Alcohol consumption—frequency, change in quantity, expenditure

D.   Attitudes towards drinking—informant, family

E.   Possible symptoms of alcohol addiciion—blackouts, attempts to cut down or stop drinking, success in cutting down or stopping drinking, ability to stop drinking after one or two drinks, morning drinking, drinking alone

F.   Family history of alcoholism

G.   Problems from alcohol abuse—total points scored, number of problems, type, drinking offences

H.   The Alcoholic At Risk Register

I.   Prevalence Rates

6.1   A. TOTALS OF CATEGORIES OF DRINKER IDENTIFIED

554 STAQs were administered, of which 8 contained insufficient information for the questionnaires to be scored. The following

Table 4   Totals of categories of drinker identified (informants)

Informant	Social Drinker (SD)			Heavy Drinker (HD)			Problem Drinker (PD)			Alcohol Addict (AA)			Not classified	Grand Total
	Present	Past	Total	Present	Past	Total	Present	Past	Total	Present	Past	Total		
Male														
No.	92	2	94	29	39	68	32	33	65	39	27	66	4	297
%	98	2	100	43	57	100	49	51	100	59	41	100		
Female														
No.	199	3	202	17	10	27	9	7	16	7	1	8	4	257
%	99	1	100	63	37	100	56	44	100	88	12	100		
Total														
No.	291	5	296	46	49	95	41	40	81	46	28	74	8	554
%	98	2	100	48	52	100	51	49	100	62	38	100		

comments are based on the 546 STAQs which were classified:

546 STAQs identified 250 informant abnormal drinkers
(HD, PD, AA), i.e. 45.8% of total.
546 STAQs identified 155 informant alcoholics (PD, AA)
i.e. 28.4% of total.

Thus the questionnaire screened an 'at risk' population and found
that almost half the individuals were abnormal drinkers, and about
one quarter were alcoholics.

Table 4 illustrates the breakdown into 'present' and 'past'
categories of informant drinker. About half the heavy drinkers
and problem drinkers were classified as *past* drinkers, as were
about a third of the alcohol addicts.

Ratio of male: female for the different categories of informant
abnormal drinker (present and past combined) were:

heavy drinkers (HD)   = 2.5:1
problem drinkers (PD)   = 4.1:1
alcohol addicts (AA)   = 8.2:1
alcoholics (PD, AA)   = 5.5:1
abnormal drinkers (HD, PD, AA)   = 3.9:1

554 STAQs were administered, of which 8 contained insufficient
information for the questionnaires to be scored. The 403 STAQs
defined in Table 5 above as 'not applicable' refer to the 8 STAQs
with inadequate information and the 395 STAQs where *no* family
member scored any points.

546 STAQs identified 140 family abnormal drinkers
(HD, PD, AA) i.e. 25.6% of total.
546 STAQs identified 123 family alcoholics (PD, AA)
i.e. 22.5% of total.

Thus the questionnaire revealed that about one quarter of the
informants had an alcoholic relative in the immediate family.

Table 5 illustrates the breakdown into 'present' and 'past'
categories of family drinker. About one quarter of the heavy
drinkers and problem drinkers were classified as *past* drinkers,
and only 3% of the alcohol addicts were similarly classified.

Ratio of male: female for the different categories of family
abnormal drinker (present and past combined) were:

heavy drinkers (HD)   = 7.5:1
problem drinkers (PD)   = 17.7:1
alcohol addicts (AA)   = 21.3:1
alcoholics (PD, AA)   = 19.5:1
abnormal drinkers (HD, PD, AA)   = 16.5:1

Table 5   Totals of categories of drinker identified (family)

Sex of Relative	Social Drinker (SD)			Heavy Drinker (HD)			Problem Drinker (PD)			Alcohol Addict (AA)			Not applicable	Grand Total
	Present	Past	Total	Present	Past	Total	Present	Past	Total	Present	Past	Total		
Male														
No.	8	3	11	11	4	15	39	14	53	61	3	64	154	297
%	73	27	100	73	27	100	74	26	100	95	5	100		
Female														
No.				2		2	1	2	3	3		3	249	257
%				100		100	33	67	100	100		100		
Total														
No.	8	3	11	13	4	17	40	16	56	64	3	67	403	554
%	73	27	100	76	24	100	71	29	100	96	4	100		

The very high ratio of males : females reflects the large proportion of husbands, fathers and brothers, who were identified as being abnormal drinkers (Tables 38 and 39, pages 108 and 109).

6.2 B. BASIC DATA

Table 6. Age distribution of male informants

Age Groups	Social Drinker (SD)		Heavy Drinker (HD)		Problem Drinker (PD)		Alcohol Addict (AA)		Not classified	
	$n = 94$		$n = 68$		$n = 65$		$n = 66$		$n = 4$	
	No.	%	No.	%	No.	%	No.	%	No.	%
15-19	2	2			3	5				
20-24	12	13	7	10	13	20	4	6		
25-29	11	12	9	13	14	22	10	15		
30-34	11	12	7	10	8	12	5	8		
35-39	11	12	8	12	7	11	12	18	1	25
40-44	7	7	10	15	9	14	8	12		
45-49	9	9	7	10	4	6	16	24	1	25
50-54	10	11	9	13	6	9	5	8		
55-59	6	6	8	12	1	1	5	8		
60-65	15	16	3	5			1	1	2	50

The *mean ages* (and standard deviation) of the different categories of *male* drinker were:

Social drinker	42 years (SD 14)
Heavy drinker	41 years (SD 12)
Problem drinker	34 years (SD 11)
Alcohol addict	41 years (SD 10)

The social drinkers and heavy drinkers tended to have a flat age distribution, but there was a tendency for the problem drinkers to be concentrated in the lower age range, and the alcohol addicts in a slightly higher age range. It is noteworthy that the mean age of the problem drinkers was 7 years lower than that for the alcohol addicts and the *same* interval was found for the *females* (Table 7).

A possible explanation of these figures is that the social drinkers and heavy drinkers together represent a very similar group of individuals with a very similar mean age and age distribution. If only a minority of them later become problem drinkers, then it would be possible for the mean age of the problem drinkers to be lower than the mean age of the social or heavy drinkers. The figures further suggest that problem drinkers tend, on the average, to progress to the stage of alcohol addiction after 7 years.

Table 7.   Age distribution of female informants

Age Groups	Social Drinker (SD) $n = 202$		Heavy Drinker (HD) $n = 27$		Problem Drinker (PD) $n = 16$		Alcohol Addict (AA) $n = 8$		Not classified $n = 4$	
	No.	%	No.	%	No.	%	No.	%	No.	%
15–19	12	6	1	4	1	6				
20–24	17	8	4	15	4	25	1	12	1	25
25–29	29	14	2	7	6	38	1	13	1	25
30–34	37	18	2	7						
35–39	18	9	5	19	1	6	3	38	1	25
40–44	19	10	4	15	2	12	2	25	1	25
45–49	25	13	2	7	2	13				
50–54	16	8	2	7						
55–59	17	8	3	11			1	12		
60–65	12	6	2	8						

The *mean ages* (and standard deviation) of the different categories of *female* drinker were:

Social drinker	39 years (SD 13)
Heavy drinker	40 years (SD 13)
Problem drinker	31 years (SD 9)
Alcohol addict	38 years (SD 10)

The mean ages were very similar to those for the males, the female mean ages tending to be slightly lower. There was the same 7 year interval between the mean ages of the problem drinkers and the alcohol addicts.

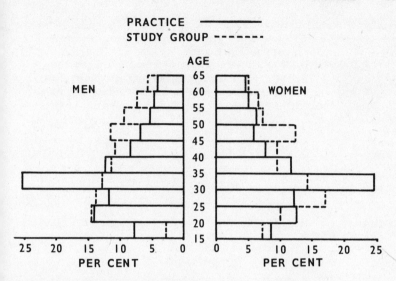

Figure 2.   Age and sex distribution of the population
(Practice, and study group)

Figure 2 illustrates the age-sex structure of the study group
compared with that of the practice population for the same age
range, 15-65 years. The study group had a lower proportion of
males and females in the 15-20 and 30-35 age groups, but a higher
proportion in the 40-65 age group. It might be expected that
there would be a few patients 'at risk' in the youngest age group,
but more 'at risk' amongst the patients in the older age groups.
The results are difficult to interpret because many of the 'at risk
factors' were particularly relevant for certain age groups, and
for either males or females.

Table 8   Social class of male informants

Social Class	Category of drinker				
	Social Drinker (SD) $n = 94$	Heavy Drinker (HD) $n = 68$	Problem Drinker (PD) $n = 65$	Alcohol Addict (AA) $n = 66$	Not classi-fied $n = 4$
	No. %	No. %	No. %	No. %	No. %
I	1　1	2　3	1　1		
II	7　7	4　6	5　8	2　3	1　25
III NM	12　13	4　6	3　5	3　4	
III M	23　25	17　25	17　26	16　24	1　25
IV	20　21	17　25	16　25	13　20	
V	14　15	19　28	15　23	21　32	
Student	8　9	1　1	4　6		
Unemployed	3　3	4　6	3　5	5　8	1　25
No information	6　6		1　1	6　9	1　25

$\chi^2 = 13.49$, d.f. $= 12$, $0.50 > p > 0.30$. Not significant at 5% level.

The results for Social Classes I and II were pooled, and the results for students, unemployed, and no information were omitted.

Table 9   Social class of female informants

Social Class	Category of drinker									
	Social Drinker (SD) $n = 202$		Heavy Drinker (HD) $n = 27$		Problem Drinker (PD) $n = 16$		Alcohol Addict (AA) $n = 8$		Not classi-fied $n = 4$	
	No.	%	No.	%	No.	%	No.	%	No.	%
I + II	9	5	2	7	1	6			1	25
III NM	30	15	4	15	3	19	1	12		
III M	7	3	1	4						
IV	47	23	8	30	1	6	1	13		
V	13	7	4	15	3	19	2	25	1	25
Student	6	3	1	4						
Housewife	69	34	5	18	4	25	3	38	1	25
Unemployed	6	3			1	6	1	12		
No information	15	7	2	7	3	19			1	25

Numbers too small for statistical tests.

There was *no* significant difference in the Social Class distribution for the different categories of *male* drinker. The numbers for the *females* were too small for statistical tests to be carried out.

The Social Classes were based on the Registrar General's classification.[391]

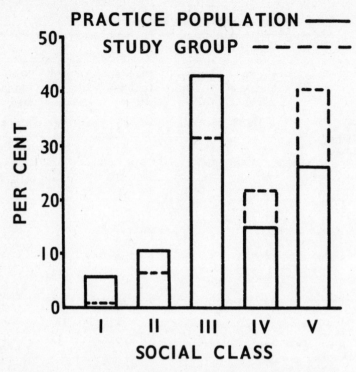

Figure 3.   Social class distribution of the population
(Practice, and study group)

Figure 3 illustrates the Social Class distribution of the study group compared with that of the practice population. In order to make a comparison meaningful, the same method for determining the Social Classes of both populations was adopted, i.e. the one used for the practice population (Chapter 5). As expected, the 'at risk' group comprised a higher proportion of the lower Social Classes (IV and V) than does the practice population.

Table 10   Marital status of male informants

Marital Status	Category of drinker									
	Social Drinker (SD) $n = 94$		Heavy Drinker (HD) $n = 68$		Problem Drinker (PD) $n = 65$		Alcohol Addict (AA) $n = 66$		Not classi- fied $n = 4$	
	No.	%	No.	%	No.	%	No.	%	No.	%
Single	32	34	28	41	28	43	19	29	1	25
Married (once)	46	49	34	50	25	39	23	35	2	50
Married (more than once)					1	2	3	4		
Divorced	5	5			4	6	9	14		
Separated	7	8	5	7	6	9	7	11	1	25
Widowed	2	2	1	2	1	1	2	3		
Single, living as married	1	1					2	3		
Other										
No information	1	1					1	1		

$\chi^2 = 10.93$, d.f. $= 6, 0.10 > p > 0.05$. Not significant at 5% level.

The test was carried out on 3 categories of marital status: single, married (once, more than once, and single living as married, pooled), and the remainder (divorced, separated, widowed). The figures for 'no information' were omitted.

Table 11   Marital status of female informants

Marital Status	Social Drinker (SD) $n = 202$		Heavy Drinker (HD) $n = 27$		Problem Drinker (PD) $n = 16$		Alcohol Addict (AA) $n = 8$		Not classi- fied $n = 4$	
	No.	%	No.	%	No.	%	No.	%	No.	%
Single	34	17	4	15	2	13	1	12	1	25
Married (once)	108	54	11	41	9	56	3	38	3	75
Married (more than once)			3	11						
Divorced	12	6	2	7	1	6				
Separated	30	15	3	11	1	6	4	50		
Widowed	11	5	2	7	1	6				
Single, living as married	3	1	1	4	2	13				
Other	3	2	1	4						
No information	1	—								

$\chi^2 = 0.38$, d.f. $= 4$, $0.99 > p > 0.98$. Not significant at 5% level.

The test was carried out on 3 categories of marital status: single, married (once, more than once, and single living as married, pooled), and the remainder (divorced, separated, widowed, other). The results for PD and AA were also pooled.

There were *no* significant differences between the different types of marital status for the different categories of *male* or *female* drinker.

Table 12 Ethnic group of male informants

Ethnic Group	Category of drinker: Social Drinker (SD) n = 94 No.	%	Heavy Drinker (HD) n = 68 No.	%	Problem Drinker (PD) n = 65 No.	%	Alcohol Addict (AA) n = 66 No.	%	Not classified n = 4 No.	%
Mainland British	61	65	45	66	49	75	40	61	2	50
Irish	16	17	19	28	11	17	22	33		
Other Whites	4	4							1	25
West Indian	2	2	1	1						
African Coloured	3	3			1	2				
Asian	5	6	1	2	2	3	1	1		
Other Coloured	3	3			1	2				
No information			2	3	1	1	3	5	1	25

$\chi^2 = 18.21$, d.f. $= 6$, $0.01 > p > 0.001$. Significant at 1% level.

The data was grouped into Mainland British and Other Whites, Irish, etc. The figures for 'no information' were omitted.

Table 13   Ethnic group of female informants

Ethnic Group	Category of drinker									
	Social Drinker (SD) $n = 202$		Heavy Drinker (HD) $n = 27$		Problem Drinker (PD) $n = 16$		Alcohol Addict (AA) $n = 8$		Not classified $n = 4$	
	No.	%	No.	%	No.	%	No.	%	No.	%
Mainland British	145	72	23	85	13	81	4	50	4	100
Irish	36	18	3	11	2	13	2	25		
Other Whites	8	4	1	4			2	25		
West Indian	3	1								
African Coloured	4	2								
Asian	2	1								
Other Coloured										
No information	4	2			1	6				

$\chi^2 = 0.92$, d.f. $= 2, 0.70 > p > 0.50$. Not significant at 5% level.

The data was grouped into Mainland British and Other Whites, Irish, etc. The figures for 'no information' were omitted.

It was a decision of the practice doctors that the ethnic group should be determined by the birthplace of the *mother* of the patients. Mainland British refers to England, Scotland and Wales. Irish refers to Northern and Southern Ireland.

There were significantly more Irish represented amongst the *male* alcohol addicts than in the other categories of drinker. *No* significant differences were found for the *females*.

Table 14   Residential unit of male informants

Residential unit	Category of drinker									
	Social Drinker (SD) $n = 94$		Heavy Drinker (HD) $n = 68$		Problem Drinker (PD) $n = 65$		Alcohol Addict (AA) $n = 66$		Not classi- fied $n = 4$	
	No.	%	No.	%	No.	%	No.	%	No.	%
Living:										
— with spouse	45	48	34	50	25	38	24	36	2	50
— with other relatives	13	14	5	7	11	17	4	6		
— alone	16	17	13	19	12	19	18	27	1	25
— in digs	9	10	13	19	6	9	4	6	1	25
— in hostel	6	6	2	3	4	6	8	12		
Other	4	4			4	6	7	11		
No information	1	1	1	2	3	5	1	2		

$\chi^2 = 6.17$, d.f. $= 6, 0.50 > p > 0.30$. Not significant at 5% level.

The data was grouped into: living with spouse, with other relatives, living alone, etc.

Table 15   Residential unit of female informants

Residential unit	Category of drinker									
	Social Drinker (SD) $n = 202$		Heavy Drinker (HD) $n = 27$		Problem Drinker (PD) $n = 16$		Alcohol Addict (AA) $n = 8$		Not classi- fied $n = 4$	
	No.	%	No.	%	No.	%	No.	%	No.	%
Living:										
— with spouse	109	54	16	59	7	44	2	25	2	50
— with other relatives	39	19	8	30	3	19	3	38		
— alone	22	11	1	4	2	12			1	25
— in digs	7	4			1	6	3	37	1	25
— in hostel	1	1								
Other	23	11	2	7	3	19				
No information	1	—								

$\chi^2 = 1.50$, d.f. $= 1, 0.30 > p > 0.20$. Not significant at 5% level.

The data was grouped into: living with spouse or with other relatives, etc. The results for the SD and HD were pooled, and for PD and AA were pooled.

There were *no* significant differences between the different types of residential unit for the different categories of *male* or *female* drinker.

6.3   C. ALCOHOL CONSUMPTION

Table 16   Frequency of drinking of male informants

	Category of drinker									
	Social Drinker (SD)		Heavy Drinker (HD)		Problem Drinker (PD)		Alcohol Addict (AA)		Not classi- fied	
Frequency of Drinking	$n = 94$		$n = 68$		$n = 65$		$n = 66$		$n = 4$	
	No.	%	No.	%	No.	%	No.	%	No.	%
Every day	5	5	22	32	20	31	29	44	1	25
More than twice a week	14	15	18	26	14	21	14	21		
Once or twice a week	35	37	18	27	20	31	9	14	1	25
Every few weeks	9	10	4	6			3	5		
Only on special occasions	15	16	1	2	5	8	2	3	1	25
Never	16	17	5	7	6	9	8	12	1	25
No information							1	1		

Kruskal Wallis' test: $\chi^2 = 43.36$, d.f. $= 3$, $p < 0.001$. Significant at 0.1% level.

Results for 'no information' omitted.

Table 17   Frequency of drinking of female informants

Frequency of Drinking	Category of drinker									
	Social Drinker (SD) $n = 202$		Heavy Drinker (HD) $n = 27$		Problem Drinker (PD) $n = 16$		Alcohol Addict (AA) $n = 8$		Not classi-fied $n = 4$	
	No.	%	No.	%	No.	%	No.	%	No.	%
Every day	4	2	8	30			7	88		
More than twice a week	9	4			4	25	1	12		
Once or twice a week	38	19	10	37	8	50				
Every few weeks	21	10	2	7	1	6				
Only on special occasions	80	40	7	26	2	13			4	100
Never	50	25			1	6				
No information										

Kruskal Wallis' test: $\chi^2 = 56.74$, d.f. $= 3, p < 0.001$. Significant at 0.1% level.

Results for 'no information' omitted.

There were significant differences, for both *males* and *females*, in the distribution of the frequency of drinking admitted; the frequency increased with increasing severity of the category of drinker. For example, 5% of male social drinkers (2% of females) admitted to drinking every day, compared with 44% of male alcohol addicts (88% of females).

Table 18 Change in quantity of drinking of male informants

	Category of drinker				
	Social Drinker (SD)	Heavy Drinker (HD)	Problem Drinker (PD)	Alcohol Addict (AA)	Not classified
Changes in Quantity of Drinking	$n = 94$	$n = 68$	$n = 65$	$n = 66$	$n = 4$
	No. %	No. %	No. %	No. %	No. %
Drinks more now	34 36	12 18	18 28	10 15	2 50
Drinks less now	16 17	30 44	28 43	33 50	
No change	44 47	26 38	19 29	23 35	2 50

$\chi^2 = 27.13$, d.f. $= 6, p < 0.001$. Significant at 0.1% level.

Table 19 Change in quantity of drinking of female informants

	Category of drinker				
	Social Drinker (SD)	Heavy Drinker (HD)	Problem Drinker (PD)	Alcohol Addict (AA)	Not classified
Changes in Quantity of Drinking	$n = 202$	$n = 27$	$n = 16$	$n = 8$	$n = 4$
	No. %	No. %	No. %	No. %	No. %
Drinks more now	76 38	6 22	7 44	4 50	3 75
Drinks less now	18 9	10 37	2 12	2 25	
No change	108 53	11 41	7 44	2 25	1 25

$\chi^2 = 1.90$, d.f. $= 2, 0.50 > p > 0.30$. Not significant at 5% level.

The results for SD and HD, and for PD and AA were pooled.

There was a significant difference in the proportions of the different categories of male drinker who admitted to a change in their quantity of drinking. 47% of the social drinkers denied any change, compared with 29% of the problem drinkers and 35% of the alcohol addicts. No significant differences were found for the females.

Table 20   Maximum weekly expenditure on alcohol now or in the past of male informants

Maximum weekly expenditure on alcohol now/past	Category of drinker				
	Social Drinker (SD) $n = 94$	Heavy Drinker (HD) $n = 68$	Problem Drinker (PD) $n = 65$	Alcohol Addict (AA) $n = 66$	Not classi-fied $n = 4$
	No. %	No. %	No. %	No. %	No. %
None					
Up to £4		22 32	18 28	4 6	
£4-8		27 40	28 43	27 41	
£8 or more		17 25	15 23	35 53	
Not applicable	94 100	2 3	4 6		4 100

$\chi^2 = 22.61$, d.f. $= 4, p < 0.001$. Significant at 0.1% level.

Results for SD omitted because of the large proportion of social drinkers who reached a cut-off point before this question was asked. Results for 'not applicable' omitted.

Table 21 Maximum weekly expenditure on alcohol now or in the past of female informants

Maximum weekly expenditure on alcohol now/past	Category of drinker									
	Social Drinker (SD) $n = 202$		Heavy Drinker (HD) $n = 27$		Problem Drinker (PD) $n = 16$		Alcohol Addict (AA) $n = 8$		Not classi- fied $n = 4$	
	No.	%	No.	%	No.	%	No.	%	No.	%
None										
Up to £4			13	48	9	56	3	38		
£4-8			7	26	1	6	3	37		
£8 or more			2	7	2	13	2	25		
Not applicable	202	100	5	19	4	25			4	100

χ^2 (Yates correction applied) $= 0$, d.f. $= 1$, $p = 1$. Not significant at 5% level.

Results for SD omitted because of the large proportion of social drinkers who reached a cut-off point before this question was asked. Results for PD and AA pooled, and results for £4-8 have been pooled with £8 or more. Results for 'not applicable' omitted.

Significant differences were found for the maximum weekly expenditure on alcohol (now or in the past) admitted by the different categories of *male* drinker. For example, 53% of the male alcohol addicts spent £8 or more per week, compared with 25% of the heavy drinkers. No significant differences were found for the females.

6.4   D. ATTITUDES TOWARDS DRINKING

Table 22   Male informant's opinion that he is drinking too much either now or in the past

Informant thinks he drinks too much now or in the past	Category of drinker				
	Social Drinker (SD) $n = 94$	Heavy Drinker (HD) $n = 68$	Problem Drinker (PD) $n = 65$	Alcohol Addict (AA) $n = 66$	Not classi-fied $n = 4$
	No. %	No. %	No. %	No. %	No. %
Yes		42 62	43 66	57 86	
No	83 88	26 38	21 32	9 14	1 25
Not applicable	11 12				
No information			1 2		3 75

$\chi^2 = 140.05$, d.f. $= 3, p < 0.001$. Significant at 0.1% level.

Results for 'no' and 'not applicable' pooled, as the latter refers to teetotal patients. Results for 'no information' omitted.

Table 23   Female informant's opinion that she is drinking too much either now or in the past

Informant thinks she drinks too much now or in the past	Category of drinker				
	Social Drinker (SD) $n = 202$	Heavy Drinker (HD) $n = 27$	Problem Drinker (PD) $n = 16$	Alcohol Addict (AA) $n = 8$	Not classi-fied $n = 4$
	No. %	No. %	No. %	No. %	No. %
Yes		11 41	8 50	7 88	1 25
No	166 82	16 59	8 50	1 12	3 75
Not applicable	36 18				
No information					

Exact test: $p < 0.000\,000\,001$. Significant at 0.1% level.

Results for 'no' and 'not applicable' pooled, as the latter refers to teetotal patients. Results for SD and HD pooled, and for PD and AA pooled. Results for 'no information' omitted.

There were significant differences for both *males* and *females* in the proportions of the different categories of drinker who think that they are drinking too much either now *or* in the past. Of the alcohol addicts 86% of the males and 88% of the females admitted to drinking too much, compared with 62% of the male heavy drinkers and 41% of the females, and none of the social drinkers (male or female).

Table 24 Opinion of family that male informant is drinking too much either now or in the past

Family opinion -whether informant drinks or drank too much now or in past	Category of drinker									
	Social Drinker (SD) $n = 94$		Heavy Drinker (HD) $n = 68$		Problem Drinker (PD) $n = 65$		Alcohol Addict (AA) $n = 66$		Not classified $n = 4$	
	No.	%	No.	%	No.	%	No.	%	No.	%
Yes	1	1	27	40	43	66	45	68	1	25
No	81	86	40	59	19	29	16	24		
Not applicable	11	12								
No information	1	1	1	1	3	5	5	8	3	75

$\chi^2 = 110.51$, d.f. $= 3, p < 0.001$. Significant at 0.1% level.

Results pooled as in Table 22.

Table 25   Opinion of family that female informant is drinking too much either now or in the past

Family opinion — whether informant drinks or drank too much now or in past	Category of drinker									
	Social Drinker (SD) $n = 202$		Heavy Drinker (HD) $n = 27$		Problem Drinker (PD) $n = 16$		Alcohol Addict (AA) $n = 8$		Not classi- fied $n = 4$	
	No.	%	No.	%	No.	%	No.	%	No.	%
Yes	1		6	22	8	50	1	13	2	50
No	163	81	21	78	8	50	6	75	2	50
Not applicable	37	18								
No information	1	1					1	12		

Exact test: $p < 0.000 006$. Significant at 0.1% level.

Results pooled as in Table 23.

There were significant differences for both *males* and *females* in the proportions of the different categories of drinker who admitted that someone in their families thinks that they are or were drinking too much, either now *or* in the past. 68% of the male alcohol addicts (37.5% of the female problem drinkers and alcohol addicts combined) admitted to this symptom, compared to 40% of the male heavy drinkers (3% of the female social drinkers and heavy drinkers combined), and only 1% of the male social drinkers.

6.5   E. POSSIBLE SYMPTOMS OF ALCOHOL ADDICTION

Table 26   Experience of blackouts by male informants

	Category of drinker								
	Social Drinker (SD) $n = 94$		Heavy Drinker (HD) $n = 68$		Problem Drinker (PD) $n = 65$		Alcohol Addicts (AA) $n = 66$		Not classi-fied $n = 4$
Blackouts	No.	%	No.	%	No.	%	No.	%	No.	%
Yes			20	29	24	37	62	94		
No	43	46	46	68	37	57	4	6		
Not applicable	51	54								
No information			2	3	4	6			4	100

$\chi^2 = 62.97$, d.f. $= 2, p < 0.001$. Significant at 0.1% level.

The results for SD were omitted because, by definition, they cannot score 2 points, which this question entails. Results for 'no information' omitted.

Table 27   Experience of blackouts by female informants

	Category of drinker								
	Social Drinker (SD) $n = 202$		Heavy Drinker (HD) $n = 27$		Problem Drinker (PD) $n = 16$		Alcohol Addict (AA) $n = 8$		Not classi-fied $n = 4$
Blackouts	No.	%	No.	%	No.	%	No.	%	No.	%
Yes			4	15	7	44	7	88		
No	92	46	22	81	8	50	1	12		
Not applicable	110	54								
No information			1	4	1	6			4	100

$\chi^2 = 14.93$, d.f. $= 2, p < 0.001$. Significant at 0.1% level.

The results for SD were omitted because, by definition, they cannot score 2 points, which this question entails. Results for 'no information' omitted.

Blackouts are an important symptom of alcohol addiction although they may occur infrequently after a heavy drinking bout in non-addicted drinkers. Significant differences for both *males* and *females* were found in the proportion of alcohol addicts admitting to having had at least one blackout compared to the other categories of abnormal drinker. 94% of the male, and 88% of the female alcohol addicts admitted to blackouts, compared to 29% of the male, and 15% of the female heavy drinkers.

Table 28   Attempt of male informants to cut down or stop drinking

Tried to cut down or stop drinking	Category of drinker									
	Social Drinker (SD) $n = 94$		Heavy Drinker (HD) $n = 68$		Problem Drinker (PD) $n = 65$		Alcohol Addict (AA) $n = 66$		Not classi-fied $n = 4$	
	No.	%	No.	%	No.	%	No.	%	No.	%
Yes	6	6	43	63	44	68	52	79		
No	38	41	23	34	17	26	14	21		
Not applicable	50	53								
No information			2	3	4	6			4	100

$\chi^2 = 3.11$, d.f. $= 2, 0.30 > p > 0.20$. Not significant at 5% level.

Results for SD omitted because of the large proportion of them who reached a cut-off point before this question was asked. Results for 'no information' omitted.

Table 29 Attempt of female informants to cut down or stop drinking

Tried to cut down or stop drinking	Category of drinker				
	Social Drinker (SD) $n = 202$	Heavy Drinker (HD) $n = 27$	Problem Drinker (PD) $n = 16$	Alcohol Addict (AA) $n = 8$	Not classi-fied $n = 4$
	No. %	No. %	No. %	No. %	No. %
Yes	6 3	11 41	6 38	5 63	
No	86 43	15 55	9 56	3 37	
Not applicable	110 54				
No information		1 4	1 6		4 100

$\chi^2 = 0.16$, d.f. $= 1, 0.70 > p > 0.50$. Not significant at 5% level.

Results for SD omitted because of the large proportion of them who reached a cut-off point before this question was asked. Results for PD and AA pooled, and those for 'no information' omitted.

There were *no* significant differences, for either males or females, in the proportions of the different categories of abnormal drinker who admitted to having tried to cut down or stop drinking.

Table 30   Success of male informants in cutting down or
              stopping drinking

Success in cutting down or stopping drinking	Category of drinker				
	Social Drinker (SD) $n = 6$	Heavy Drinker (HD) $n = 43$	Problem Drinker (PD) $n = 44$	Alcohol Addict (AA) $n = 52$	Not classi- fied $n = 4$
	No. %	No. %	No. %	No. %	No. %
Succeeded	6 100	41 96	42 95	31 60	
Did not succeed		1 2	2 5	21 40	
No information		1 2			4 100

$\chi^2 = 33.04$, d.f. $= 2, p < 0.0005$. Significant at 0.1% level.

Results for no information omitted. Results for SD and HD pooled.

Tables 30 and 31 relate to those informants who admitted that
they had tried to cut down or stop drinking. The figures of those
informants who did not try to cut down or stop drinking were
enumerated in Tables 28 and 29.

Table 31   Success of female informants in cutting down or
              stopping drinking

Success in cutting down or stopping drinking	Category of drinker				
	Social Drinker (SD) $n = 6$	Heavy Drinker (HD) $n = 11$	Problem Drinker (PD) $n = 6$	Alcohol Addict (AA) $n = 5$	Not classi- fied $n = 4$
	No. %	No. %	No. %	No. %	No. %
Succeeded	6 100	8 73	6 100	2 40	
Did not succeed		3 27		3 60	
No information					4 100

Exact test: $p = 0.88$. Not significant at 5% level.

Results for no information omitted. Results for SD and HD, and
for PD and AA pooled.

Significant differences were found for the *males*, in the proportions of the different categories of drinker who had tried *and*
succeeded in cutting down or stopping drinking. 60% of the male
alcohol addicts had tried *and* succeeded, compared with 100%
of the male social drinkers. No significant differences were
found for the females.

Table 32   Stopping drinking by male informants after one or two
drinks

Stop drinking after one or two drinks	Category of drinker									
	Social Drinker (SD) $n = 94$		Heavy Drinker (HD) $n = 68$		Problem Drinker (PD) $n = 65$		Alcohol Addict (AA) $n = 66$		Not classi-fied $n = 4$	
	No.	%	No.	%	No.	%	No.	%	No.	%
No			4	6	3	5	35	53		
Yes	43	46	62	91	56	86	31	47		
Not applicable	51	54								
No information			2	3	6	9			4	100

$\chi^2 = 56.74$, d.f. $= 2, p < 0.001$. Significant at 0.1% level.

The results for SD were omitted because, by definition, they
cannot score 2 points which this question entails. Results for
'no information' omitted.

Table 33   Stopping drinking by female informants after one or
two drinks

Stop drinking after one or two drinks	Category of drinker								
	Social Drinker (SD) $n = 202$		Heavy Drinker (HD) $n = 27$		Problem Drinker (PD) $n = 16$		Alcohol Addict (AA) $n = 8$		Not classi- fied $n = 4$
	No.	%	No.	%	No.	%	No.	%	No.	%
No			4	15			4	50		
Yes	90	45	22	81	14	88	4	50		
Not applicable	112	55								
No information			1	4	2	12			4	100

$\chi^2 = 0.07$, d.f. $= 1, 0.80 > p > 0.70$. Not significant at 5% level.

The results for SD were omitted because by definition, they
cannot score 2 points which this question entails. Results for
'no information' were omitted, and those for PD and AA pooled.

53% of the male alcohol addicts admitted that they cannot control
their drinking, which was a significantly higher proportion than
that found in the other categories of abnormal drinker. No
significant differences were found for the females.

Table 34   Morning drinking by male informants

Drinks alcohol in the morning	Category of drinker				
	Social Drinker (SD)	Heavy Drinker (HD)	Problem Drinker (PD)	Alcohol Addict (AA)	Not classi-fied
	$n = 94$	$n = 68$	$n = 65$	$n = 66$	$n = 4$
	No. %	No. %	No. %	No. %	No. %
Yes		3 4	1 2	23 35	
No	44 47	63 93	60 92	43 65	
Not applicable	50 53				
No information		2 3	4 6		4 100

$\chi^2 = 36.04$, d.f. $= 2$, $p < 0.001$. Significant at 0.1% level.

The results for SD were omitted because, by definition, they cannot score 2 points which this question entails. Results for 'no information' omitted.

Table 35   Morning drinking by female informants

Drinks alcohol in the morning	Category of drinker				
	Social Drinker (SD)	Heavy Drinker (HD)	Problem Drinker (PD)	Alcohol Addict (AA)	Not classi-fied
	$n = 202$	$n = 27$	$n = 16$	$n = 8$	$n = 4$
	No. %	No. %	No. %	No. %	No. %
Yes		2 7		4 50	
No	92 46	24 89	15 94	4 50	
Not applicable	110 54				
No information		1 4	1 6		4 100

Exact test: $p = 0.55$. Not significant at 5% level.

The results for SD were omitted because, by definition, they cannot score 2 points which this question entails. Results for PD and AA pooled, and 'no information' omitted.

35% of the *male* alcohol addicts admitted to morning drinking which was significantly greater than the proportions found in the other categories of abnormal drinker. No significant difference was found for the females.

Table 36   Preference by male informants for drinking alone

Prefers to drink	Social Drinker (SD) n = 94 No.	%	Heavy Drinker (HD) n = 68 No.	%	Problem Drinker (PD) n = 65 No.	%	Alcohol Addict (AA) n = 66 No.	%	Not classi-fied n = 4 No.	%
Alone			6	9	2	3	22	33		
Alone or in company	3	3	10	15	11	17	11	17		
In company	38	41	47	69	45	69	30	45		
Not applicable	53	56								
No information			5	7	7	11	3	5	4	100

$\chi^2 = 26.10$, d.f. $= 4$, $p < 0.001$. Significant at 0.1% level.

Results for SD omitted as in Table 28. Results for 'no information' omitted.

Table 37   Preference by female informants for drinking alone

Prefers to drink	Category of drinker									
	Social Drinker (SD) $n = 202$		Heavy Drinker (HD) $n = 27$		Problem Drinker (PD) $n = 16$		Alcohol Addict (AA) $n = 8$		Not classified $n = 4$	
	No.	%	No.	%	No.	%	No.	%	No.	%
Alone	1	1	2	7			4	50		
Alone or in company	6	3	5	19	3	19	2	25		
In company	83	41	19	70	12	75	2	25		
Not applicable	112	55								
No information			1	4	1	6			4	100

Exact test: $p = 0.55$. Not significant at 5% level.

Results for SD omitted and for PD and AA pooled as in Table 29. Results for 'alone or in company' pooled with 'in company'. Results for 'no information' omitted.

33% of the *male* alcohol addicts admitted to drinking alone, which was significantly greater than the proportions found in the other categories of abnormal drinker. No significant differences were found for the *female* abnormal drinkers.

6.6   F. FAMILY HISTORY OF ALCOHOLISM

Table 38   Family history of alcoholism admitted by male informants

Family alcoholics	Male Informant—category of drinker			
	Social Drinker (SD) $n = 94$	Heavy Drinker (HD) $n = 68$	Problem Drinker (PD) $n = 65$	Alcohol Addict (AA) $n = 66$
Family—category of drinker →	PD+AA $n = 6$	PD+AA $n = 5$	PD+AA $n = 12$	PD+AA $n = 11$
	No. %	No. %	No. %	No. %
Father	1 17	2 40	6 50	4 36
Mother				
Wife	1 16			1 9
Husband				
Brother	3 50	2 40	5 42	4 37
Sister				1 9
Son				
Daughter		1 20		
Other relative	1 17		1 8	
Cohabitant				
No information				1 9

$\chi^2 = 8.34$, d.f. $= 3$, $0.05 > p > 0.02$. Significant at 5% level.
Results for all relatives pooled, and for no information omitted.

Table 38 illustrates the family history of alcoholics (PD + AA) elicited by questioning the *male* informants. There was a significant difference in the proportions of the different categories of male drinker who admitted to having an alcoholic relative. 19% of the alcoholic informants (PD + AA) had an alcoholic relative (PD + AA) compared with 6% of the social drinker informants. 83% of the alcoholic relatives of alcoholic informants were fathers or brothers, and only one alcoholic informant admitted to having an alcoholic wife.

Table 39   Family history of alcoholism admitted by female informants

Family alcoholics	Female Informant—category of drinker							
	Social Drinker (SD) $n = 202$		Heavy Drinker (HD) $n = 27$		Problem Drinker (PD) $n = 16$		Alcohol Addict (AA) $n = 8$	
Family—category of drinker →	PD+AA $n = 62$		PD+AA $n = 13$		PD+AA $n = 11$		PD+AA $n = 2$	
	No.	%	No.	%	No.	%	No.	%
Father	9	15	1	8	2	18		
Mother	2	3						
Wife								
Husband	38	61	7	54	7	64	1	50
Brother	8	13	2	15	1	9		
Sister								
Son	1	2	1	8			1	50
Daughter								
Other relative					1	9		
Cohabitant	4	6	2	15				

$\chi^2 = 11.98$, d.f. = 3, $0.01 > p > 0.001$. Significant at 1% level. Results for all relatives pooled.

Table 39 illustrates the family history of alcoholics (PD + AA) elicited by questioning the *female* informants. There was a significant difference in the proportions of the different categories of female drinker who admitted to having an alcoholic relative. 54% of the alcoholic informants (PD + AA) had an alcoholic relative (PD + AA) compared with 31% of the social drinker informants. 61% of the alcoholic relatives of alcoholic informants were husbands, and 68% of the alcoholic relatives of the social drinker informants were husbands or cohabitants.

6.7   G. PROBLEMS FROM ALCOHOL ABUSE

Table 40   Total points scored by male informants

	Category of drinker				
Total points scored	Social Drinker (SD) n = 94	Heavy Drinker (HD) n = 68	Problem Drinker (PD) n = 65	Alcohol Addict (AA) n = 66	Not classi-fied n = 4
	No. %	No. %	No. %	No. %	No. %
None	56 60				
1	38 40				
2		16 24	1 1		
3—5		37 54	18 28		1 25
6—9		15 22	28 43	15 23	
10—19			18 28	33 50	
20—34				18 27	
No information					3 75
Mean score	0.4	4.1	7.8	15.7	

Table 41   Total points scored by female informants

Total points scored	Social Drinker (SD) $n = 202$		Heavy Drinker (HD) $n = 27$		Problem Drinker (PD) $n = 16$		Alcohol Addict (AA) $n = 8$		Not classi- fied $n = 4$	
	No.	%	No.	%	No.	%	No.	%	No.	%
None	149	74							1	25
1	53	26								
2			11	41	1	6				
3—5			14	52	6	38				
6—9			2	7	5	31	1	12		
10—19					4	25	5	63		
20—28							2	25		
No information									3	75
Mean score	0.3		3.2		7.1		14.6			

Tables 40 and 41 detail the distribution of the total points scored by the different categories of male and female drinker. It should be noted that, by definition, a social drinker can score 0 or 1 point, the minimum score for a heavy drinker is 2 points, for a problem drinker is 2 points and for an alcohol addict is 6 points.

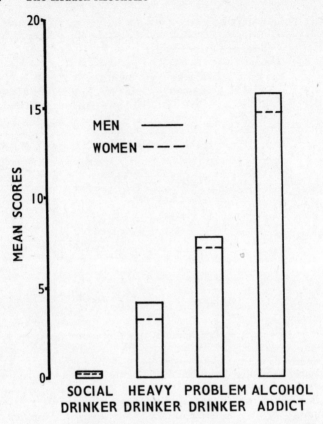

Figure 4.   Mean point scores for different categories
            of informant drinker.

Figure 4. Illustrates the disparity between the scores of the
different categories of both male and female drinker.

Table 42 Number of problems admitted by male and female informant problem drinkers and alcohol addicts

| Number of Problems | MALES n=131 | | | | FEMALES n=24 | | | |
| | Problem Drinker (PD) n = 65 | | Alcohol Addict (AA) n = 66 | | Problem Drinker (PD) n = 16 | | Alcohol Addict (AA) n = 8 | |
	No.	%	No.	%	No.	%	No.	%
None			15	23			2	25
One	48	74	10	15	5	31	3	38
Two	10	15	9	13	9	57		
Three	3	5	11	17	1	6	1	12
Four	2	3	10	15			1	13
Five	2	3	11	17	1	6	1	12

The results were analysed by the Mann Whitney U-test to determine whether there was any difference between the informant problem drinkers and alcohol addicts in the number of problems admitted due to drink. All the results refer to the standard normal distribution.

Males

Result = 3.653, $p = 0.0003$.
Significant at 0.1% level.

As expected, the alcohol addicts tended to admit to more problems than the problem drinkers.

Females

Result = 0.29, $p = 0.75$. Not significant at 5% level

No significant differences were found for the females, which was probably due to the female problem drinkers admitting to more problems than might be expected (*see* below).

Comparison of Males and Females

The male and female results for the number of problems admitted by the problem drinkers and alcohol addicts were compared using the Mann Whitney U-test.

(a) Problem drinkers: Result = 2.378, p = 0.0017. Significant at 0.01% level.

The test indicated that the female problem drinkers tended to admit to more problems than the male problem drinkers which was an unexpected finding.

(b) Alcohol addicts: Result = 1.628, p = 0.10. Not significant at 5% level.

There was *no* significant difference between the number of problems admitted by the male and female alcohol addicts.

Table 43   Type of problems admitted by male and female informant problem drinkers and alcohol addicts

Type of Problem	MALES n=131				FEMALES n=24			
	Problem Drinker (PD) n = 65		Alcohol Addict (AA) n = 66		Problem Drinker (PD) n = 16		Alcohol Addict (AA) n = 8	
	No. (a)	$\%\frac{(a)}{65}$	No. (b)	$\%\frac{(b)}{66}$	No. (c)	$\%\frac{(c)}{16}$	No (d)	$\%\frac{(d)}{8}$
Health	29	45	37	56	6	38	4	50
Arguments	31	48	36	55	14	88	5	63
Drunken Offences	15	23	28	42	3	19	2	25
Money	12	18	27	41	6	38	2	25
Work	8	12	28	42	2	13	2	25

Statistical tests were carried out to determine if there were any significant differences between the proportions of informant problem drinkers and alcohol addicts who admitted to each of the 5 types of problem, for males and females.

Males

(a) Health

χ^2 = 1.72, d.f. = 1, 0.20 > p > 0.10. Not significant at 5% level.

(b) Arguments

$\chi^2 = 0.62$, d.f. $= 1$, $0.50 > p > 0.30$. Not significant at 5% level.

(c) Drunken offences

$\chi^2 = 5.56$, d.f. $= 1$, $0.02 > p > 0.01$. Significant at 2% level.

(d) Money

$\chi^2 = 7.89$, d.f. $= 1$, $0.01 > p > 0.001$. Significant at 1% level.

(e) Work

$\chi^2 = 14.90$, d.f. $= 1$, $p < 0.001$. Significant at 0.1% level.

The results indicate that there were no significant differences for *males*, in the proportions of problem drinkers and alcohol addicts who admitted to health problems or arguments in the family about their drinking. However, for the more serious problems of drunken offences, and money and work problems due to drinking, significant differences were found.

Females

(a) Health

χ^2 (Yates correction applied) $= 0.021$, d.f. $= 1$,
$0.90 > p > 0.80$. Not significant at 5% level.

(b) Arguments

Exact test: $p = 0.37$. Not significant at 5% level.

(c) Drunken offences

χ^2 (Yates correction applied) $= 0$, d.f. $= 1$, $p = 1$. Not significant at 5% level.

(d) Money

χ^2 (Yates correction applied) $= 0.023$, d.f. $= 1$,
$0.90 > p > 0.80$. Not significant at 5% level.

(e) Work

χ^2 (Yates correction applied) $= 0.038$, d.f. $= 1$,
$0.90 > p > 0.80$. Not significant at 5% level.

The results indicate that for *females, no* significant differences were observed between the proportion of problem drinkers and alcohol addicts who admitted to any of the five problems.

Table 44   Number of offences committed under the influence of drink by male informants

Number of offences committed under the influence of drink	Category of Drinker									
	Social Drinker (SD) $n = 94$		Heavy Drinker (HD) $n = 68$		Problem Drinker (PD) $n = 65$		Alcohol Addict (AA) $n = 66$		Not classified	
	No.	%	No.	%	No.	%	No.	%	No.	%
None	83	88	68	100	50	77	37	56	1	25
One					6	9	8	12		
Two					2	3	5	8		
Three or more					7	11	16	24		
Not applicable	11	12							3	75

$\chi^2 = 70.90$, d.f. $= 3, p < 0.0005$. Significant at 0.1% level.

Results for SD and HD, and not applicable omitted. Results for 'one' and 'two' offences pooled.

Table 45   Number of offences committed under the influence of
drink by female informants

| Number of offences committed under the influence of drink | Category of Drinker | | | | |
| | Social Drinker (SD) $n = 202$ | Heavy Drinker (HD) $n = 27$ | Problem Drinker (PD) $n = 16$ | Alcohol Addict (AA) $n = 8$ | Not classified $n = 4$ |
	No. %	No. %	No. %	No. %	No. %
None	165 82	27 100	13 82	6 75	4 100
One			1 6		
Two			1 6		
Three or more			1 6	2 25	
Not applicable	37 18				

Exact test: $p = 0.000023$. Significant at 0.1% level.

Results for SD and HD, and not applicable omitted. Results for 'one' and 'two' offences pooled.

Significant differences were found for both males and females, in the proportions of problem drinkers and alcohol addicts who admitted to offences committed while under the influence of drink. 24% of male alcohol addicts and 25% of the female admitted to at least 3 offences, compared with 11% of male problem drinkers (6% of the females).

Table 46   Alcoholic At Risk Register

		Social Drinker (SD) $n=296$		(c)	%
		M	F	All	$\dfrac{(c)}{296}$
		(1)	(2)	(3)	(4)
1.	Physical diseases	28	10	38	12.8
2.	Mental diseases	36	120	156	52.7
3.	Alcoholic symptoms	1		1	0.3
4.	Occupations	6	12	18	6.1
5.	Work problems	2	4	6	2.0
6.	Accidents	7		7	2.4
7.	Criminal offences	2	1	3	1.0
8.	Family problems	3	26	29	9.8
9.	Help asked for treatment of alcoholism		3	3	1.0
10.	Patient smelling of drink	1	2	3	1.0
11.	Marital status	22	45	67	22.6
12.	Living in hostel for destitutes	4		4	1.4
13.	Known alcoholic				
14.	Family history of abnormal drinking	1	5	6	2.0
15.	Interviewed because another member of family had previously received STAQ	9	30	39	13.2
16.	Other reason	3	5	8	2.7
	Total	125	263	388	131.1
	Number of patients	94	79	296	
	Average 'at risk' factors per patient	1.33	3.33	1.31	

Columns 4, 8, 12 and 15, refer to the proportions of social drinkers, heavy drinkers, problem drinkers and alcohol addicts combined, and all drinkers who were identified as possessing a particular AARR category.

Categories of AARR items possessed by male and female informant drinkers

Heavy Drinker (HD) $n = 95$				Problem Drinker and Alcohol Addict (PD + AA) $n = 155$				All $n = 546$		
		(d)	%			(a)	%	(b)	%	%
M	F	All	$\frac{(d)}{95}$	M	F	All	$\frac{(a)}{155}$		$\frac{(a)}{(b)}$	$\frac{(b)}{546}$
(5)	(6)	(7)	(8)	(9)	(10)	(11)	(12)	(13)	(14)	(15)
34	2	36	37.9	53	4	57	36.8	131	43.5	24.0
20	19	39	41.1	41	13	54	34.8	249	21.7	45.6
3		3	3.2	33	4	37	23.9	41	90.2	7.5
7	8	15	15.8	11	4	15	9.7	48	31.3	8.8
4		4	4.2	11		11	7.1	21	52.4	3.8
11	3	14	14.7	12	1	13	8.4	34	38.2	6.2
2		2	2.1	24	4	28	18.1	33	84.8	6.0
5	2	7	7.4	12	7	19	12.3	55	34.5	10.1
				8	4	12	7.7	15	80.0	2.7
3	1	4	4.2	19	1	20	12.9	27	74.1	4.9
22	9	31	32.6	45	6	51	32.9	149	34.2	27.3
2		2	2.1	10		10	6.5	16	62.5	2.9
				9	2	11	7.1	11	100.0	2.0
2	2	4	4.2	7	1	8	5.2	18	44.4	3.3
4	2	6	6.3	7	3	10	6.5	55	18.2	10.1
5	1	6	6.3	6		6	3.9	20	30.0	3.7
124	49	173	182.1	308	54	362	233.5	923	39.2	169.0
68	27	95		131	24	155		546	28.4	
1.82	1.81	1.82		2.35	2.25	2.34		1.69		

Column 13 refers to the total number of patients identified as possessing a particular AARR category.
Column 14 refers to the proportion of patients identified as possessing a particular AARR category who were classified as alcoholics (PD + AA).

6.8   H. THE ALCOHOLIC AT RISK REGISTER (AARR)

Data is presented in Tables 46 and 47 to illustrate the relative
importance of the different items on the Alcoholic At Risk Register as predictors of alcoholism. It should be noted that any one
patient may have been identified as possessing more than one
'at risk' item; the 546 patients with usable questionnaires possessed a total of 923 'at risk' items. The average number of 'at
risk' items per patient was 1.31 for the social drinkers, 1.82
for the heavy drinkers, and 2.34 for the alcoholics (problem
drinkers and alcohol addicts).

The Tables illustrate three characteristics for each item or
group of items (categories) all of which are relevant in assessing
the value of the items. Table 46 summarises the characteristics
for informant drinkers of the 16 categories of the AARR.

(a)   The proportion of alcoholics (PD and AA) who were identified as possessing a particular item or group of items is shown
in vertical column 12

The most useful categories were:

>   Physical diseases 36.8%
>   Mental diseases 34.8%
>   Marital status 32.9%
>   Alcoholic symptoms 23.9%
>   Criminal offences 18.1%

(b)   The proportion of patients identified as possessing a particular item or group of items who were classified as alcoholics is
shown in vertical column 14.

All the groups were useful in this respect, except for the one
relating to patients interviewed because a member of the family
had previously received a STAQ. The categories in which over
50% of the patients were classified as alcoholics were:

>   Known alcoholics 100.0%
>   Alcoholic symptoms 90.2%
>   Criminal offences 84.8%
>   Help asked for treatment of alcoholism 80.0%
>   Smelling of drink 74.1%
>   Living in a hostel 62.5%
>   Work problems 52.4%

(c)   The proportion of patients completing usable questionnaires
who were identified as possessing a particular item or group of
items is shown in vertical column 15.

The most useful categories in the Alcoholic At Risk Register were:

Mental diseases 45.6%
Marital status 27.3%
Physical diseases 24.0%

Table 47 details the characteristics for informant drinkers of all the 64 items in the AARR.

1. Physical diseases

Peptic ulcer and gastritis were the most useful items from the point of view of numbers of patients interviewed and the pick-up of alcoholics. The diagnosis of peptic ulcer was made clinically, not always with supporting radiographic evidence, and so I consider it justifiable to consider these two items together. (No patient was identified as possessing both of these items.) Of the patients with one of these items, 41.3% were alcoholics and together they contributed to 29.1% of the total number of alcoholics identified.

Although figures were small, it is noteworthy that the three patients with cirrhosis of the liver and the three patients presenting with epilepsy for the first time at age 25 years or over were classified as alcoholics. There were 11 male obese patients of whom 5 were alcoholics and 5 heavy drinkers.

2. Mental diseases

Anxiety state and depression were the most useful items from the point of view of numbers of patients interviewed and the pick up of alcoholics. It is not always easy in general practice to diagnose patients as having anxiety *or* depression, many patients having features of both, and the diagnosis is often influenced by the doctor's personal judgment. As some patients were categorised as having both of these conditions it is not possible to summate the results. About 20% of the patients with either of these diagnoses were classified as alcoholics. Of all the alcoholics 13.5% had an anxiety state and 18.1% had depression. It should be noted that these items were included to detect alcoholic spouses as well as alcoholic informants.

Only four patients presented with attempted suicide but three of them were classified as alcoholics and the fourth as a heavy drinker.

Table 47 Alcoholic at risk register

| AARR Factors | Social Drinkers (SD) $n = 296$ | | | |
	M	F	All (c)	% $\frac{(c)}{296}$
	(1)	(2)	(3)	(4)
1. **Physical diseases**				
Pancreatitis				
Cirrhosis of liver				
Peptic ulcer	13	6	19	6.4
Gastritis	14	4	18	6.1
Peripheral neuritis				
Tuberculosis				
Congestive heart failure of unknown origin				
Epilepsy—1st time 25 years and over				
Malnutrition				
Obesity (men)	1		1	0.3
Total No.	28	10	38	12.8
2. **Mental diseases**				
Anxiety state	16	39	55	18.6
Depression	13	77	90	30.4
Attempted suicide				
Other	7	4	11	3.7
Total No.	36	120	156	52.7

Individual AARR items possessed by male and female informant drinkers

Heavy Drinkers (HD) $n = 95$				Problem Drinkers and Alcohol Addicts $n = 155$ (PD + AA)				All	%
M	F	All	%	M	F	All	%		
		(d)	$\frac{(d)}{95}$			(a)	$\frac{(a)}{155}$	(b)	$\frac{(a)}{(b)}$
(5)	(6)	(7)	(8)	(9)	(10)	(11)	(12)	(13)	(14)
				2	1	3	1.9	3	100.0
12	1	13	13.7	16	1	17	11.0	49	34.7
14		14	14.7	26	2	28	18.1	60	46.7
1		1	1.1					1	
2		2	2.1	1		1	0.7	3	33.3
	1	1	1.0					1	
				3		3	1.9	3	100.0
5		5	5.3	5		5	3.2	11	45.5
34	2	36	37.9	53	4	57	36.8	131	43.5
10	11	21	22.1	18	3	21	13.5	97	21.6
8	7	15	15.8	20	8	28	18.1	133	21.1
	1	1	1.1	2	1	3	1.9	4	75.0
2		2	2.1	1	1	2	1.3	15	13.3
20	19	39	41.1	41	13	54	34.8	249	21.7

AARR Factors	Social Drinkers (SD) $n = 296$			
	M	F	All	%
			(c)	$\frac{(c)}{296}$
	(1)	(2)	(3)	(4)
3. Alcoholic Symptoms				
The shakes	1		1	0.3
Blackouts				
Delirium tremens				
Alcoholic epilepsy				
Other				
Total No.	1	—	1	0.3
4. Occupations				
Catering Trade	4	2	6	2.0
Publicans and others	1	8	9	3.1
Travelling salesmen	1		1	0.3
Journalists				
Entertainers		2	2	0.7
Executives				
Printing industry				
Market porter				
Seamen				
Miners				
Total No.	6	12	18	6.1
5. Work Problems				
Three or more jobs		2	2	0.7
Three or more spells of absence off work		1	1	0.3
Request for certificate? genuine	2	1	3	1.0
Total No.	2	4	6	2.0

Heavy Drinkers (HD) n = 95				Problem Drinkers and Alcohol Addicts n = 155 (PD + AA)				All	%
M	F	All	%	M	F	All	%		
		(d)	$\frac{(d)}{95}$			(a)	$\frac{(a)}{155}$	(b)	$\frac{(a)}{(b)}$
(5)	(6)	(7)	(8)	(9)	(10)	(11)	(12)	(13)	(14)
				14	2	16	10.3	17	94.1
2		2	2.1	16	1	17	11.0	19	89.5
				2		2	1.3	2	100.0
1		1	1.1		1	1	0.6	2	50.0
				1		1	0.7	1	100.0
3		3	3.2	33	4	37	23.9	41	90.2
1	2	3	3.2	3		3	1.9	12	25.0
4	3	7	7.4	5	2	7	4.5	23	30.4
1		1	1.0	1		1	0.6	3	33.3
	3	3	3.2		1	1	0.7	6	16.7
					1	1	0.7	1	100.0
1			1.0	2		2	1.3	3	66.7
7	8	15	15.8	11	4	15	9.7	48	31.3
				2		2	1.3	4	50.0
1		1	1.0	4		4	2.6	6	66.7
3		3	3.2	5		5	3.2	11	45.5
4		4	4.2	11		11	7.1	21	52.4

AARR Factors	Social Drinkers (SD) $n = 296$			
	M	F	All	%
			(c)	$\frac{(c)}{296}$
	(1)	(2)	(3)	(4)
6. Accidents				
At work	4		4	1.4
At home				
Road traffic	3		3	1.0
Total No.	7		7	2.4
7. Criminal Offences				
Drunken offences				
Others	2	1	3	1.0
Total No.	2	1	3	1.0
8. Family Problems				
Neglected children		1	1	0.3
Family disharmony	3	23	26	8.8
Mentally disturbed children		2	2	0.7
Total No.	3	26	29	9.8
9. Help asked for treatment of alcoholism by:				
Patient				
Wife		3	3	1.0
Ancillary staff or social agency				
Total No.		3	3	1.0

Heavy Drinkers (HD) $n = 95$				Problem Drinkers and Alcohol Addicts $n = 155$ (PD + AA)				All	%
M	F	All	%	M	F	All	%		
		(d)	$\frac{(d)}{95}$			(a)	$\frac{(a)}{155}$	(b)	$\frac{(a)}{(b)}$
(5)	(6)	(7)	(8)	(9)	(10)	(11)	(12)	(13)	(14)
6	1	7	7.4	3		3	1.9	14	21.4
4	2	6	6.3	5	1	6	3.9	12	50.0
1		1	1.0	4		4	2.6	8	50.0
11	3	14	14.7	12	1	13	8.4	34	38.2
				20	4	24	15.5	24	100.0
2		2	2.1	4		4	2.6	9	44.4
2		2	2.1	24	4	28	18.1	33	84.8
1		1	1.1	1		1	0.7	3	33.3
4	2	6	6.3	8	6	14	9.0	46	30.4
				3	1	4	2.6	6	66.7
5	2	7	7.4	12	7	19	12.3	55	34.5
				6	2	8	5.1	8	100.0
				1	1	2	1.3	5	40.0
				1	1	2	1.3	2	100.0
				8	4	12	7.7	15	80.0

AARR Factors	Social Drinkers (SD) $n = 296$			
	M	F	All	%
			(c)	$\frac{(c)}{296}$
	(1)	(2)	(3)	(4)
10. Patient smelling of drink				
Total	1	2	3	1.0
11. Marital Status				
Single, male, 40 yrs or over	10		10	3.4
Married more than once		1	1	0.3
Divorced	5	12	17	5.7
Separated	7	32	39	13.2
Total	22	45	67	22.6
12. Living in Hostel for destitutes				
Total	4		4	1.4
13. Known Alcoholic				
Total				
14. Family history of abnormal drinking				
Total	1	5	6	2.0
15. Interviewed because member of family had previously received STAQ				
Total	9	30	39	13.2
16. Other Reason				
Total	3	5	8	2.7

Heavy Drinkers (HD $n = 95$)				Problem Drinkers and Alcohol Addicts $n = 155$ (PD + AA)				All	%
M	F	All	%	M	F	All	%		
		(d)	$\frac{(d)}{95}$			(a)	$\frac{(a)}{155}$	(b)	$\frac{(a)}{(b)}$
(5)	(6)	(7)	(8)	(9)	(10)	(11)	(12)	(13)	(14)
3	1	4	4.2	19	1	20	12.9	27	74.1
17		17	17.9	15		15	9.7	42	35.7
	3	3	3.1	3		3	1.9	7	42.9
	2	2	2.1	13	1	14	9.0	33	42.4
5	4	9	9.5	14	5	19	12.3	67	28.4
22	9	31	32.6	45	6	51	32.9	149	34.2
2		2	2.1	10		10	6.5	16	62.5
				9	2	11	7.1	11	100.0
2	2	4	4.2	7	1	8	5.2	18	44.4
4	2	6	6.3	7	3	10	6.5	55	18.2
5	1	6	6.3	6		6	3.9	20	30.0

3. Alcoholic symptoms

Of the 17 patients identified as exhibiting 'the shakes' one was classified as a social drinker. Of the two patients identified as having the symptoms of alcoholic epilepsy, one of them was classified as a heavy drinker. These apparent errors may have been due to misdiagnosis, or denial of other symptoms by the patients concerned. Of the 19 patients with blackouts, two of them were classified as heavy drinkers. However, blackouts can occur in nonalcoholics (*see* Chapter 7).

4. Occupations

As expected, a large proportion (72.9%) of the 48 individuals 'at risk' in this category worked in the drink industry or the catering trade. 28.6% of the patients in these occupations were classified as alcoholics.

5. Work problems

It was not surprising that 52.4% of the patients 'at risk' in this category were classified as alcoholics. It is noteworthy that of the 11 patients who were considered to have requested sickness certificates for dubious reasons, five were classified as alcoholics and a further three as heavy drinkers.

6. Accidents

This category was useful as a predictor of alcoholism, 38.2% of those identified being classified as alcoholics. Accidents in the home are not generally recognised as possible symptoms of a drinking problem, but of the 12 patients who presented with this item, six were alcoholics (one female) and the other six were heavy drinkers (two female).

7. Criminal offences

This category was very important as shown above with reference to Table 46 (page 118).

8. Family problems

The most important item in this category was family disharmony which accounted for 83.6% of the 55 patients identified as having a family problem.

I suspect that the number of patients identified as being 'at risk' in the above four categories is an underestimate of the true situation. Information on these categories is not as readily available as on the other categories.

9. *Help asked for treatment of alcoholism*

Only eight patients personally sought help and all of them were classified as alcoholics. Four wives were interviewed because they asked for help for their husband and one of the wives herself was classified as an alcoholic. One husband attended at his wife's request and was an alcoholic. Only two patients were interviewed at the request of a health visitor and social worker and both of them were classified as alcoholics.

10. *Patient smelling of drink*

This category was very important as shown above with reference to Table 46 (page 118).

11. *Marital status*

All the items in this category were important as predictors of alcoholism. About one-third of the 149 patients interviewed were found to be alcoholics. This category was included in the AARR to detect alcoholic spouses as well as alcoholic informants.

12. *Living in a hostel for destitutes*

Sixteen patients were identified in this category, of whom 62.5% were classified as alcoholics. These patients were living in a Church Army Hostel situated within the practice area.

13. *Known alcoholic*

As expected, all 11 patients were classified as alcoholics.

14. *Family history of abnormal drinking*

Of the 18 patients identified in this category, 44.4% were found to be alcoholics. More patients were 'at risk' in this category than were identified but this was not known until the family sections of the questionnaires had been completed.

15. *Interviewed because a family member had previously received a STAQ*

As expected, this category was not important as a predictor of alcoholism, as some of these informants were relatives of alcoholics. This category is considered in detail in Chapter 11.

16. *Other reasons*

Twenty patients received STAQs because the doctor suspected that they might be abnormal drinkers for reasons other than those listed in the AARR. The reasons recorded for the six alcoholics were: red face (two patients), volunteered drinking information, involved in a fight, dyspnoea at night only when patient stops drinking, and gruff voice.

17. Interviewed as relative of suspected alcoholic

No patients received questionnaires because of this category.

The Family Alcoholics

An analysis of the relative importance of the different 'at risk' items as predictors of alcoholism in family members of the informants has been described in detail elsewhere.[390] As expected the most useful items were: anxiety state, depression, family disharmony, separation, divorce, family history of abnormal drinking, and a history of another family member having received a STAQ. These items had been included in the AARR specifically to detect alcoholic spouses as well as informants.

6.9   I. PREVALENCE RATES FOR THE PRACTICE

There are a number of difficulties in calculating accurate prevalence rates for abnormal drinkers in the practice population.

1.   As in all studies from general practice, there is the problem of assessing the population at risk.[83,84] (a) The practice population did not remain stable throughout the survey year. The quarterly returns from the Manchester Executive Council were as follows:

1 July 1970	1 October 1970	1 January 1971	1 April 1971	1 July 1971
11 729	11 624	12 233	12 262	12 194

The mean of these figures, i.e. 12 008, was taken as the baseline. However, it is known that the turnover rate per annum for the practice is about 22% (compared to a national average of 9%).[84] Consequently there were 14 650 patients who were registered for at least a part of the survey year and so were potential candidates to receive a questionnaire. (b) The Executive Council figures may be 'inflated' e.g. dead patients had not been notified to the Executive Council, or patients left the practice without the knowledge of the doctor or the Executive Council. In Manchester, the Executive Council report that 98.9% of the population are registered with a general practitioner, so that any inflation is likely to be of small magnitude.[392]

2. In the present study, the age range of patients 'at risk' was restricted to 15-65 years, which corresponded to 77.4% of the practice population. The adjusted figure on which all the prevalence rates were based was therefore 77.4% of 14 650 i.e. 11 339 patients.

There are further potential sources of error relevant to this particular research, all of which could lead to an underestimate of the true prevalence rate.

3. Patients may have denied symptoms, and so be classified incorrectly as nonalcoholics.

4. STAQs were administered only to those patients who were identified as possessing one or more AARR factors. Some patients may not have been identified because of ignorance of their 'at risk' status.

5. There may have been patients who did *not* possess any AARR factors, but were alcoholics, as shown by the study of 179 'not at risk' patients (Chapter 8).

6. STAQs were administered only to patients who actually attended the surgery, and not to those seen on home visits, or who did not consult the doctor at all. Nationally, about 70% of patients consult their doctor in any one year.[84] In the Cambridgeshire survey, only 40.5% of the known alcoholics consulted their general practitioner because of their alcoholism, or conditions attributable to alcoholism. However, it is not known how many consulted for other reasons.[94]

If this error was allowed for, the prevalence estimates would be increased significantly. It is not known whether alcoholics tend to visit their family doctors more or less than the average patient; if they have physical or mental disease they will presumably visit more, but otherwise they are known to avoid their family doctor. It was therefore considered unjustifiable to calculate a rate using some theoretical figure representing the non-attendance rate of alcoholics.

7. The prevalence rates only refer to the practice population, and do not take into account those alcoholics in the practice area who are not registered. It is probable that a proportion of alcoholics are not registered with any family doctor.

8. The age limit of 65 years may have led to a small proportion of older alcoholics not being interviewed. Although this will not affect the prevalence rate as defined in 2. above, it should be emphasised that a prevalence rate relating to individuals 15-65 years of age is not directly comparable with those rates in other studies which have no age limit. In the Cambridgeshire survey, 9% of the

Table 48   Figures on which the prevalence rates were based

	Heavy Drinker (HD) n = 119				Problem Drinker (PD) n = 108				Alcohol Addict (AA) n = 99			
	Present n = 62		Past n = 57		Present n = 55		Past n = 53		Present n = 71		Past n = 28	
	M	F	M	F	M	F	M	F	M	F	M	F
	n = 39	n = 23	n = 46	n = 11	n = 46	n = 9	n = 43	n = 10	n = 62	n = 9	n = 27	n = 1
(1) informants	29	17	39	10	32	9	33	7	39	7	27	1
(2) family DHHC	4	2	2		13		8	1	23	1		
(3) NAR informants	6	4	4	1	1		2	2				
(4) NAR family DHHC			1							1		

(1) Refers to informants identified by the STAQ in the main study.
(2) Refers to family members identified by the STAQ in the main study who were registered at the Darbishire House Health Centre (DHHC).
(3) Refers to informants identified by the STAQ in the 'not at risk' group (NAR) (*see* Chapter 8).
(4) Refers to family members identified by the STAQ in the 'not at risk' group who were registered at the DHHC.

known alcoholics were 65 years and older.[94] Other reported figures range from 5-12% in the over-60 years age group.[150,282,393]

9.   It is not possible to estimate what credence to give to those
patients who only admitted to problems in the *past*. Most prevalence studies have reported the rates for present *and* past
alcoholics combined. This would seem to exaggerate the true
extent of morbidity, although I consider that many of the *past*
abnormal drinkers as classified by the STAQ were denying their
current status (*see* Validation Study in Chapter 9).

10. Finally, the criticism has often been made that prevalence
studies adopt various definitions of the 'alcoholic', leading to
difficulty in comparing different rates. In the present study,
prevalence rates for males and females were estimated for the
following categories of abnormal drinker as defined in Chapter 5.

    heavy drinkers (HD)
    problem drinkers (PD)
    alcohol addicts (AA)
    'alcoholics' (PD + AA)
    'abnormal drinkers' (HD + PD + AA)

A range will be given, the minimum referring to the number of
present drinkers, and the maximum to the combined total of present *and* past drinkers.

The total population at risk = 11 339 patients aged 15-65 years.
    Males at risk   = 6 234   "   "   "
    Females at risk   = 5 105   "   "   "

The proportion of **males** and females was estimated from the
known proportions of a 50% sample of the practice population
for the year October 1969-October 1970.

Table 49   Prevalence Rates of the different categories of
abnormal drinkers registered in the practice

	MALES	FEMALES	TOTAL
	per 1000 of male population, 15-65 years	per 1000 of female population, 15-65 years	per 1000 of total population, 15-65 years
Heavy drinkers (HD)	6.3-13.6	4.5-6.7	5.5-10.5
Problem drinkers (PD)	7.4-14.3	1.8-3.7	4.8-9.5
Alcohol addicts (AA)	9.9-14.3	1.7-2.0	6.3-8.7
'Alcoholics' (PD + AA)	17.3-28.6	3.5-5.7	11.1-18.2
'Abnormal drinkers' (HD + PD + AA)	23.6-42.2	8.0-12.4	16.6-28.7

As mentioned above, the minimum figures refer to the present
drinkers, and the maximum figures to the combined present and
past drinkers.

These prevalence rates will be discussed in relation to those of
other English studies in Chapter 7.

7 Discussion

'Priest and prophet are addicted to wine and bemused with
wine; clamouring in their cups, confirmed topers hiccuping
in drunken stupor; '

Isaiah: 28, 7

7.1 PATIENTS AND METHOD

7.1.1 The Patients

Although the response rate from the patients questioned was
virtually 100%, it is a valid criticism that the patients 'at risk'
to receive a questionnaire did not comprise the total practice
population.

The age limits were 15-65 years. I considered it unwise to
administer STAQs to children, and not relevant except for the
purpose of detecting an alcoholic relative. Although a small
proportion of questionnaires administered to patients over 65
years would have detected alcoholics, the majority would have
been negative and thus wasteful of time.

Patients on home visits were excluded. It seemed unreasonable
to expect my colleagues to carry questionnaires into patients'
homes, and sit down with an ill patient for 7 minutes, asking
what to the patient would appear to be irrelevant questions.

Not all patients consulted during the survey year. Facilities were
not available to interview a sample of patients who did not consult at all during the survey year.

It is likely that there were some patients who possessed 'at risk'
factors but who were not recognised as such. Most of the AARR
factors were probably identified, but information on some of
them, such as criminal offences or repeated job changes, was not
readily available. It was considered unjustifiable to question
every patient to determine if they possessed an 'at risk' factor.
Reliance was placed on the presenting symptoms, and the data
contained in the records.

Finally, there may have been some patients who were alcoholics
but who did not possess any of the defined 'at risk' factors. The
AARR was deliberately designed to elicit the maximum amount
of information with the least expenditure of time. Although 64

items were listed it was not feasible to include every known 'at
risk' factor, and indeed there may be some not yet described
in the literature.

7.1.2   The Interviewers

The main difficulty of the study was the circumstances in which it
took place. For a period of 52 weeks, busy general practitioners
not experienced in this type of research, completed questionnaires
during the course of normal surgery sessions. Naturally, my own
enthusiasm and motivation were not shared by all, and this was
reflected in the results. There was no obvious reason why the
patients I interviewed should be more 'at risk' than the others,
but despite a practice list of about 20% of the total practice
population, I administered 36% of all the questionnaires. If the
response rate from my colleagues had equalled my own, which
could not reasonably be expected, it is likely that more abnormal
drinkers would have been detected. Before the survey began, and
throughout the year, deliberate efforts were made to maintain
the cooperation of all the interviewers (Chapter 5).

7.1.3   The Questionnaire

The questionnaire took a maximum of 7-8 minutes to complete in
the case of an abnormal drinker, but considerably less time if
most of the answers were in the negative (because of the cut-off
points). Nevertheless, if a doctor administered three STAQs
during the course of a surgery, this could have added 25 minutes
to a 2-hour session. The questionnaire could have been shortened
by reducing the number of alcohol-related questions but in the
context of a study partially aimed at determining some of the
characteristics of the community based alcoholic, this was
rejected. Alternatively, an undisguised approach could have
been adopted and questions restricted only to directly relevant
ones. I considered that this would have significantly lowered the
proportion of truthful responses.

The questionnaire could have been self-administered, the patient
completing it before leaving the Health Centre, or returning it by
post. It would be surprising if either method, especially the
latter, would have produced a response rate anywhere near
approaching the 99.8% actually achieved. The questionnaire
could have been administered by a specially appointed research
worker, or a member of the health team (e.g. secretary, practice
nurse, health visitor, social worker), but facilities were not
available.

I consider that the method adopted was the most suitable one for a research project, but for general application the use of a short self-administered questionnaire might be considered.

7.2   RESULTS

The results will be discussed within the framework of the original aims of the study.

The main aims of the study were, firstly, to study the prevalence of the abnormal drinker in general practice in those patients identified as having a condition or risk factor which previous studies have shown to have an association with alcoholism, and secondly, by virtue of these findings, to construct a list of the most commonly associated factors seen in general practice, in order to increase the possibility of recognition of the abnormal drinker in the practice population as a whole.

The results of the 'at risk' group showed that approximately one quarter of all the questionnaires identified an alcoholic informant (problem drinker or alcohol addict).

A closer examination of the AARR suggests that it would be possible to reduce it in size without seriously affecting the number of alcoholics detected. A balance has to be created between the desire to identify as many alcoholics as possible, and the construction of a list of 'at risk' items which can be readily memorised.

Tables 46 and 47 relate to any patient identified as possessing at least one of the AARR factors. Some of the patients had a combination of factors which will be the subject of future analysis. The average number of risk factors per alcoholic informant was found to be 2.34. A total of 546 patients possessed 923 at risk factors. With the results as presented, it is not possible to predict accurately which group of factors would detect the largest proportion of alcoholics. However, by considering the characteristics of the AARR detailed in the Tables, a modified version can be constructed.

These comments are based on the informant results as no item was found to be significant for family members which was not also significant for informants. Additionally, from a practical point of view, the management of the informant alcoholic is likely to be more successful than that of the family member who had not been seen by the general practitioner.

Any item which carried a prevalence rate for alcoholics of about 50% or higher was included. However, a rate of 25% or above was considered adequate if sufficient patients had been inter-

viewed to contribute a reasonable proportion (at least 10%) of all
the alcoholics identified. These arbitrary rules acted as a guide
in the construction of a modified AARR. In addition, the evidence
reported in the literature was strong enough to justify inclusion
of some items (e.g. accidents at work, publicans) even though they
did not meet the broad criteria outlined above.

Any AARR devised must be based on a personal judgement which
attempts to balance certain opposing principles. I consider that
the one detailed below is an improvement for practical application by busy general practitioners, compared with the original
64 item AARR which was constructed as a research tool.

7.2.1   Modified Alcoholic At Risk Register

1. Physical diseases

    (i)   Cirrhosis of the liver
    (ii)   Peptic ulcer
    (iii) Gastritis
    (iv)   Epilepsy for first time at 25 years or over from no
           apparent cause
    (v)   Obesity (men)

2. Mental diseases

    (i)   Anxiety
    (ii)   Depression
    (iii) Attempted suicide

3. Alcoholic Symptoms

    (i)   The shakes
    (ii)   Blackouts
    (iii) Delirium Tremens
    (iv)   Alcoholic epilepsy

4. Occupations

    (i)   Catering trade
    (ii)   Publicans and others working in a pub, or the drink
           industry
    (iii) Seamen

5. Work Problems

    (i)   Three or more jobs in year preceding consultation
    (ii)   Three or more spells of absence off work in year
           preceding consultation for three days or less
    (iii) Patient requesting certificate for absence from work
           for conditions which are possibly not genuine

6. Accidents

    (i)   At work
    (ii)   At home
    (iii) Road traffic

7. Criminal Offences

    (i)   Drunk and disorderly/incapable, and/or drunken driving, and/or offence committed while under influence of drink
    (ii)   Any other

8. Family Problems

    (i)   Children suffering from neglect
    (ii)   Family disharmony
    (iii) Children with mental or psychosomatic disease

9. Help asked for treatment of alcoholism by

    (i)   Patient
    (ii)   Father of suspected alcoholic
    (iii) Mother of suspected alcoholic
    (iv) Wife of suspected alcoholic
    (v)   Husband of suspected alcoholic
    (vi) Brother of suspected alcoholic
    (vii) Sister of suspected alcoholic
    (viii) Son of suspected alcoholic
    (ix) Daughter of suspected alcoholic
    (x)   Other relative of suspected alcoholic
    (xi) Member of ancillary staff or social agency.

10. Patient smelling of drink at consultation

11. Marital status

    (i)   Single, male, 40 years or over
    (ii)   Married more than once
    (iii) Divorced
    (iv) Separated

12. Living in a hostel for destitutes

13. Known alcoholic (confirmed by psychiatrist)

14. Family history of abnormal drinking

7.2.2 Prevalence

Rates were calculated for males and females, separately and together, for present and past heavy drinkers, problem drinkers, and alcohol addicts, per 1000 of the practice population aged 15-65 years. Comparisons with other studies are difficult because of the different definitions of alcoholic used, and the varying populations at risk with reference to age, sex and source of the data. Nevertheless, how do the prevalence rates in the present study compare with those reported from other English studies?

The present study produced prevalence rates for problem drinkers and alcohol addicts separately. For present drinkers, the ratio of problem drinkers to alcohol addicts was 0.8:1, and for past drinkers the ratio was 1.9:1. There have apparently only been two English studies which differentiated addicts from nonaddicted problem drinkers. Hensman et al.[95] in a survey of general practitioner estimates in London reported a 1:1 ratio. Edwards et al.[22, 96] in their household survey of the same area tentatively suggested that the ratio of male problem drinkers to addicts was 4:1. The former study found a prevalence rate for addicts of 1.7 per 1000 of the population aged 20 years and over, and the latter study suggested that for males it might be 12 per 1000 of the male population aged 18 years and over. We found a rate for present and past alcohol addicts of 8.7 per 1000 of the population aged 15-65 years.

The male:female ratios are discussed in Section 7.2.3

It is a matter of opinion which prevalence rate is used for comparison with other English studies. Whether one uses the above figures for alcohol addicts, or includes those for present problem drinkers suggesting a rate of 13.5 per 1000, or adds also the past problem drinkers to produce a rate of 18.2 per 1000 of the population aged 15-65 years, the rates are all far higher than most reported English studies, with four exceptions. The hospital population surveyed by Gaind[99] and the visitors to a health exhibition concerning alcoholism interviewed by Searle-Jordan[98] clearly do not represent comparable populations with the general practice patients. However, it is interesting that Patterson,[113] in a questionnaire survey of general practice patients, reported a prevalence rate of 15 per 1000 adults with a 'serious drinking problem'. Edwards et al.[96] in a household survey found that 31.3 per 1000 of the population aged 18 years and over had a 'notable drinking problem'. It is noteworthy that our results are comparable with the World Health Organisation estimate, using the Jellinek formula,[23] of 11 per 1000 of the population aged 20 years and over.

It should be emphasised that the practice population is not representative of the country as it contains a high proportion of lower social class patients living in a densely urbanised area with a high turnover of patients. These are factors which would tend to produce a higher rate than a typical cross-section of the community. On the other hand, for reasons described elsewhere (*see* Chapter 6) I believe that the prevalence rates are indeed an underestimate of the true situation. Our figures suggest that the World Health Organisation estimate is far closer to the truth (and is possibly an underestimate) than the much lower figures suggested by previous studies.

7.2.3   Characteristics of the Alcoholic

The two subsidiary aims of the study were, firstly, to analyse some of the characteristics of the abnormal drinker detected in general practice and compare these findings with those of cases treated in hospital; and secondly, to illustrate the potential for research by full time general practitioners who only have limited access to research facilities. I consider that both these aims were realised.

The work in administering the questionnaires was absorbed during normal consulting sessions without too much difficulty. Expenses were limited to the cost of paper and punching of the cards. The regular secretarial staff of the practice carried out the typing and duplicating of the STAQs.

However, I gratefully acknowledge the considerable help given by the two psychiatrists in one of the validation studies (Chapter 9), and the work of the Department of Community Medicine in the coding and analysis of the results. Although this study was conducted in a University Department of General Practice, it could equally well have been carried out in a 'nonacademic' general practice.

Basic Data

Age (Tables 6 and 7 pages 79 and 80). The mean ages of the problem drinkers were 34 years ± 11 for the males and 31 years ± 9 for the females. The mean ages of the alcohol addicts were 41 years ± 10 for the males and 38 years ± 10 for the females. These results suggest that problem drinkers tend, on the average, to progress to the stage of addiction after about 7 years.

The figures for alcohol addicts are similar to those reported from other series of alcoholics. The mean age for men and women in 15 Alcoholism Treatment Units in England and Wales in 1972 was 42 years ± 12.1 and 40.3 ± 9.7 respectively. [394] The mean age of members of Alcoholics Anonymous was 45.7 years for males and 45.6 years for females [150], and for clients of Alcoholism Information Centres 43.1 years for males and 44.9 years for females. [149]

The study found that 47% of male problem drinkers (69% female) and 21% of male alcohol addicts (25% female) were under the age of 30 years. These figures are higher than those reported from hospital[282,294] and some Alcoholism Information Centres[287,290] where 8-15% were under the age of 30 years. However, they are similar to those found in a series of alcoholics attending the Coventry and Warwickshire Alcoholism Information Centre in 1969-73. There were 26% males and 22% females under the age of 30 years. [395] In recent years, the proportion of young alcoholics treated in hospital has been increasing, and is likely to continue to do so if family doctors can identify them in the early stages.

Sex (Table 4 page 76). The ratio of males to females was for heavy drinkers 2.5:1, problem drinkers 4.1:1, and alcohol addicts 8.2:1. These results suggest that females are less likely to suffer from the severe forms of alcohol abuse, or are more reluctant to admit to them.

Varying ratios have been reported from different sources. The highest proportion of females was found in two studies from general practice. Parr[87] reported a ratio of 2.2:1 and Hensman *et al*.[95] one of 3:1. Recent figures from Alcoholism Information Centres suggested a ratio of about 4 or 5:1 [287,290,395] and similar results have been reported from members of Alcoholics Anonymous[150], hospitals[276,282,340], the multi-source surveys in Cambridgeshire[94] and London[96] and a general practice study.[90] However a study of three Alcoholism Information Centres in 1966[345] found a ratio of 7:1, and a household survey in London[396] in 1972 suggested a possible ratio of 8:1.

The conflicting results probably serve to emphasise the difficulty of detecting female alcoholics. Their stigma is undoubtedly greater than for males and so they are more likely to deny any symptoms. The high proportion of female heavy drinkers identified in our study confirm the need to regard female alcohol abuse as a significant problem which cannot be ignored.

Social Class (Tables 8 and 9, pages 82 and 83). There were significantly more alcoholics (problem drinkers and alcohol addicts) in Social Classes IV and V than would be expected from the proportions in the practice population. The distribution was 7% Social Classes I and II, 35% Social Class III, 25% Social Class IV and 33% Social Class V. There is no typical alcoholic Social Class pattern. A higher proportion of alcoholics in Social Classes I and II compared with the general population has been found in a study of alcoholics in Alcoholism Treatment Units[394] and members of Alcoholics Anonymous.[150] However, the lower Social

Classes were over-represented in surveys of a large general mental hospital,[342] a Reception Centre,[348] and drunkenness offenders.[321]. It is interesting that the distribution of male alcoholics attending Alcoholism Information Centres more closely parallels the social class distribution of the general population.[149] There have been no studies from general practice to indicate whether patients in the higher Social Classes are less likely to approach their family doctors for help with a drinking problem.

Marital Status (Tables 10 and 11 pages 85 and 86). No significant differences were found for males or females in the marital status of the different categories of drinker. The distribution for the male alcoholics (females in brackets) was single 36% (12.5%), married 40% (50%), divorced or separated 20% (25%), widowed 2% (4%) and single living as married 1.5% (8%). Although practice figures are not yet available for comparison the proportion of divorced or separated is far higher than found in the general population. These results confirm the findings of other studies that there is a significant degree of marital breakdown amongst alcoholics (*see* Chapter 3).

Ethnic Group (Tables 12 and 13 pages 87 and 88). Of the male alcohol addicts 33% were Irish, which was a significantly greater proportion than the 17% of male social drinkers. The ethnic origins of the practice population are not yet known but the proportion of Irish is believed to be higher than that found in the general population. This is suggested by the figure of 9% of the 'not as risk' group who were Irish (Table 53). The results were not surprising as there is considerable evidence of a higher rate of alcoholism in Eire than in England.[56] A study of male clients attending Alcoholism Information Centres found that 9% were born in Northern Ireland or Eire.[149] A comparison of Irish-born patients with a matched control group of English-born patients, obtained from the Camberwell Cumulative Psychiatric Register in South London, showed that 18% of the Irish patients, compared with 3% of the English patients, had received a primary diagnosis of alcoholism.[397]

Consideration was given to including Irish patients as an item in the AARR but it was omitted because the large proportion of Irish in the practice would have necessitated too many STAQ interviews.

Residential Unit (Tables 14 and 15 pages 89 and 90). No significant differences were found in the proportions of the different categories of drinkers living in different types of residential unit. The 7% of the male 'at risk' group who lived in a hostel reflects its inclusion in the AARR, and the existence of a hostel within the practice area (*see* Chapter 3).

Alcohol Consumption

Frequency (Tables 16 and 17 pages 91 and 92). There were significant differences for both males and females in the distribution of the frequency of drinking admitted; the frequency increased with increasing severity of the category of drinker. For example, 44% of male alcohol addicts (88% female) admitted to drinking every day compared with 5% of male social drinkers (2% female). Daily drinking is by no means necessarily abnormal drinking behaviour nor is it a feature of all alcohol addicts. Some addicts only drink at weekends and others in bouts every few months. There is a remarkable lack of published data to compare our figures with those of hospitalised addicts.

Change in quantity (Tables 18 and 19, page 93). As expected, a change in the quantity of alcohol consumed was admitted by a greater proportion of the addicts compared with the social drinkers, at least for males. 47% of the social drinkers denied any change, compared with 29% of the problem drinkers and 35% of the alcohol addicts. No significant differences were found for the females. This may be due to their reluctance to admit to drinking more or less than before, and so implying that drink might be a problem for them.

It is suggested that any change may be significant. Those who are drinking more are obviously at risk of having or developing a problem with drink. Those who are drinking less may have recognised that their drinking is becoming harmful to them. Additionally, in the late stages of alcohol addiction there is a fall in tolerance, and alcoholics are unable to drink as much as previously. 50% of the male alcohol addicts admitted to drinking less, which was a higher proportion than that found in the other categories of drinker. In one hospital series, 50% of male alcoholics (56% of females) reported a decrease in tolerance. [319]

Expenditure (Tables 20 and 21 pages 94 and 95). It would not have been surprising if patients had been reluctant to admit to spending heavily on alcohol. Nevertheless 53% of the male alcohol addicts admitted to spending a maximum weekly of £8 or more either now or in the past. This was significantly greater than the 25% of male heavy drinkers with the same alcohol expenditure. The differences for the females were not significant although 25% of female addicts admitted to this degree of expenditure.

Edwards *et al.* [22] reported that 56% of 25 problem drinkers identified in a household survey in South London admitted to drinking more than 25 pints of beer per week (costing about £3) compared with 7% of 383 non-problem drinkers. No hospital figures are available for comparison.

Attitudes Towards Drinking

Opinion of Informant (Tables 22 and 23 page 96). An indication of a potential or actual drinking problem is the realisation by the individual that he or she is drinking too much. There were significant differences in the proportions of the different categories of male and female drinkers who thought that they were drinking too much either now or in the past. 86% of the male alcohol addicts (88% female) admitted to drinking too much, compared with 62% of the male heavy drinkers (41% female) and none of the social drinkers (male or female). Hospital data is not available for comparison.

Opinion of Family (Tables 24 and 25 pages 97 and 98). It was considered likely that the alcoholic might more readily admit that someone in the family thought that the drinking was excessive, than give a personal admission. This was not found to be so, although there were significant differences in the proportions of the different categories of male and female drinkers who gave positive answers to this question. 68% of the male alcohol addicts (37.5% of the female problem drinkers and alcohol addicts combined) admitted this symptom, compared with 40% of the male heavy drinkers (3% of the female heavy and social drinkers) and only 1% of the male social drinkers. Hospital data is not available for comparison.

Possible Symptoms of Alcohol Addiction

Blackouts (Tables 26 and 27 page 99). 94% of male alcohol addicts (88% female) admitted to having experienced at least one blackout which was significantly higher than found in the other categories of drinker. These figures are comparable to those reported from hospital, [282,319] Alcoholics Anonymous[150] and Alcoholism Information Centres.[149] However, it is interesting that 37% of male problem drinkers (44% female) and 29% of male heavy drinkers (15% female) also admitted to blackouts.

The view of Jellinek[24] that the frequent occurrence of blackouts after only medium alcohol intake 'marks the beginning of the prodromal phase of alcohol addiction' is generally accepted. An exception is Goodwin *et al*.[398] who reported that blackouts were a *late* manifestation of alcoholism. Nevertheless it is known that blackouts may occur on rare occasions in a nonaddictive drinker when he drinks intoxicating amounts in a state of physical or mental exhaustion. Edwards *et al*.[22] found that 17% of a random sample of male householders in South London had experienced at least one blackout at some time. Rowntree[399] reported that 20% of a random sample of male apprentices admitted to having had at least one blackout.

It should be noted that the question was worded to refer to an *'ever'* occurrence of *any* blackouts. The relatively high proportions for the nonaddictive drinkers may reflect the rare occurrence of a blackout, denial of other symptoms of addiction, or misunderstanding of the question.

Attempt to cut down or stop drinking (Tables 28 and 29 pages 100 and 101). 79% of the male alcohol addicts (63% female) admitted to having tried to cut down or stop their drinking, compared with 6% of the male social drinkers (3% female). These differences were not statistically significant as about half the social drinkers did not answer this question due to completion of the questionnaire at an early cut-off point. These patients were therefore not included in the statistical test. It is very probable that if they had answered the question a highly significant difference would have been shown.

Success in cutting down or stopping drinking (Tables 30 and 31 page 102). Of those who had attempted to cut down or stop their drinking, 100% of the male social drinkers had succeeded, compared with 60% of the male alcohol addicts. The differences for the females were not significant. It is particularly interesting that so many addicts said they had managed to reduce their drinking. Even if some of the addicts were lying, and some were not true addicts, the proportion is still high. 21% of the male addicts stated that they did not try to control their drinking (Table 28) so the proportion of all male addicts who had controlled (or at least reduced) their drinking was 47%.

It has been a generally accepted belief that alcoholics can never return to social drinking, but in recent years there have been at least 15 reports that 7-37% of treated alcoholics had managed to control their drinking. In England, Davies[400] found that 7% of 93 alcohol addicts had become social drinkers after 7-11 years' follow-up. There has been considerable criticism of these reports—for example, that the patients were not true addicts or that their drinking behaviour was still abnormal. There have also been surveys of *un*treated alcoholics suggesting that 3-9% become social drinkers. [273,401]

It is not suggested that almost half of the alcohol addicts detected in this study are now social drinkers—the question wording does not permit this conclusion. Nevertheless, the results highlight the need for further follow-up study of the drinking behaviour of alcohol addicts.

Ability to stop drinking after one or two drinks (Tables 32 and 33 pages 103 and 104). 53% of the male alcohol addicts (50% female) admitted to being unable to stop drinking after taking one or two drinks, which for the males was a significantly greater proportion than that found in the other categories of drinker. Loss of control is the hallmark of alcohol addiction, of which the communest types are 'inability to abstain' (the alcoholic who must drink every day but rarely becomes drunk) and 'inability to stop' (the alcoholic who, once he has had a single drink, cannot stop voluntarily). This question was designed to detect the latter groups, to which most English hospitalised alcoholics belong. However, in a study of 100 hospitalised alcoholics in Edinburgh, 42% were classified as 'inability to abstain' addicts and an equal number as 'inability to stop' addicts, the remainder not fitting clearly into either pattern. [282]

It is possible that about half the study alcohol addicts were of the 'inability to abstain' type or alternatively were lying or not true addicts. 5% of the male problem drinkers admitted to loss of control and these individuals may be alcohol addicts who admitted to no other symptoms of addiction.

Morning Drinking (Tables 34 and 35 page 105). 35% of the male alcohol addicts (50% female) admitted to drinking alcohol in the morning, which for the males was significantly higher than the proportions found in the other categories of drinker. Morning drinking to relieve 'the shakes' i.e. withdrawal symptoms, is a recognised feature of alcohol addiction. The incidence of morning drinking or the shakes is usually reported as occurring in about 70-80% of alcohol addicts. [282,149,150] The lower figure found in the study may reflect denial, or that the study alcohol addicts are at an earlier stage of addiction when morning drinking is less likely to occur.

Drinking alone (Tables 36 and 37 pages 106 and 107). A preference for drinking alone is recognised as a characteristic drinking pattern of some alcohol addicts but it is not an essential component of the addictive state. 33% of the male alcohol addicts (50% female) admitted this preference compared with none of the male social drinkers (1% female) which for the males was statistically significant. A study of young alcohol addicts (under 30 years of age) in Edinburgh found that 57% of them regularly drank alone compared with none of a control group. [282]

Family History of Alcoholism

Family History (Tables 38 and 39 pages 108 and 109). 19% of the male alcoholics (54% female) admitted to having an alcoholic relative in the immediate family compared with 6% of the male social drinkers (31% female) the difference being statistically significant. Many of the wives were 'at risk' to have alcoholic husbands because of marital breakdown or mental disease, thus accounting for the relatively high incidence amongst the female social drinkers. The results are comparable with those reported from hospital series (*see* Chapter 3).

Problems from Alcohol Abuse

Comparison of the mean scores of the different categories of drinkers (Tables 40 and 41 pages 110 and 111). The total point score of a patient was a summation of the points awarded for positive answers to questions in the four areas of alcohol consumption, attitudes to drinking, problems from drink, and symptoms of alcohol addiction. The total score is thus one way of grading the severity of an individual's drinking problem. The mean scores for the male drinkers (female in brackets) were: social drinkers 0.4 (0.3), heavy drinkers 4.1 (3.2), problem drinkers 7.8 (7.1) and alcohol addicts 15.7 (14.6).

The marked differences are an artifact to some extent as the definitions of each category of drinker are basd on predetermined minimum scores. Nevertheless the results do suggest that the classification into four grades is a valid one. It is particularly striking that the mean score of the addict is double that of the problem drinker.

Number of Problems (Table 42 page 113). The male alcohol addicts tended to admit to more problems from alcohol abuse than the male problem drinkers. For example, 49% of the addicts admitted to three or more problems compared with only 11% of the problem drinkers. It is not possible, by definition, for a problem drinker to have no problems, but 23% of the addicts denied any problems from alcohol abuse. Although an 'ever' prevalence was sought, this figure probably reflects the abstaining alcoholic's suppression of his previous problems, or denial by the active alcoholic.

No significant differences were found for the females, which was probably due to the female problem drinkers tending to admit to more problems than the males. This was an unexpected finding. It would seem unlikely that females would have, or indeed admit to more problems than the males.

Types of Problems (Table 43 page 114). Questions were asked of problems from alcohol abuse in the five areas of health, arguments within the family about drinking, drunken offences, money, and work. There were no significant differences in the proportions of male problem drinkers and alcohol addicts who admitted to health problems or arguments in the family about their drinking. Both of these problems were admitted by about half of the problem drinkers and addicts. However for the more serious problems of drunken offences, and money and work problems due to drinking, significant differences were found. This was strikingly shown for work problems which were admitted by 42% of the addicts, compared with 12% of the problem drinkers.

There were no significant differences in the proportions of female problem drinkers and alcohol addicts admitting to any of the five types of problem. Apart from arguments about drinking which were admitted by 80% of the female alcoholics, the proportions of females admitting to problems were lower than the males. This may reflect the female's unwillingness to admit to problems or that the female alcoholics were less seriously affected.

Drunken Offences (Tables 44 and 45 pages 116 and 117). Patients who admitted to drunken offences were asked how many they had committed. Both male and female alcohol addicts had significantly worse criminal records than the problem drinkers. Three or more offences were admitted by 24% of the male addicts (25% females) compared with 11% of the male problem drinkers (6% females). These figures are lower than those reported for hospitalised addicts (*see* Chapter 3). The study addicts may be at an earlier stage of addiction or may be reluctant to admit criminal offences to the general practitioner.

PART FOUR

Subsidiary studies

'The nations have drunk of her wine and that has made them mad.'

Jeremiah: 51, 7.

8 Validation Studies of the Alcoholic at Risk Register

'But the vine answered:
What, leave my new wine which gladdens
Gods and men to come and hold sway over the trees'.

Judges: 9.13.

Two studies are described. In the first, patients considered to be 'not at risk' received questionnaires during the survey year. In the second, a group of general practitioners who had referred a patient to the Alcoholism Treatment Unit were asked what factors had suggested the diagnosis to them.

8.1 ADMINISTRATION OF STAQ TO 'NOT AT RISK' GROUP

One of the hypotheses of the study was that the Alcoholic At Risk Register (AARR) is a valid predictor of the abnormal drinker, i.e. patients possessing one of the AARR factors are more likely to have a drinking problem than patients 'not at risk'. A group of patients believed to be 'not at risk' received questionnaires during the survey year to test this hypothesis.

8.1.1 Patients and Methods

A different consecutive day each week was chosen for administering a STAQ to one 'not at risk' patient. I considered it unwise to ask my colleagues to devote any more time to this control group as it might have led to a reduction in the number of 'at risk' patients interviewed. Before the survey began an estimate was made, based on the pilot studies, of the likely prevalence rate of abnormal drinkers that might be found in the 'at risk' group. It was decided in consultation with a statistician that sufficient numbers would probably be obtained by selecting only one 'not at risk' patient per week per doctor. It was estimated that this would allow a meaningful comparison to be made between the 'at risk' and 'not at risk' groups.

Patients were selected from morning surgeries which tend to be less busy than those in the evening. The records of the 10.00 a.m. appointment (of the 9-10.30 a.m. session) and the midday appointment (of the 11-12.30 a.m. session) for each doctor holding one of these sessions were personally scrutinised to check if the patient possessed any 'at risk' factors. If he or she appeared to be 'not at risk' and was aged 15-65 years, an action marker was inserted in the records, and the appointment list appropriately marked to indicate that a questionnaire should be administered. If no 10.00 a.m. or midday appointment had been booked, or the patient was 'at risk', successive records were examined until a 'not at risk' patient was found. If no patients were allocated from the morning sessions, a similar procedure was adopted for the evening session beginning with the first appointment.

There was a possibility that certain types of patient might deliberately choose the first or last appointment of a surgery session. It was considered a better random selection to select initially a patient about halfway through the morning session. The first appointment of the evening session was chosen so that the doctor might administer the questionnaire at his least busy time.

If, on interview or during the administration of the question-naire, it appeared that the patient did not fit the 'not at risk' criteria, the doctor was asked to transfer the action marker to the next suitable patient on the appointment list. If no other patient could be selected from that session, the action marker was inserted in the records of the first applicable evening appointment.

The procedures adopted were designed to obtain a satisfactory random group of 'not at risk' patients within the limits of prac-ticalities, especially the anticipated cooperation of all the doctors. It was not considered feasible to match the 'not at risk' patients with the 'at risk' group for age, sex, social class, etc. The very nature of the AARR would be likely to produce patients with specific characteristics which could not be matched in a control group.

The questionnaires were analysed as for the 'at risk' group, and prevalence rates calculated for the different categories of abnormal drinker.

8.1.2   Results

179 questionnaires were administered and classified. The re-sponse rate was 100%.

Basic Data

Table 50   Age-Sex distribution of 'not at risk' group

Age groups	Male $n = 75$	%	Female $n = 104$	%	Total $n = 179$	%
15-19	7	9	10	10	17	9
20-24	21	28	21	20	42	24
25-29	7	9	17	16	24	13
30-34	4	5	14	13	18	10
35-39	7	9	5	5	12	7
40-44	5	7	8	8	13	7
45-49	6	8	8	8	14	8
50-54	5	7	5	5	10	6
55-59	7	9	7	7	14	8
60-64	6	8	5	5	11	6
Unknown			4	4	4	2

Comparison of the sex distribution of the 'not at risk' group (Table 50 above) with that of the 'at risk' group (Tables 6 and 7, pages 79 and 80) shows that the former had a significantly lower proportion of males. * This is not surprising as many of the AARR factors are particularly applicable to males.

There was no significant difference in the age group distribution between the 'not at risk' and the 'at risk' groups for the females.** However, there was a significantly higher proportion of males in the 15-24 age range of the 'not at risk' group. †
This may be because students predominate in this group, and there are more male than female students.

---

* $\chi^2 = 7.42$, d.f. $= 1, 0.01 > p > 0.001$. Significant at 1% level.
** $\chi^2 = 13.15$, d.f. $= 9, 0.20 > p > 0.10$. Not significant at 5% level.
† $\chi^2 = 28.35$, d.f. $= 9, p < 0.001$. Significant at 0.1% level.

Table 51 Marital Status of Male and Female 'not at risk' group

Marital Status	Male n = 75	%	Female n = 104	%	Total n = 179	%
Single	37	49	37	36	74	41
Married	33	44	59	57	92	51
Widowed	1	1	3	3	4	2
Single living as married			2	2	2	1
Unknown	4	6	3	3	7	4

Comparison of the distribution of the types of marital status in the 'not at risk' group (Table 51 above) with that in the 'at risk' group (Tables 10 and 11 pages 85 and 86) show that, as expected there were significant differences for both males* and females†. There were no divorced or separated patients in the 'not at risk' group as, by definition, they were 'at risk'. There was a significantly higher proportion of single males and females in the 'not at risk' group.

Table 52 Social Class of Male and Female 'not at risk' group.

Social Class	Male n = 75	%	Female n = 104	%	Total n = 179	%
I	2	3	5	5	7	4
II	13	17	9	9	22	12
III	36	48	46	44	82	46
IV	6	8	10	10	16	9
V	13	17	19	18	32	18
Unknown	5	7	15	14	20	11

* $\chi^2 = 13.43$, d.f. $= 2, 0.01 > p > 0.001$. Significant at 1% level. Figures for marital status other than single and married pooled together because of smallness of numbers.
† $\chi^2 = 40.09$, d.f. $= 2, p < 0.001$. Significant at 0.1% level. Grouping as for males.

The Social Class distribution of the 'not at risk' group (Table 52 above) has been compared with that of the 'at risk' group (Appendix 6) using the method of classification adopted for the practice population (Chapter 5). The 'not at risk' group had a significantly higher proportion of patients in social classes I, II and III for both the males* and females†. This was as expected because the 'at risk' group of potential alcoholics would be likely to have a higher proportion of the lower social classes (IV and V).

Table 53   Ethnic Group of Male and Female 'not at risk' group

Ethnic Group	Male $n = 75$	%	Female $n = 104$	%	Total $n = 179$	%
Mainland British	52	69	76	73	128	72
Irish	7	9	13	12	20	11
Other Whites	4	5	2	2	6	3
West Indian	2	3	5	5	7	4
African Coloured			2	2	2	1
Asian	5	7	1	1	6	3
Other Coloured	3	4	1	1	4	2
No Information	2	3	4	4	6	3

Definitions of Ethnic Groups as for Tables 12 and 13 (pages 87 and 88)

Comparison of the ethnic group of the *males* in the 'not at risk' group (Table 53 above) with that in the 'at risk' group (Tables 12 and 13) shows that there is a significantly higher proportion of Irish in the latter group.**

The results for females were not significantly different.††

---

* $\chi^2 = 33.97$, d.f. $= 4$, $p < 0.001$. Significant at 0.1% level.
† $\chi^2 = 25.10$, d.f. $= 4$, $p < 0.001$. Significant at 0.1% level.
** $\chi^2 = 12.24$, d.f. $= 3$, $0.01 > p > 0.001$. Significant at 1% level. Figures of groups other than British, Irish and Other Coloured pooled together because of smallness of numbers.
†† $\chi^2 = 5.99$, d.f. $= 3$, $0.20 > p\ 0.10$. Not significant at 5% level. Grouping as for males.

These results were as expected because the 'at risk' group of potential alcoholics is likely to contain more Irish male patients.[56]

STAQ classification of the abnormal drinkers

Of the 179 STAQs completed for the 'not at risk' patients:

159 revealed *no* abnormal drinkers in the informants

20 revealed that the informant was an abnormal drinker

171 revealed no abnormal drinkers in the immediate family

8 revealed that there *was* an abnormal drinker in the immediate family

The details of those scoring as abnormal drinkers on the STAQ are shown in Table 54. The family member group is subdivided into those who are registered with a doctor at Darbishire House Health Centre (DHHC).

Table 54　STAQ Classification of Informants and Family Members (179 STAQs completed)

STAQ Classification of Abnormal Drinkers	Informant			Family					
				Total			DHHC Registered		
	Present	Past	Total	Present	Past	Total	Present	Past	Total
	$n = 11$	$n = 9$	$n = 20$	$n = 5$	$n = 3$	$n = 8$	$n = 1$	$n = 1$	$n = 2$
Heavy Drinker	10	5	15		2	2		1	1
Problem Drinker	1	4	5	1	1	2			
Alcohol Addict				4		4	1		1

If one considers that the 'alcoholics' are the present and past problem drinkers and alcohol addicts combined, then, out of a total of 179 STAQs administered, there were 5 (2.8%) alcoholic informants, and 6 (3.3%) alcoholics in the family; 1 (0.6%) was registered at Darbishire House.

The proportions in the 'not at risk' group of the following categories of abnormal drinker were significantly *lower* than in the 'at risk' group (*see* Chapter 6):

Informant heavy drinkers ($\chi^2 = 8.52$, d.f. $= 1$, $0.01 > p > 0.001$. Significant at 1% level).
Informant alcoholics ($\chi^2 = 51.35$, d.f. $= 1$, $p < 0.001$. Significant at 0.1% level).

Family alcoholics registered at DHHC ($\chi^2 = 12.50$, d.f. $= 1$, $p < 0.001$. Significant at 0.1% level).

Family alcoholics not registered at DHHC ($\chi^2 = 17.19$, d.f. $= 1$, $p < 0.001$. Significant at 0.1% level).

Differences were *not* significant for the following categories of abnormal drinker:

Family heavy drinkers registered at DDHC ($\chi^2 = 0.32$, d.f.$= 1$, $0.70 > p > 0.50$. Yates correction applied. Not significant at 5% level).

Family heavy drinkers not registered at DHCC ($\chi^2 = 0.32$, d.f. $= 1$, $0.70 > p > 0.50$. Yates correction applied. Not significant at 5% level).

Thus in the 'not at risk' group there was a significantly *lower* proportion of heavy drinkers and alcoholics in the informants, and of alcoholics in the family members. This supports the hypothesis that the Alcoholic At Risk Register is an important tool for detecting abnormal drinkers in the practice population.

However, there was *no* significant difference in the proportion of heavy drinkers in the family. Family abnormal drinkers may be detected for three reasons. The informant who is an abnormal drinker may have a family member who is an abnormal drinker. Secondly, the informant may be interviewed because he is 'at risk' to have an abnormal drinker in the family. Finally, there is the element of chance. The first two reasons are perhaps more likely to appertain to the problem drinkers and alcohol addicts than the heavy drinkers who only require to score two points to be thus classified. Therefore the element of chance might equally apply in both groups and so no differences be noted.

The National Health Service records of the 20 informants who were abnormal drinkers were scrutinised for evidence of possible 'at risk' factors that may have been present either before or after the STAQ was administered.

Of the 20 patients who were revealed as informant abnormal drinkers (12 male, 8 female) there were 8 (6 male, 2 female) whose records revealed significant information.

Male Heavy Drinker: Works in a bakery (known associationship with alcoholism)

Male Heavy Drinker: Gastritis diagnosed, 5 months after completing STAQ

Male Heavy Drinker: Depression diagnosed, 2 months after completing STAQ

Male Problem Drinker: Gastritis diagnosed, 5 months after completing STAQ

Male Problem Drinker: Accident at work, 17 months before completing STAQ

Male Problem Drinker: Irish building labourer (known associationship with alcoholism)

Female Heavy Drinker: Anxiety and depression treated 2 years and 6 months before completing STAQ

Female Heavy Drinker: Anxiety treated 11 months before completing STAQ, and 9 months after

Thus of the 20 *informant* abnormal drinkers, 6 fulfilled the criteria of being 'at risk' at some time, and 2 possessed recognised 'at risk' factors which were not included in the AARR. It is possible that a similar proportion of the 159 social drinkers possessed 'at risk' factors at some time, but these records were not examined.

The relationships to the informants of the 8 abnormal drinkers in the family were 3 fathers, 1 mother, 1 husband, and 3 brothers. Only 2 were registered at Darbishire House, and their records were missing.

8.2   STUDY OF REASONS FOR REFERRAL TO AN ALCOHOLISM TREATMENT UNIT

As yet, the usefulness of the Alcoholic At Risk Register has not been tested by other general practitioners in a prospective study similar to the present one. However, the opportunity was taken in a separate study of the prevalence and management of alcoholism by general practitioners in the Greater Manchester area[403] to make a crude assessment retrospectively of the value of the AARR.

8.2.1   Method

One hundred and ninety-two general practitioners who had referred at least one alcoholic to the Regional Alcoholism Treatment Unit (Springfield Hospital, Manchester) in a two year period (1971-72) were circulated with a semi-structured questionnaire. One of the questions asked what presenting factors had suggested the diagnosis to the general practitioner. The complete list of the AARR factors was not itemised. The respondent was asked to detail which, if any, physical diseases, mental diseases, symptoms of alcohol addiction, and occupation, were considered

significant. In addition, the following were listed: work problems,
criminal offences, family disharmony, help requested by a
relative and smelling of drink. Two items not included in the
AARR were also specifically mentioned: aggressive behaviour
towards friends, relatives, etc., and drinking leading to debt.
The general practitioner was given the opportunity of adding
any other factors not detailed in the questionnaire.

8.2.2   Results

One hundred and ninety-two questionnaires were sent out relating
to 154 male and 38 female alcoholics. Of these, 123 were returned, a response rate of 64%. However, only 101 (53%) contained data suitably completed for analysis.

Table 55 details the percentage of patients presenting with the
factors mentioned by the general practitioners in the same order
as the AARR. The results are compared with the findings in the
current study, but AARR items not detailed by the general practitioners are excluded from the Table.

As the methodologies of the two studies were dissimilar a detailed comparative analysis would not be justified. However, certain
trends emerge in relation to the usefulness of the AARR.

Aggressive behaviour was noted in 24.7% of patients and drinking leading to debt in 17.8%. These two items would appear to
be useful additions to the Alcoholic At Risk Register. Most of
the AARR items were found to have varying degrees of usefulness.
One would not expect general practitioners who are not specialists
in alcoholism to mention such items as marital status, children
suffering from neglect or mental disturbance. It is interesting
that living in a hostel and accidents were not mentioned by any
of the respondents.

8.2.3   Conclusion

A total of 179 questionnaires were administered to patients
judged to be 'not at risk' as abnormal drinkers, or to have
abnormal drinkers in the immediate family. The results strongly
suggest that the Alcoholic At Risk Register is a useful predictor
of alcoholism. This is shown by the finding that only 2.8% of
the 'not at risk' group were classified as alcoholics compared
with 28.4% of the 'at risk' group. One possible source of interviewer error should be noted. 'There is a danger that the
intensity with which an interviewer probes the answers, and
perhaps his interpretation of the response, might be affected by
his prior knowledge of whether the respondent was a case or a

Table 55 Percentage of Alcoholics in Greater Manchester and Health Centre Study identified as possessing certain factors

The Factors	Percentage of Alcoholics with factor	
	Greater Manchester $n = 101$	Health Centre $n = 155$
1. Physical Diseases		
02 Cirrhosis of the liver	2.0	1.9
03 Peptic ulcer	3.0	11.0
04 Gastritis	11.9	18.1
05 Peripheral Neuritis	4.0	
— Excessive fatigue	4.0	
— Pneumonia	3.0	
— Fractured rib	1.0	
— Persistent diarrhoea	1.0	
2. Mental diseases		
01, 02 Anxiety and/or Depression	12.9	31.6
03 Attempted suicide	4.9	1.9
3. Alcoholic Symptoms		
01, 02 The Shakes	3.0	10.3
03 Delirium Tremens	2.0	1.3
4. Occupations		
02 Publicans and others	4.0	4.5
03 Travelling salesmen	1.0	0.6
09 Seamen	1.0	1.3
5. Work Problems	35.6	7.1*
7. Criminal Offences	15.8	18.1
8. 02 Family disharmony	52.5	9.0
9. 02 Help asked by wife/relatives	47.5	1.3
10. Smelling of alcohol	28.7	12.9
— Debts	17.8	
— Aggressive behaviour	24.7	

* 40.5% on answering the STAQ admitted to work problems.

control'.[402] How important is this possible source of bias cannot be assessed but it is unlikely that it would significantly alter the trend of the results.

The study of the reasons for referral to an Alcoholism Treatment Unit suggest that the AARR, with the addition of the items of aggressive behaviour and debts, is likely to be a satisfactory instrument for identifying possible alcoholics in general practice.

9 Validation Studies of the Questionnaire

'Shame on you! you who rise early in the morning
to go in pursuit of liquor
and draw out the evening inflamed with wine'.

Isaiah: 5.11.

Two studies are described which attempted to ascertain whether
the questionnaire correctly classifies patients as alcoholic or not.
In the first, two psychiatrists interviewed a sample of the patients,
and their clinical assessments were compared with the questionnaire classifications. In the second, a group of known hospitalised alcoholics received questionnaires and their results were
compared with those of the alcohol addicts identified in the study
population.

9.1   PSYCHIATRIC ASSESSMENT

9.1.1   Review of the Literature

The validity of a response has been defined as 'its closeness to
the truth which one is trying to ascertain'.[404] The difficulty lies
in defining what is 'the truth'.

The problem of validation in psychiatric studies in general is
two-fold: the nature of mental disease has the effect that 'there is
no clear "natural" separation between wellness and illness'[408]
and this in itself introduces into the diagnosis a degree of sub-
jectivity, which is exacerbated by the difficulty in classifying
psychiatric morbidity in exact terms that are generally accepted.[405-407] Several studies have illustrated the extent to
which individual psychiatrists may differ in their assessment of
the same patients.[409-411]

Notwithstanding these obstacles to the validation of psychiatric
questionnaires with a generally accepted external criterion,[412]
the current situation is that 'in psychiatry, the clinical interview
is still the final arbiter of morbidity'.[413] Instead of the usually
relatively unstructured type of clinical interview, attempts have
been made to design a standardised one which would have a similar reliability when used by different psychiatrists.[414]

There have been three main categories of validation test used in mental health surveys described as content, criterion-orientated, and construct validity. [415—416] The type most relevant to the present study is criterion-orientated validity which essentially measures the correlation between two different criteria of the same characteristic. In surveys of psychiatric illness, the results of a questionnaire are usually compared with those of clinical interview of the same individuals.

9.1.2   Validation of Alcoholism Questionnaires

Most of the major community surveys to detect alcoholism have ignored the standard concepts of validation methodology, and reliance has been placed on face validity as the criterion for 'truth'. This concept, known also as logical validity, refers to an opinion based on common sense, that 'on the face of it', the results must be true. Cynics have referred to this as 'faith validity'.

The problems of universally accepted definitions of 'alcoholism', and the validity of the clinical interview remain the stumbling blocks to accurate validation studies. A further difficulty is the well known propensity of the alcoholic to deny his symptoms (*see* Chapters 10 and 11).

Cisin[361] has argued that in surveys of drinking behaviour the criterion is not the absolute precise measurement of individual behaviour, but measurement sufficiently exact to allow the correct placing of the individual in one of a number of fairly broad categories: 'The question of validity ought not to be asked about the truthfulness of any individual statements, but about the resultant summary classification of any individual'. Some alcoholism surveys have been criticised for dividing the population into only two groups of 'alcoholic' and 'nonalcoholic'. Bruun[417] has suggested using two or three categories 'thereby indicating the vagueness of our definitions'.

Some questionnaires have been validated by administering them to known institutionalised alcoholics. However, this method begs the question that the only definition of an alcoholic is one who is admitted to an institution. [418] Other research workers have used, as an external criterion of validity, the responses from members of the immediate family (*see* Chapter 11). In some community surveys, the individual alcoholics detected have been 'checked' by reference to records of such agencies as hospitals and probation officers. [117]

Mulford and Miller[363] in their comprehensive Iowa community study utilised other external criteria to test the validity of four different scales that were administered to individuals. They concluded that there was sufficient evidence to suggest the validity of one of the scales termed the Iowa Scale of Preoccupation with Alcohol. Firstly, the prevalence rate produced from a certain cut-off point was the same as would be expected from the Jellinek formula. This presumes the validity of the Jellinek estimation which has been disputed (*see* Chapter 1). Secondly, the authors considered that the Preoccupation Scale had a logically expected association with the three other measures that they had devised. Thirdly, the Scale was found to identify medically diagnosed alcoholics in up to 90% of cases. Finally, it repeatedly identified a small segment of the population with similar sociocultural characteristics. Clearly each of these criteria is open to criticism, but taken together they may be considered to provide a reasonable validation.

In view of all the difficulties it is perhaps not surprising that most studies have relied on face validity including the direct interview surveys carried out in England (*see* Chapter 1). Despite the criticisms reviewed above I considered it necessary to attempt a validation of the questionnaire by two methods. Firstly, a random sample of patients were re-interviewed by a psychiatrist, and the clinical assessment correlated with the STAQ classification. Secondly, the questionnaire was administered to hospitalised alcoholics to check its ability to identify the established alcohol addict.

9.1.3 Patients and Methods

Over a period of 16 weeks (21 June-11 October, 1971) the Consultant-in-Charge of the Alcoholism Treatment Unit at Springfield Hospital, Manchester (Dr Brian Hore) and his Registrar (Dr Jan Alsafar), interviewed patients who had previously received questionnaires, at weekly sessions of $1\frac{1}{2}$ hours each. The interview was a semi-structured one lasting about 10 minutes and was designed to elicit the drinking status of the informant at the time of interview, and whether there had been a change in recent years. At the pilot interviews, an attempt was made to determine the drinking status at the time of completion of the STAQ, but this was later rejected because of the difficulties of making an accurate assessment.

The psychiatrists were given only the Index Number of the informant, and were not provided with the informant's name or STAQ classification. This work was carried out in the spare time of the psychiatrists, and a prearranged period was agreed upon in which to complete the study.

Originally, a variety of stratified random sampling techniques were considered, but these had to be rejected because of the poor attendance figures, and ultimately, *every* heavy drinker, problem drinker and alcohol addict was invited to attend for interview in addition to a simple random sample of social drinkers.

Initially, a table of random numbers referring to the Index Number of the patient was used to select patients for interview. The patient's National Health Service record card was then extracted to ascertain whether the patient was still registered at the Health Centre, his present address, and whether he appeared well enough to attend the surgery. A note was made of patients who were not eligible for interview because of death, not being registered, or because their records were not available.

A cyclostyled letter was sent to the patient inviting him to attend to answer some more questions on his spare time activities, and a stamped addressed envelope with a slip for returning was enclosed. The patient's name was not mentioned on the letter, but only the Index Number to suggest confidentiality, and the letter was signed *per pro*. the doctor with whom the patient was registered.[390] About half way through the validation study, a less formal letter was devised in an attempt to improve the attendance rate.[390]

If a patient returned the slip stating that he could not or would not attend, another patient was sent for that session and, depending on the circumstances, the patient was sent for again on a later occasion.

Records were kept of envelopes returned by the Post Office because of address unknown, patient unknown, house demolished, et

For the convenience of the interviewers, sessions were held on a week day from 5.00-6.30 p.m. for the first 9 weeks. For the remainder of the period, the psychiatrists agreed to attend evening sessions from 7.00-9.00 p.m., but there was no improvement in attendance figures. Initially, 5 patients were sent for each session, and an appointment time given to the patient. Later, this was increased to 8 and then 10, and ultimately 50 patients were sent for each session with no fixed appointment being stated.

None of these devices appeared to improve the attendance rate. Consequently, the social worker attached to the practice (Mrs Eileen Ineson) agreed to visit the homes of a random sample of nonattenders to interview the patient, relative or neighbour to find out the reason for nonattendance, and if possible offer a fresh appointment. If access to the home was not possible, a letter was left suggesting another appointment.[390]

A random sample of problem drinkers and alcohol addicts who did not attend on the first invitation were sent second appointments, and three appointments were sent to one of each of the 4 categories of drinker whose replies suggested they might attend.

Those patients who attended were not told by the psychiatrists the true purpose of the interview, although most of the questions naturally related to drinking.

9.1.4   Results

Response to invitations

Table 56 analyses the responses to the first invitation. A total of 231 patients received at least one invitation to attend for interview, but only 42 (18%) attended in response to the first letter. It is noteworthy that 13 patients did not reply to the letter but attended for interview, and a further 12 replied saying they *would* attend, but did not. A total of 171 patients (74%) did not even reply to the letter, of which 15 letters were returned unopened by the Post Office because the patient was not living at the address to which they were sent. Only 6 patients replied saying they could not or would not attend on any occasion, of which only 1 gave no reasonable explanation. Thirteen patients replied stating they could not attend on the day suggested but were prepared to come on another occasion. Three patients arrived too late for the interview and had not replied to the letter.

Table 57 analyses the responses to the second invitation. In answer to the *first* letter, a total of 28 patients either replied in the affirmative but did not attend, were willing to come on another occasion, or arrived late for the appointment. It was intended to send second letters to all these patients, but only 13 received second invitations, as some of the first letters were sent towards the end of the interviewing sessions, and the psychiatrists had placed a limit on the number of sessions they were able to attend. A further random sample of 42 patients who did not reply to the first letter and did not attend were sent second letters, making a total of 55 patients who received second invitations. Fourteen patients (27%) attended in response to the second request.

Table 56   Response to the first invitation

| Response to first invitation | STAQ Classification | | | | | | | | Total |
| | Present (n = 136) | | | | Past (n = 95) | | | | |
	SD n = 31	HD n = 39	PD n = 31	AA n = 35	SD n = 2	HD n = 40	PD n = 34	AA n = 19	n = 231
No reply and no attendance	13	23	18	25	1	26	22	12	140
No reply but did attend	2	2	0	3	0	4	1	1	13
Replied in affirmative and attended	8	8	5	2	1	2	3	0	29
Replied in affirmative but did not attend	2	2	4	0	0	1	2	1	12
Replied in negative for given appointment	2	2	2	0	0	4	2	1	13
Cannot or will not attend ever	1	2	0	0	0	1	0	2	6
Letter returned to sender	3	0	1	3	0	2	4	2	15
Arrived too late for interview (and no reply)	0	0	1	2	0	0	0	0	3

Key: SD = Social Drinker   HD = Heavy Drinker
       PD = Problem Drinker   AA = Alcohol Addict

Table 57   Response to the second invitation

Response to second invitation	STAQ Classification								Total
	Present (n = 26)				Past (n = 29)				
	SD	HD	PD	AA	SD	HD	PD	AA	
	n = 4	n = 6	n = 8	n = 8	n = 0	n = 7	n = 17	n = 5	n = 55
Attended	1	2	1	4	0	2	2	2	14
Did not attend	3	4	7	4	0	5	15	3	41
First appointment—nonreply and nonattendance	3	4	5	7	0	5	14	4	42
First Appointment—nonattendance for given appointment	1	2	0	0	0	1	2	1	7
First Appointment—replied in affirmative but did not attend	0	0	2	0	0	1	1	0	4
First Appointment—arrived too late	0	0	1	1	0	0	0	0	2

Key as for Table 56

Table 58   Response to the third invitation

STAQ Classification	Response to FIRST invitation	Response to SECOND invitation	Response to THIRD invitation
Social Drinker (present)	No reply or attendance	Forgot	Attended
Heavy Drinker (past)	No reply or attendance	Unable to attend	Attended
Problem Drinker (present)	No reply or attendance	No reply or attendance in response to social worker	Nonattendance
Alcohol Addict (present)	No reply or attendance		Nonattendance

As shown in Table 58, four patients who did not reply or attend in response to the first letter received three invitations. One patient forgot to attend the second appointment, and one was unable to attend, and they both attended on the third occasion. Two patients did not reply or attend in response to the letter from the Social Worker, and were sent a third appointment in error, but neither attended. A grand total of 290 letters were sent out to 231 patients.

As shown in Table 59, initially, 286 patients were selected to receive letters, but 55 patients could not be sent appointments. A total of 44 patients (15%) were found to have left the practice (off list). The proportions of the different categories of drinker found to be 'off list' were 8% social drinkers, 15% heavy drinkers, 17% problem drinkers, and 18% alcohol addicts. A total of 10 patients' National Health Service records could not be traced because they were either mislaid, were temporary residents whose records had been returned to the Executive Council, or who had only attended the surgery on one occasion and had not been registered. None of these patients were social drinkers. One alcohol addict had died.

Table 60 summarises the four previous tables, and includes the percentages of the different categories of drinkers with classified questionnaires who were selected for interview.

Table 59 Patients selected for interview but not sent letter

STAQ Classification	Off List n = 44	No trace n = 10	Dead n = 1	Total n = 55	Grand Total n = 286
Social Drinker	3	0	0	3	36
Heavy Drinker	14	2	0	16	95
Problem Drinker	14	2	0	16	81
Alcohol Addict	13	6	1	20	74

Table 60 Summary Table of patients selected for interview

STAQ Classification	Sent for on ONE occasion only n = 172	Sent for on TWO occasions n = 55	Sent for on THREE occasions n = 4	Could not be sent for interview n = 55	TOTAL Selected n = 286	Classified STAQs	
						TOTAL n = 546 interview	% selected for interview
Social Drinker	28	4	1	3	36	296	12
Heavy Drinker	65	13	1	16	95	95	100
Problem Drinker	39	25	1	16	81	81	100
Alcohol Addict	40	13	1	20	74	74	100

'Classified STAQs' refers to the 546 questionnaires from a total of 554 administered which contained sufficient information to allow a classification of category of drinker to be made.

Although 52% of all patients were selected for interview, this comprised 100% of all heavy drinkers, problem drinkers, and alcohol addicts, and a random sample of 12% of the social drinkers.

Table 61   Visits by Social Worker

	Number
Patients' homes visited	32
Homes found to be demolished	5
Interviews with informants	2
Interviews with relatives	4
Interviews with household occupiers	4

The social worker was given the known addresses of a random sample of 32 patients (Table 61). The homes of 5 patients were found to be demolished, and their present addresses were unobtainable. Appointments were left for the remaining 27 patients.

In only 2 cases was the patient at home when visited. One was suffering from chronic illness and could not leave the house. The other was already attending her general practitioner regularly, and did not want to make a special visit for the psychiatric interview. She was prepared to be interviewed if it could be arranged at the same time as her appointment with her general practitioner (not possible).

In 4 cases, a relative was interviewed. One wife knew nothing about her husband's appointment, and another wife said that her husband never came home before 7.30 p.m. except on one day a week (attended for the new appointment). One father said his son was on holiday, and so a fresh appointment was made on his return but he never attended. One father said his son had now left the Manchester area.

In 4 cases the social worker interviewed someone living in the household who was not a relative, and left a letter offering an appointment. In one of these cases it was discovered that the informant had left the country to visit his sick mother.

Thus, from 32 visits, it was only possible to make fresh appointments for 27 patients. In only 6 cases was the informant or a relative personally interviewed. Three patients had genuine reasons why they could not attend. Four patients actually attended the new appointment. Three were alcohol addicts (including the patient who had left the Manchester Area), and one was a heavy drinker.

The *attendance rate,* based on the 32 homes visited, was therefore only 12.5%.

Attendance Rates

Table 62   Attendance Rates for all categories of drinker separately

STAQ Classification		Number sent for	Attendance		Classified STAQs	
			Number	Rate %	Total No.	% attended
Present	SD	31	12	39	291	4
	HD	39	12	31	46	26
	PD	31	6	19	41	15
	AA	35	9	26	46	19
	TOTAL	136	39	29	424	9
Past	SD	2	1	50	5	20
	HD	40	9	22	49	18
	PD	34	6	18	40	15
	AA	19	3	16	28	11
	TOTAL	95	19	20	122	16
GRAND TOTAL		231	58	25	546	11

(Key as for Table 56).

Table 62 summarises information contained in the previous tables relating to the attendance rate of the different categories of drinker; in addition it relates the attendance rates to the total number of classified questionnaires.

The overall attendance rate from patients sent letters was 25%, which represented 11% of the total number of classified questionnaires. There were no significant differences (at the 5% level) in the attendance rate:

1. for the different categories of *present* drinker as a proportion of those called for interview

    ($\chi^2 = 3.8$, d.f. $= 3, 0.40 > p > 0.30$)

2. for the different categories of *past* drinkers as a proportion of those called for interview

    ($\chi^2 = 0.47$, d.f. $= 2, 0.80 > p > 0.70$)

3. for *all present* drinkers pooled together compared with *all past* drinkers pooled together, as a proportion of those called for interview

    ($\chi^2 = 2.24$, d.f. $= 1, 0.30 > p > 0.20$)

    However, it should be noted that there was a significant difference in the different classifications of present and past drinkers ($\chi^2 = 23.85$, d.f. $= 3, p < 0.0005$) and so a simple comparison is not very meaningful.

4. between present and past drinkers of the different categories as a proportion of those called for interview

    Social drinkers: $p = 0.99$ (exact test)
    Heavy drinkers: $\chi^2 = 1.49$, d.f. $= 1, 0.30 > p > 0.20$
    Problem drinkers: $\chi^2 = 0.03$, d.f. $= 1, 0.90 > p > 0.80$
    Alcohol addicts: $\chi^2 = 0.24$, d.f. $= 1, 0.70 > p > 0.60$

5. between present and past categories of drinkers as a proportion of the total number of STAQ's administered to the different categories.

    Social drinkers: $p = 0.404$ (exact test)
    Heavy drinkers: $\chi^2 = 0.43$, d.f. $= 1, 0.60 > p > 0.50$
    Problem drinkers: Inspection clearly showed no significant difference.
    Alcohol addicts: $\chi^2 = 0.46$, d.f. $= 1, 0.50 > p > 0.40$.

Table 63   Attendance Rates for present and past drinkers combined

STAQ Classification	Number sent for	Attendance		Classified STAQs	
		Number	Rate	Total Number	% attended
SD	33	13	39	296	4
HD	79	21	27	95	22
PD	65	12	18	81	15
AA	54	12	22	74	16
TOTAL	231	58	25	546	11

(Key as for Table 56)

As shown in Table 63, the overall attendance rate for all drinkers as a proportion of those called for interview was 25%. There was no significant difference in the attendance rates for the different categories of drinkers, present and past pooled, as a proportion of those called for interview. ($\chi^2 = 5.43$, d.f. $= 3, 0.20 > p > 0.10$)

However, there were significant differences in the attendance rates for the different categories of drinker, present and past pooled, as a proportion of the STAQs administered to each category ($\chi^2 = 29.24$, d.f. $= 3, p < 0.005$). This was to be expected as a 12% random sample of social drinkers were selected for interview compared to 100% of the other categories.

Psychiatric Assessment

Table 64   Psychiatric Assessment—Heavy Drinkers

STAQ Classification	Number interviewed	Psychiatric Classification			
		Not Abnormal	Prodromal Problem Drinker	Problem Drinker	Alcohol Addict
Heavy Drinker	21	10	10	0	1

The psychiatric assessment of the heavy drinker is considered separately as the psychiatrists considered they could not assess this category at clinical interview. The psychiatrists were, however, asked to interview these patients to test the hypothesis that patients classified as heavy drinkers may, in fact, be problem drinkers or alcohol addicts.

Twenty-one patients were interviewed and 10 of them (48%) were designated as prodromal problem drinkers (*see* below) by the psychiatrists, and 1 was considered an alcohol addict (Table 64).

Table 65   Psychiatric Assessment—Social Drinkers, Problem Drinkers, Alcohol Addicts

STAQ Classification	Number interviewed	Psychiatric Classification			
		Not Abnormal	Prodromal Problem Drinker	Problem Drinker	Alcohol Addict
Social Drinker	13	13	0	0	0
Problem Drinker	12	2	2	3	5
Alcohol Addict	12	2	3	0	7
TOTAL	37	17	5	3	12

A total of 37 social drinkers, problem drinkers and alcohol addicts were interviewed by the psychiatrists (Table 65) who defined their classifications of patients as follows:

Not Abnormal Drinker. A patient who is either teetotal, or is a social drinker, with no evidence of any problems related to alcohol abuse.

Prodromal Problem Drinker. A patient whose drinking would appear, whilst not at the moment to be creating severe problems, to be very likely to do so in the future—for example, the patient whose efficiency at work has fallen off through drinking, but who has not yet actually been in trouble over this. A similar example might apply to a wife, who, whilst disturbed about her husband's drinking, has not yet made this a serious issue between them, but again, it appears very likely that this will be so.

Problem Drinker. A patient whose drinking quite clearly creates problems in any area of his life, whether it is medical, social etc., and who, despite this, continues drinking.

Alcohol Addict. A patient who shows one or more of the following symptoms:

> Drinking pattern of the 'loss of control' or 'inability to abstain' type
>
> Change in tolerance
>
> Presence of withdrawal symptoms, e.g. morning shakes

There was 100% correlation between the psychiatric and STAQ classification of the social drinkers.

There was correlation in only 3 out of the 12 problem drinkers, but if one considers the prodromal problem drinkers as mild problem drinkers as suggested by the psychiatric definition, then out of 12 problem drinkers there was correlation in 5 cases, and a further 5 were designated as alcohol addicts.

There was correlation in 7 out of the 12 alcohol addicts: 3 were designated as prodromal problem drinkers, and 2 as 'not abnormal drinkers'. One of these 'not abnormal drinkers' had been diagnosed as having 'alcoholic peripheral neuropathy' by a consultant physician 20 years previously, and his first wife left him because of his drinking. The other patient often attended the surgery smelling strongly of drink, assaulted his wife while drunk on a number of occasions, and she left him twice because of this.

If one classifies as 'alcoholic' the problem drinkers and alcohol addicts, then of the total 24, there was correlation by the psychiatrists in 15 cases (62.5%). If one considers the prodromal problem drinker as a variety of problem drinker, then there was correlation in 20 cases (83.3%).

The sensitivity and specificity of the screening test, defining the 'alcoholic' as the problem drinkers and alcohol addicts combined, was:

$$\text{Sensitivity} = \frac{\text{No. of psychiatrically diagnosed alcoholics with correct STAQ classification}}{\text{All psychiatrically diagnosed alcoholics}}$$

$$= \frac{15}{15}$$

$$= 100\%.$$

$$\text{Specificity} = \frac{\text{No. of psychiatrically diagnosed nonalcoholics with correct STAQ classification}}{\text{All psychiatrically diagnosed nonalcoholics}}$$

$$= \frac{13}{22}$$

$$= 59.1\%.$$

If the purpose of the STAQ is not to diagnose 'the alcoholic', but to detect those patients with a mild or severe drinking problem who require advice, then it is justifiable to include the prodromal problem drinker in the analysis. In this case,

$$\text{Sensitivity} = \frac{20}{20}$$

$$= 100\%.$$

$$\text{Specificity} = \frac{13}{17}$$

$$= 76.5\%.$$

Unfortunately, the numbers interviewed were small so that any analysis can only suggest trends, and must be considered in the light of the total number interviewed.

Table 66 comprises the psychiatric assessment (at the time of psychiatric interview) of the 19 patients whose STAQ classification was of a *past* drinker.

These results were examined to consider the possibility that some of the patients who admitted to problems in the past might be denying their current drinking status. As the psychiatrists did not interview at the same time as the STAQ was administered, the figures must be interpreted with caution.

Nine past heavy drinkers were interviewed by the psychiatrists who assessed one as a prodromal problem drinker and one as an alcohol addict. Three of the six past problem drinkers were considered to be alcohol addicts. It is unlikely that in the intervening period of 3-16 months these patients had suddenly developed symptoms of alcohol addiction. The three past alcohol addicts were classified as alcohol addicts. However, two of them were currently abstaining, but in the terminology of the psychiatric definition were assessed as 'alcohol addicts'.

9.1.5   Discussion

The most important aspect of this validation study was the poor response rate of 25%. It is not surprising that patients did not attend in any great numbers as there was nothing apparently to motivate them. An unsatisfactory response rate was anticipated, and unfortunately was not improved, despite deliberate tactics incorporated in the original design and a number of modifications made as the study proceeded.

It could be argued, that those alcoholics who did not recognise they had a problem would tend to stay away, whereas those who

Table 66 Current Psychiatric Assessment of STAQ-Classified PAST Drinkers

STAQ Classification		Number Inter-viewed	Psychiatric Assessment (current)				
			Not Abnormal Drinker	Prodromal Problem Drinker	Problem Drinker	Alcohol Addict
	Social Drinker	1	1	0	0	0
PAST	Heavy Drinker	9	7	1	0	1
	Problem Drinker	6	3	0	0	3
	Alcohol Addict	3	0	0	0	3
TOTAL		19	11	1	0	7

wanted help would grasp the opportunity to speak to a doctor. Although the letter offering an appointment made no mention of drinking, the questionnaire was referred to; the more severe a problem drinker, the more questions on drinking would have been answered by the patient, and the purpose of the questionnaire realised. It is interesting that one alcohol addict who had moved out of Manchester made a special effort to attend, and another alcohol addict took time off work to come from Liverpool for interview.

Response rates to questionnaires to alcoholics even from well motivated groups such as members of Alcoholics Anonymous have been reported as being only 10-47%.[360,419-420] This compares with a response rate of 60% from a questionnaire study of nonalcoholic psychiatric patients.[421] In community surveys to identify alcoholics, Mulford and Miller[363] found that 20.7% of the sample population refused to be interviewed whilst Cahalan and Cisin[422] found that 22% of heavy drinkers refused to be interviewed compared with 12.15% of those not classified as heavy drinkers.

From these studies it would appear that alcoholics are less likely than other groups to reply to questionnaires, and to be more reluctant to be interviewed.

Ideally, the patient on completing the questionnaire should have been offered an interview at the same surgery session. However, the present study relied on psychiatrists who kindly agreed to conduct interviews in their spare time and were not able to be present at all surgery sessions.

If one accepts that the purpose of the STAQ is to identify patients with a mild or severe drinking problem who may be potential or actual alcoholics, then the misclassification rate, i.e. proportion of patients incorrectly classified by the questionnaire, was 10.8%. The sensitivity was 100% and the specificity was 76.5%. These results compare very favourably with those of 8 other studies of a psychiatric questionnaire administered in general practice and reviewed by Goldberg.[79] However, if one excludes the 'prodromal problem drinker' from the analysis, the sensitivity is 100%, the specificity is 59.1% and the misclassification rate is 24.3%. All the results detailed above are based on a definition of 'the alcoholic' as the problem drinkers and alcohol addicts pooled. General practitioners have been criticised because they miss cases. This study has shown that *no* patient identified by the psychiatrists as being an 'alcoholic' was not also identified as such by the questionnaire. In other words, none of the STAQ-classified social drinkers were considered to be alcoholics by the psychiatrists.

Although the figures are regrettably small, the findings merit a more detailed analysis. One of the problems in classifying the categories of abnormal drinker was the meaning that should be given to the 'heavy drinkers'. It is interesting to note that of the 21 interviewed, 10 were considered prodromal problem drinkers, and one an alcohol addict. The results suggest that this group of abnormal drinkers is worth picking out from the social drinkers as patients 'at risk' to have or develop a drinking problem.

It should be reiterated that, during the course of their normal work, psychiatrists usually encounter established alcohol addicts, and a few severe problem drinkers. They have little, if any, experience of 'heavy drinkers' or even of alcoholics in the community as detected by the STAQ, perhaps many years before they would normally be seen at hospital. These observations must affect the likely validity of the psychiatric assessment, and account for the definition of prodromal problem drinker they developed in the early weeks of the validation study. In this connection, it is interesting that 2 out of the 12 STAQ-classified problem drinkers were assessed as prodromal problem drinkers despite the fact that in the questionnaire one of the patients admitted to a drinking offence, and the other patient admitted to health problems because of drink. A further 2 problem drinkers were assessed by the psychiatrists as being 'not abnormal drinkers'; both of these patients admitted, in the questionnaire, to arguments in the family about their drinking, and one of them said both he and his family thought he drank too much. Five of the problem drinkers were classified as alcohol addicts; one admitted to 2 problems and blackouts, one to health problems and drinking every day, one to a drunkenness offence, one to health problems, blackouts, and spending over £4.00 a week on alcohol, and one to arguments about drinking and spending over £4.00 a week on alcohol. It is not unexpected that a proportion of the STAQ-classified problem drinkers denied their addiction when answering the questionnaire, but were revealed at clinical interview to be alcohol addicts.

Of the 3 correctly classified problem drinkers, 2 of them admitted to 3 or more problems when answering the questionnaire. It would therefore appear that most of the misclassifications are due to the psychiatrists' understanding of a 'prodromal problem drinker' as a mild problem drinker, and a 'problem drinker' as a more severe problem drinker.

Considering the STAQ-classified alcohol addicts, the psychiatrists assessed 2 of them as being 'not abnormal drinkers'. As mentioned, there is evidence from the records and from the family doctor strongly suggesting that these patients were in fact, alcohol addicts who successfully lied to the psychiatrists. The three patients classified as prodromal problem drinkers all scored over 10 points and admitted to at least 3 symptoms of alcohol addiction in the questionnaire; their misclassification cannot be explained.

It is suggested that, although numbers are small, the validation study does appear to indicate that the STAQ is a satisfactory screening instrument for identifying, with a reasonable degree of accuracy, a segment of the population who are potential or actual alcoholics. In any future study, I would suggest that funds be made available to allow psychiatric interviews to take place immediately following the administration of the questionnaire.

9.2   ADMINISTRATION OF QUESTIONNAIRE TO KNOWN HOSPITALISED ALCOHOLICS

9.2.1   Introduction

Another method of validating the questionnaire was to administer it to a sample of known alcoholics and to determine the resulting STAQ classifications. Ideally, the sample should contain known nonalcoholics and the interviewer should not have prior knowledge of the drinking status of the patients. Unfortunately such a group could not be selected.

Another difficulty is that the characteristics of hospitalised alcoholics are likely to be different from those of alcoholics seen in the community who do not have hospital in-patient treatment.[21,149] Despite these two important criticisms, it was considered necessary to carry out the subsidiary validation study to confirm or otherwise the contention that hospitalised alcoholics would score high points on the questionnaire.

9.2.2   Patients and Methods

The questionnaire was administered to the 14 male and 1 female alcohol addicts who were in-patients at the Alcoholism Treatment Unit at Springfield Hospital, Manchester on one day in December 1971. There was a 100% response. As all the patients were abstinent at the time of interview, the questions were directed to their drinking behaviour immediately prior to admission.

9.2.3   Results

1.   Age Range: 31-61 years (mean 39 years)

2.   Sex: 14 males, 1 female

3. Marital Status: Single   2
                      Married   7
                      Divorced   4
                      Separated   2

4. Social Status: Social Class I   1
                                  II   0
                                  III   3
                                  IV   5
                                  V   6

5. Ethnic Group: British   11
                    Irish   2
                    European   2

6. STAQ Classification: All alcohol addicts

7. Range of scores: 12-26 (mean 18).

9.2.4 Discussion

The results were as expected. There was only one female (the unit has only 2 female beds), the mean age was 39 years, and 25% were separated or divorced. 73% were social class IV or V which is the distribution normally found at this Alcoholism Treatment Unit, although it is not typical of the country. 73% were of British origin. Only two patients were Irish.

All the patients were classified as alcohol addicts, and noone scored less than 12 points. The mean score was 18 points, compared with 16 points in the practice survey.

The defects of this study have been outlined above. Nevertheless, the results strongly suggest that those patients classified as alcohol addicts in the practice survey are correctly classified.

9.2.5 Conclusion

A validation study is described in which two psychiatrists interviewed a sample of patients classified by the STAQ as one of four categories of drinker. The results suggest that patients identified by the STAQ as being 'alcoholics' are likely to be similarly classified by the psychiatrists.

In the second study, 15 known hospitalised alcoholics received a STAQ. All the patients were correctly classified by the questionnaire, and the mean score was 18 points compared with 16 points scored by the alcohol addicts in the main survey. It is suggested that the results indicate that the STAQ classification of 'alcohol addict' is valid.

10 Reliability Study of the Questionnaire

'It is not for kings, O Lemuel, not for kings to drink wine nor for princes to crave strong drink; if they drink, they will forget rights and customs and twist the law against their wretched victims.'

Proverbs 31, 4-5.

This chapter describes a Reliability Study in which 41 patients received a questionnaire on two separate occasions

10.1 REVIEW OF THE LITERATURE

'A measuring instrument is *reliable* to the extent that repeat measurements made with it under constant conditions will give the same result (assuming no change in the basic characteristic being measured)'.[404] There are three methods generally used to measure reliability.

The *test-retest* technique involves the repeating of the same questions to the same people using the same methods, and the results are compared. The difficulties of this method are that the first questioning may have made respondents think more about the questions; they may try to be consistent in their two replies; they may make less effort the second time to give accurate answers, or they may deliberately falsify their answers on the second occasion. The interviewer may be biased if he remembers the original responses.

A second technique (*multiple form*) employs the use of two questionnaires believed to be equivalent, being administered successively to the same individuals. Although there is less risk of the first questioning affecting answers on the subsequent occasion, there is still the possibility that the characteristic itself has genuinely changed between the two occasions. If the two questionnaires are sufficiently correlated, then their connection may well be obvious to the subject. Also, differences between the two sets of answers will be a mixture of unreliability and differences between the items used.

The third technique (*split-half*) is generally considered to be the most accurate one. Only one questionnaire is used on one occasion, and it is assumed that any randomly selected part will fairly represent the whole. Respondents are asked to answer all the test items, and these items are then split into two halves by some random procedure, and the correlation between the total scores on the two 'sub-scales' is taken as a measure of reliability. This technique is only useful if there is empirical demonstration that the scale is a unity, so that either half may be taken as adequately representative of the whole, and that each half scale contains sufficient items to be reliable itself.

10.1.1 Alcoholism Surveys

In the field of alcoholism surveys, Elinson remarked in 1967[423] that 'it is hard to believe that there has been only one study reported of individual reliability'. This was the work of Bailey *et al.* [424] in New York who administered questionnaires in 1960-61, and gave an almost identical questionnaire to the same respondents in 1963-64. As the questions were not identically worded, and the second questionnaire used an embedding technique, the reliability of individual items could not be analysed, but only the classification of alcoholic determined by the two questionnaires. Of the 132 *alcoholics* identified in the first study, they were able to trace 99 who were re-interviewed. They reported that 25 of these 99 cases failed to confirm their problem drinking in the second study. Both questionnaires elicited a lifetime prevalence, and so the poor reliability was not due to a change in circumstances. In the first study, 343 were classified as presumed *nonalcoholics*, and in the second study 29 of them (8.5%) now admitted to drinking problems. The authors considered that at least 19 of the 29 newly discovered alcoholics had certainly had problems which long antedated the time of the original study. Thus both studies revealed considerable under-reporting, and it is not surprising that Bailey[368] concluded that 'the reliability of alcoholism survey data leaves a great deal to be desired'.

More recently, this view has been supported by three other surveys. Summers[425] interviewed 15 males who gave a lifetime drinking history when admitted to an in-patient alcoholism programme. On re-interview, 2 weeks later, 14 of them had changed their responses to 50% of the questions. Half of the respondents gave a more severe history, and half a less severe history. The answer to a history of blackouts and delirium tremens was changed in each case by 9 patients. The drinking pattern over the previous year was reported differently by 8 patients, and 4 patients altered their responses to the question asking how many years drinking had been a problem.

In 1971 Guze and Goodwin[426] reported the results of re-interview with 176 male criminals who were asked the same 17 questions

8-9 years previously with the aim of eliciting a lifetime prevalence of alcoholism. Of those classified as 'definite' or
'questionable' *alcoholics* at the first interview, 27% were classified as nonalcoholic at the second interview. Of those originally
classified *nonalcoholics,* 32% were classified as 'definite' or
'questionable' alcoholics at the second interview. The authors
considered that deliberate denial may have occurred in some
cases but was unlikely to have been the rule. There were too
many men who denied alcoholism symptoms at follow-up but *did*
admit to drug abuse, homosexuality and other socially undesirable
features, to conclude that they tried to picture themselves in a
more favourable light only with regard to alcoholism. Also, the
failure to receive a follow-up diagnosis of drug abuse etc. after
receiving one of these diagnoses originally, was the same for the
inconsistent alcoholics as for the consistent ones. Interviewer
bias was also not believed to be an important factor. However,
the authors concluded from a detailed analysis of the results
that 'the *more extensive* the original drinking problem, the more
likely the subject is to be consistent in his answers at follow-up'.
It should be noted that the subjects were prisoners, and the
results may not be applicable to all alcoholics.

Edwards *et al.* [427] have pointed out that if respondents are re-
interviewed after a comparatively short time lapse they may
remember their original answers, whereas with a longer time
interval there may have been a real change in drinking behaviour.
In both types of study there is a difficulty in assessing the degree
of reliability. They reported a preliminary survey in which 80
subjects were re-interviewed 2-3 months later with a shortened
version of the original questionnaire. Answers about drinking
behaviour generally showed about 70% consistency. On the second
occasion, 8% admitted fewer drinking problems.

These studies confirm the generally accepted opinion that 'it is
part of the pattern of an established alcoholic's behaviour to
deceive, confabulate and exaggerate'.[428]

Chalke and Prys Williams[429] concluded that 're-approach at a
later date is "scientifically" useless, because there is no means
of knowing if, and how far, the respondent has been conditioned—
in memory and even as to performance—by the process of completing the first interview'.

It is not surprising, therefore, that there have been so few reliability studies of alcoholism questionnaires. Nevertheless, despite
the difficulties, it was considered useful to carry out a Reliability
Study in the general practice setting.

Table 67 Original and Reliability STAQ classification of informant

Classification		Number of Patients		
Original	Reliability	Male (*n* = 22)	Female (*n* = 19)	Total (*n* = 41)
SD	SD	7	18	25
SD	HD	0	0	0
SD	PD	1	0	1
SD	AA	1	0	1
HD	SD	2	1	3
HD	HD	2	0	2
HD	PD	0	0	0
HD	AA	0	0	0
PD	SD	2	0	2
PD	HD	2	0	2
PD	PD	2	0	2
PD	AA	0	0	0
AA	SD	1	0	1
AA	HD	1	0	1
AA	PD	0	0	0
AA	AA	1	0	1

SD = Social Drinker HD = Heavy Drinker PD = Problem Drinker AA = Alcohol Addict

10.2 PATIENTS AND METHOD

A test-retest technique was used. At the conclusion of the survey year, in the subsequent 12 weeks, I administered a questionnaire to all patients who consulted in my own surgery sessions whose record cards were marked to indicate they had previously received a questionnaire. It was considered impractical to ask my colleagues to participate in this study.

10.3   RESULTS

The varying timespan (1-12 months) between completing the Original and Reliability STAQs, and the small numbers, gave rise to difficulty in assessing what meaning to assign to the *present* and *past* categories of drinker. The results for both categories were therefore combined.

Comparisons between the two questionnaire classifications were made by calculating the Serious Disagreement Rates (adapted from Kendell *et al*.).[410]

The *Serious Disagreement Rate* is defined as the proportion of alcoholics classified in the Original STAQ who were re-classified as nonalcoholics in the Reliability STAQ, and vice versa. An 'alcoholic' is defined as a problem drinker or alcohol addict, and a 'nonalcoholic' as a social drinker or heavy drinker, as classified by the STAQ.

Table 67 details the STAQ classification for thé *informant,* from the Original and the Reliability STAQ.

Table 68   Serious Disagreement Rates for social drinker informants. Comparison of Males with Females

Sex	No. of patients	Serious disagreement (by Reliability STAQ)
Male	9	2 (22%)
Female	18	0 (0%)

A comparison of serious disagreement rates between male and female informants was carried out for social drinkers only, since the numbers in the other 3 categories were small (Table 68). The difference was *not* significant (exact test. $p = 0.21$; not significant at 5% level).

Table 69   Serious Disagreement Rates between Reliability and Original STAQ classification of nonalcoholic and alcoholic informants

Original Classification	No. of patients	Serious Disagreement (by Reliability STAQ)
Nonalcoholic	32	2 (6%)
Alcoholic	9	6 (67%)

Table 69 compares the serious disagreement rates between the Reliability STAQ classification and the Original STAQ classification of informants classified in the Original STAQ as nonalcoholic (SD or HD) or alcoholic (PD or AA). The difference between the serious disagreement rates of 6% of nonalcoholics and 67% of alcoholics was significant (exact test: $p = 0.0009$; significant at 0.1% level).

Table 70   Original and Reliability STAQ classification of Family

Classification		Number of Patients		
Original	Reliability	Male $(n = 22)$	Female $(n = 19)$	Total $(n = 41)$
NA	NA	19	9	28
SD	SD	0	0	0
SD	HD	0	0	0
SD	PD	0	1	1
SD	AA	0	0	0
HD	SD	1	0	1
HD	HD	0	0	0
HD	PD	0	0	0
HD	AA	0	0	0
PD	SD	0	1	1
PD	HD	0	2	2
PD	PD	0	3	3
PD	AA	1	1	2
AA	SD	1	0	1
AA	HD	0	0	0
AA	PD	0	1	1
AA	AA	0	1	1

SD = Social Drinker   HD = Heavy Drinker   PD = Problem Drinker   AA = Alcohol Addict
NA = not applicable (refers to those STAQs where no points were scored in the family section of either the original or Reliability STAQ).

Table 70 details the STAQ classification for the family member, from the Original and the Reliability STAQ.

3 patients (HD, PD, AA) identified in family section of Original STAQ, received *no* points in the Reliability STAQ. In Table 70 above, they are considered as SD in the Reliability classification.

Table 71   Serious Disagreement Rates between Reliability and Original STAQ classification of nonalcoholic and alcoholic family members

Classification	No. of Patients	Serious Disagreement (by Reliability STAQ)
Nonalcoholic	30	1 (3%)
Alcoholic	11	4 (36%)

Table 71 compares the serious disagreement rates between the Reliability STAQ classification and the Original STAQ classification of family members classified in the Original STAQ as non-alcoholic (SD or HD) or alcoholic (PD or AA). The difference between the serious disagreement rates of 3% for nonalcoholics and 36% for alcoholics was significant (exact test: $p = 0.028$; significant at 1% level)

Table 72   Comparison of Serious Disagreement Rates relating to Informants and Family Members

	No. of Cases	Serious Disagreement
Informant	41	8 (19%)
Family	41	5 (12%)

Table 72 compares the total serious disagreement rates (between the Original and the Reliability STAQ) for the informants and the family members. There was no significant difference between the breakdown into nonalcoholic and alcoholic (Original STAQ) in the informants and family members $\chi^2 = 0.066$; d.f. = 1; $0.80 > p > 0.70$; not significant at 5% level). It is therefore permissible to pool the nonalcoholics and alcoholics in the two groups, and compare the total serious disagreement rates. The difference between the groups was not significant (Yates correction: $\chi^2 = 0.365$, d.f. = 1, $0.60 > p > 0.50$; not significant at 5% level).

10.4   DISCUSSION

10.4.1   Patients and Method

It should be pointed out that the Reliability STAQs were administered only by myself to those patients seen at my consulting
sessions over a period of 12 weeks. Consequently, the majority
of the patients were registered with me, and in some cases I was
aware of their likely drinking status. This observer bias might
have tended to *increase* the number of agreements between the
Original and Reliability STAQ classifications, and does not
explain the serious disagreement rates obtained. As in any test-
retest technique, the possibility of respondent bias due to
memory of the Original STAQ has to be considered.

Another problem is the conscious or subconscious suppression of
past problems from drink in those patients who had reduced or
stopped drinking in the intervening period between completing the
two questionnaires.

Additional respondent bias was potentially introduced in those
few patients who had been interviewed by a psychiatrist before
completing the Reliability STAQ.

It would be difficult to improve the reliability of the STAQ other
than by substantially increasing its length. The more questions
included, the greater the likelihood of obtaining an accurate
assessment of the drinking status of the individual. Guze and
Goodwin[426] observed that if the alcoholic was asked sufficient
questions, he might deny different symptoms at different times,
but there would be enough positive responses to enable a correct
diagnosis to be made. In this way, an attempt could be made to
allow for the fact that the 'very nature of the condition has
written into it the probability of the patient's often attempting to
deny his problem'.[95]

Despite the difficulties inherent in such a study, and the relative
smallness of numbers, the results provide some important information.

10.4.2   Results

A comparison between the Original and Reliability STAQ classifications of the *informants* showed that 6% of 32 *nonalcoholics*
(Original STAQ) were classified as alcoholics in the Reliability
STAQ. This was a significantly smaller proportion than the 67%
of 9 *alcoholics* (Original STAQ) who were classified as nonalcoholics in the Reliability STAQ.

It is possible that the originally classified alcoholics who denied
symptoms later had genuinely altered their drinking pattern in

response to the doctor's advice, and did not admit to their *past* problems in the Reliability STAQ. However, it should be noted that even if the patient had meanwhile become teetotal, the Reliability STAQ classification should have indicated that the patient was a *past* alcoholic.

An alternative explanation is that the alcoholics, realising the purpose of the questionnaire, deliberately falsified their responses in the Reliability STAQ. As reported in the Bailey *et al.* [424] study, the nonalcoholics had considerably *less* serious disagreement, perhaps because they felt no need to alter their answers. It is possible that the 2 originally classified non-alcoholics had became alcoholics in the intervening few months but this is unlikely. It is more probable that they had decided to reveal their true drinking status at the second interview.

A comparison between the Original and Reliability STAQ classifications of the *family members* showed that 3% of the 30 *non-alcoholics* (Original STAQ) were classified as alcoholics in the Reliability STAQ. This was a significantly smaller proportion than the 36% of 11 *alcoholics* (Original STAQ) who were classified as nonalcoholics in the Reliability STAQ. The same arguments apply as for the informants.

There was no significant difference between the total serious disagreement rates for the informants and the family members. It would appear, therefore, that the informants felt no need to reassess themselves and their families differently. The results of both informants and their families follow the same trend of a greater degree of serious disagreement with the originally classified *alcoholics* compared to the nonalcoholics. This was also found in the Bailey *et al.* [424] survey but not in the Guze and Goodwin[426] study of alcoholic criminals.

The results illustrate the difficulty of calculating accurate prevalence rates. A total of 41 patients were interviewed on both occasions. Only three alcoholics were identified from the two questionnaires, and eight alcoholics were identified from one of the questionnaires. The Original STAQ suggested that there were nine alcoholics, but the Reliability STAQ suggested that there were only five. It is unlikely that individuals would admit to being alcoholics if they are not, and the Validation Study of the Questionnaire (Chapter 9) confirmed that no false positives were reported. Thus any prevalence rate obtained is almost certainly an underestimate.

10.5   Conclusion

The Reliability Study illustrates the difficulty of detecting alcoholics by means of a screening questionnaire and confirms the importance of the factor of denial by the alcoholic. Nevertheless the possible identification of an alcoholic on any occasion is very likely to be significant even if he later denies his symptoms when re-questioned.

11 Family Correlation Study

'A man who loves wine and oil will never grow rich'

Proverbs 21, 17.

This chapter describes the results obtained from comparing the STAQ classification of an individual with that obtained from information given by a member of the family.

11.1 REVIEW OF THE LITERATURE

There have been four American studies where information on drinking behaviour reported by the subject has been correlated with that given by a close relative. That 'denial is often an essential component of the syndrome of alcoholism'[430] is widely accepted, and a comparison of 'self' and 'proxy' reports is obviously of considerable value. Unfortunately, denial is a common feature not only of the alcoholic, but also of the family, who may attempt to protect the alcoholic in their midst because of the social stigma still attached to the disease.

A comparison of self and proxy reports on 20 drinking-history items was reported by Guze *et al.*[431] for a sample of 90 male criminals (including 29 known alcoholics) and their relatives. The results conflict with the accepted view of denial being a *very* common feature, as the degree of disagreement between the alcoholics and the relatives averaged 26% of all questions asked, although the disagreement for the total sample was 15%. It was felt that 'the higher percentage in the alcoholics might be explained, in part, by the lower percentage of negative answers from both subjects and relatives'. In cases where the subject and relative disagreed on an item, about 80% involved a positive answer from the subject, and a negative answer from the relative. This was true in the entire sample of 90 as well as in the 29 identified alcoholics.

This study of alcoholic criminals can be compared with the extensive Iowa household survey of Mulford and Wilson[118] in which individuals were interviewed both about themselves and all other members of the household who were at least 21 years old or married. The prevalence of problem drinking indicated by self and proxy reports was examined. The analysis of self versus proxy responses among known alcoholics revealed that 'in households containing known alcoholics, proxies were more likely than the alcoholic himself to report trouble in the household' and were more inclined to rate the alcoholic higher on the scales of alcoholism used.

Another household study in Washington Heights, New York City, by Bailey *et al.*[424] also compared self and proxy data for each member of the households chosen. They reported that the wife was generally the informant for a whole family. It was found that respondents were 'slightly more apt to admit their own drinking problems and to deny those of other members'. Males living alone were more likely to be respondent-identified, and females living alone, or only with children under 16 years of age, 'tended to deny their drinking problems'. The tendency to conceal other problem drinkers in the family was especially marked when the respondent was a mother, and the drinker was an adult son.[432]

Room[442] reported the preliminary findings from the California Drinking Practices Study of 320 couples in a general sample of San Francisco, in which both spouses were interviewed about their own and their spouse's drinking behaviour. The results indicated that 'both of the possible patterns of disagreement occurred with some frequency, but that a respondent is a little more likely than his spouse to indicate problems with his drinking'.

The findings from 3 of the 4 studies reviewed suggest that the family members of the alcoholic are more likely to deny the existence of the problem than the alcoholic himself.

11.2   PATIENTS AND METHOD

Every patient interviewed in the present survey answered questions about members of his or her immediate family. Any known family member who later attended the surgery during the survey year also received a questionnaire. For a total of 63 patients, two STAQ classifications could be compared, one based on the patient's own assessment, and the other on information provided by the spouse.

In a smaller number of cases, it was possible to compare information given by a family member other than the spouse. These results are considered elsewhere.[390]

11.3   RESULTS

The varying time span (1-12 months) between completion of the questionnaire by informant and spouses, and the small numbers involved, gave rise to difficulty in assessing what meaning to assign to *present* and *past* categories of drinker. The analysis of the results therefore does not differentiate between present and past drinkers.

Comparison between the pairs of classifications was made by calculating Serious Disagreement Rates.

The *Serious Disagreement Rate* was defined as the proportion of patients where the two classifications differed as to whether the patient was an 'alcoholic' (problem drinker or alcohol addict) or 'nonalcoholic' (social drinker or heavy drinker).

In the Tables, 'self-classification' relates to information obtained from an individual personally.

Table 73 Husbands: Self-classification and Wife's classification

STAQ Classification of HUSBAND		Number of Patients ($n = 32$)
by Self	by Wife	
SD	SD	11
SD	HD	1
SD	PD	1
SD	AA	0
HD	SD	4
HD	HD	1
HD	PD	1
HD	AA	1
PD	SD	4
PD	HD	2
PD	PD	0
PD	AA	0
AA	SD	1
AA	HD	0
AA	PD	4
AA	AA	1

SD = Social Drinker HD = Heavy Drinker PD = Problem Drinker AA = Alcohol Addict

Table 73 compares the *husband's* STAQ classification of himself with the wife's STAQ classification of him in the family section of her STAQ. The wife's STAQ classification of her husband was recorded as social drinker when *no* points were scored in her family section.

Table 74   Serious Disagreement Rate (relating to Table 73)

HUSBAND's Self-Classification	No. of Patients	Serious Disagreement (by WIFE)
Nonalcoholic	20	3 (15%)
Alcoholic	12	7 (58%)

Table 74 compares the serious disagreement rates between the wife's classification of her husband (proxy) with that of her husband's self-classification, of *husbands* who classify themselves as either nonalcoholic (SD or HD) or alcoholic (PD or AA).

The results indicate that the wife seriously disagreed with her husband's STAQ classification of himself as a nonalcoholic in 15% of cases, compared to 58% of cases where the husband's STAQ classification of himself was alcoholic. This difference was significant (exact test: $p = 0.031$. Significant at 1% level).

Table 75   Wives: Self-classification and Husband's classification

STAQ Classification of WIFE		Number of Patients ($n = 31$)
by Self	by Husband	
SD	SD	27
SD	HD	1
SD	PD	1
SD	AA	0
HD		0
PD	SD	2
PD	HD	0
PD	PD	0
PD	AA	0
AA		0

Table 75 compared the *wife's* STAQ classification of herself with her husband's STAQ classification of her in the Family Section of his STAQ. The husband's STAQ classification of his wife was recorded as social drinker when no points were scored in his family section. There is one less correlation pair considered in this Table compared to Table 73 as the informant section of one wife's STAQ was incomplete, and the patient could not be classified.

Table 76 Serious Disagreement Rate (relating to Table 75)

WIFE's Self-Classification	No. of Patients	Serious Disagreement by HUSBAND
Nonalcoholic	29	1 (3%)
Alcoholic	2	2 (100%)

Table 76 compares the serious disagreement rates between the husband's classification of his wife (proxy) with that of his wife's self-classification, of *wives* who classify themselves as either nonalcoholic (SD or HD) or alcoholic (PD or AA).

The results indicate that the husband seriously disagreed with his wife's STAQ classification of herself as a nonalcoholic in 3% of cases, compared to 100% of cases where the wife's STAQ classification of herself was alcoholic. This difference was significant (exact test: $p = 0.01$. Significant at 1% level).

11.4 DISCUSSION

11.4.1 Patients and Method

The basic assumption was made that if an informant admitted to being an alcoholic, and the family denied it, then it was very likely that the informant's answers were nearer to the truth. Again, if an informant denied that he was an alcoholic, but the family considered that he was, it was very likely that the family's answers were nearer to the truth.

It is possible that the family might exaggerate the informant's problems deliberately because of their attitude to alcohol in general or the informant in particular. However, this is unlikely to be a significant factor.

Another point to be considered is the possibility of collusion between the family members, as the questionnaires were answered at different times. The individual who answered the questionnaire on the later occasion may have known what answers the member of his family had previously given.

A further reason why there might be disagreement is the insufficient knowledge that the family might have of the alcoholic member. There is some evidence from a family morbidity survey (not concerned with alcoholism) that wives report that their husbands have a lower incidence of morbidity than that admitted personally by the husbands.[433]

It is considered that none of these possible sources of error seriously affect the trends suggested by the results.

11.4.2   Results

The results indicate that, of these patients who personally admitted to being alcoholics, 64% of the spouses did not reveal that a problem of alcoholism existed in the family. On the other hand, of those patients who denied they were alcoholics, 8% of the spouses considered that this was not true. This difference was statistically significant.

Contrary to what one might expect, it is the *spouse* who covers up for the alcoholic partner, rather than the alcoholic himself. Thus family doctors seeking to detect alcoholism cannot, on the basis of this study, hope for more success from questioning the spouses of suspected alcoholics, than from questioning the suspected alcoholic himself. These results confirm three of the four American studies described earlier.

12 Conclusions

'Do not gulp down the wine, the strong red wine when the
droplets form on the side of the cup; in the end it will bite
like a snake and sting like a cobra.'

Proverbs 23, 31-32.

The alcoholic is often 'hidden' because he suffers from a disease
of denial—by himself, his family, society, and sometimes, the
medical profession.

Self-recognition of the illness in its early stages is rare; admitting
it to others is still rarer. Of the 155 alcoholics identified in the
survey, only eight consulted specifically for help with their drinking problem. Admittedly, many early alcoholics do not appreciate
that alcohol is harming them. However even when they realise
the true situation they are unlikely to hurry to their family
doctor for help. The middle-aged man who has slight chest pain
does not wait till his third coronary thrombosis before seeking
medical aid. How unlike the alcoholic. He may have an operation
for peptic ulcer, criminal convictions for drunken driving, and his
wife may leave him before he is ready to admit he has a drinking
problem. Even if symptoms are acknowledged when completing a
questionnaire, we found that two-thirds of such people will deny
alcohol abuse when re-interviewed.

Regrettably, we cannot rely on the family to suggest the diagnosis.
Only four wives requested help for their husbands' alcoholism.
Of twelve alcoholic husbands who admitted their illness, seven
wives when interviewed did not mention that they had an alcoholic
spouse. Were they protecting their husbands, or did they not
know?

Denial by society is the root cause of denial by the alcoholic and
his family. It was only in 1962 that alcoholism was officially
recognised as a disease by the medical profession. Despite the
excellent work of the Alcoholism Information Centres and public-
ity in the media, alcoholism is still a disease of stigma and
shame. The medical student and general practitioner of yesterday,
but perhaps not of today, received little if any instruction in the
recognition and management of the condition. Unless he has a
high index of suspicion he is unlikely to spot the alcoholic who
presents in the consulting room with a variety of symptoms.
Some of us deny that alcoholism is a medical problem or, if ad-

mitting that it is, assert that it is not worth expending the time and energy in detecting and treating it. As one general practitioner writes: 'it is doubtful whether he should ever go searching through his practice to discover hitherto undetected cases, for on this road lies disillusionment, disappointment and downright damage'.[434] It is to be hoped that this view is held only by a minority.

The general practitioner is faced with the daunting prospect of recognising the alcoholic through a smokescreen of denial erected by the patient and his family. This book describes the use of a screening instrument, a disguised questionnaire, to detect alcoholics by administering it to selected 'at risk' patients. In practical terms, what do the results suggest? For one year, a general practitioner need spend only about 15 minutes a week interviewing patients specifically to detect alcoholism. If he has an average list of 2500 patients living mainly in an overcrowded urban area, he may originally be aware of about three alcoholics. One year later, he will probably have detected at least another thirty. In succeeding years with even less effort, this figure would probably increase. The prevalence rates suggested by the study are certainly underestimates. Whether they are an accurate reflection of the extent of alcoholism elsewhere, cannot yet be assessed. Other workers are preparing a slightly modified version of the project to be carried out in two other general practices in England and Scotland.

The present study strongly suggests that the Spare Time Activities Questionnaire is a simple yet useful means of considerably increasing the general practitioner's knowledge of the alcoholics in his practice. Recognition is the essential prerequisite to offering treatment. But knowledge of the illness obtained in a devious way is certainly no guarantee that the patient will accept the diagnosis and the treatment offered. Only time will tell whether the disease has been arrested or even reversed. It is to be hoped that the problem drinkers will develop no new problems and not become physically dependent, and that the alcoholic addicts will become abstinent and remain so for a greater or lesser period of time. A particularly interesting group are the heavy drinkers: will they cut down their drinking or progress to alcoholism? Will the 'at risk' social drinkers eventually become alcohol abusers to a greater extent than the 'not at risk' social drinkers? Can these two groups be shown to be different personality types? The answers to these questions must await further research.

The most significant feature of this survey is that a group of patients have been labelled as abnormal drinkers. The diagnosis may not be accepted the first time it is offered to the patient.

But on every occasion he consults for whatever reason, whether he has changed to another practitioner or not, the information will be available in the records. Sooner or later, the general practitioner with sympathy and understanding will be able to persuade the alcoholic that he needs guidance.

Surely the time is near when the 'hidden alcoholic' will no longer feel the 'leper of the modern day world'.[435] A general practitioner wrote with reference to alcoholism: 'Why it is even suggested that this should be the responsibility of the general practitioner is surrounded by a certain mystery'.[120] I sincerely hope that this study provides a clue to solving this apparent mystery.

Appendix One

SPARE TIME ACTIVITIES QUESTIONNAIRE (STAQ 2)

I. THE INFORMANT

A. INFORMANT PROFILE

Doctor completes:- Ringed items (1) (4) (11) (12)
                  If married more than once, ring 7, no. 3

(1.) Surname............ Forename..........

2. Index number   1-4   ☐☐☐☐

3. Patient Serial Number   5-11   ☐☐☐☐☐☐☐

(4.) Date of Interview   12-17   ☐☐☐☐☐☐

5. Date of Birth   18-23   ☐☐☐☐☐☐

6. Sex   1. Male 2. Female 24   ☐

7. Marital Status:-   25   ☐
        1. Single
        2. Married (once)
        3. Married (More than once)
        4. Divorced
        5. Separated
        6. Widowed
        7. Single (living as married)
        8. Other
        0. No information

8. Social Status:-   26   ☐
        0. No information

9. Occupation................... 27-29 ☐☐☐

205

10. Ethnic Group:-   30   ☐
    1. Mainland British (B)
    2. Irish (I)
    3. Other whites (E)
    4. West Indian (W)
    5. African coloured (A)
    6. Pakistan or Indian (P)
    7. Other coloured (O)
    8. No information

⑪ Residential Unit:-   31   ☐
    1. Living with spouse
    2. Living with cohabitant
    3. Living with other adult relatives
    4. Living with dependent children
    5. Living alone
    6. Digs
    7. Hostel for destitutes
    8. Student Hall of Residence
    9. Other
    0. No Information

⑫ Doctor completing questionnaire   32   ☐

B.   THE QUESTIONNAIRE

Ring the relevant numbers. Do *not* fill in the boxes. If patient refuses to
answer any question, draw diagonal line through question. If patient
refuses to answer questionnaire, draw diagonal line through patient profile, and write name.

1. Food—Do you consider yourself:-
    1. Poor eater
    2. Average eater
    3. More than average eater

2. Cigarettes—Do you smoke:-   33   ☐
    3. Never
    2. 20 or less/day
    1. More than 20/day
    0. Don't know

3. Television—Do you watch television:-
    1. Rarely or never
    2. Occasionally (< 3 evgs/week)
    3. Regularly (3 evgs/wk or more)

4. Do you drink alcohol:-
    6. Never
    5. Only on special occasions
    4. Every few weeks
    3. Once or twice a week
    2. More than twice a week
    1. Every day
    0. Don't know

(1)

34 ☐

5. Are you drinking the same, or more, or less,
    than you used to:-
    1. Same
    2. More (1)
    3. Less (1)
    4. Don't know
    5. Not applicable

35 ☐ 2/3=1

(if never drinks alcohol now or in past, go to family questionnaire)

6. Have you ever taken any drugs such as cannabis or L.S.D.? (Open)
    1. No
    2. Cannabis
    3. L.S.D. Group
    4. Amphetamine Group
    5. Opiate Group
    6. Other drugs of dependence
    7. Taken more than one drug of
       dependence

36 ☐

7. Have you ever had problems with your health because of the
    following:-
    Eating too much
       2. Yes   3. No   4. Don't know
    Smoking too much
       2. Yes   3. No   4. Don't know
    Overworking
       2. Yes   3. No   4. Don't know
    Drinking
       2. Yes   3. No   4. Don't know

(2)

37 ☐

8. Have there ever been arguments in your family about yourself
    because of the following:-
    Work
       2. Yes   3. No   4. Don't know   38 ☐
    Gambling
       2. Yes   3. No   4. Don't know   39 ☐

Friends
    2. Yes   3. No   4. Don't know
In-laws
    2. Yes   3. No   4. Don't know

(2)

Drinking
    2. Yes   3. No   4. Don't know   40 ☐

Trouble with Police
    2. Yes   3. No   4. Don't know   41 ☐

If 'YES' have you been in trouble with
Police:-
    1. Once
    2. Twice
    3. 3 or more times   42 ☐

What were the offences? (open)

Drunk and disorderly/incapable and/or
Drunken driving and/or offence   43 ☐
committed while under the influence of
drink
    0 1 2 3 or more times
Other offences 0 1 2 3 or more times   44 ☐

9.   Do you think that you now or in the past:-

Eat too much
    1. Yes   2. No   3. Don't know
Smoke too much
    1. Yes   2. No   3. Don't know
Drink too much

(1)

        now
    1. Yes   2. No   3. Don't know   45 ☐

Drank too much

(1)

    in the *past*
    1. Yes   2. No   3. Don't know   46 ☐

10. Does anyone in your family think that you now or in the past:-

Eat too much
    1. Yes   2. No   3. Don't know
Smoke too much
    1. Yes   2. No   3. Don't know
Drink too much

(1)

        now
    1. Yes   2. No   3. Don't know   47 ☐

Drank too much

(1)

    in the *past*
    1. Yes   2. No   3. Don't know   48 ☐

(If denies problems or heavy drinking, go to family questionnaire)

11. Have you ever had serious money problems because of the following:-

Illness
    2. Yes   3. No   4. Don't know   49 ☐

Unemployment
    2. Yes   3. No   4. Don't know   50 ☐

                                 (2)

Drinking
    2. Yes   3. No   4. Don't know   51 ☐

Gambling
    2. Yes   3. No   4. Don't know   52 ☐

12. Have you ever lost a job or got into trouble at work, such as arriving late, or being off work for a few days, because of the following:-

Illness
    2. Yes   3. No   4. Don't know   53 ☐

Disagreement with people at work
    2. Yes   3. No   4. Don't know   54 ☐

                                 (2)

Drinking
    2. Yes   3. No   4. Don't know   55 ☐

13. When you smoke, do you prefer to smoke:-
    1. Alone
    2. In company
    3. Either
    4. Not applicable

14. When you drink, do you prefer to drink:-
    1. Alone
    2. In company
    3. Either   56 ☐   1AA

15. Have you ever woken up in the morning after some drinking the night before and found you could not remember a part of the previous evening, even though you weren't incapable?

    2. Yes   3. No   4. Don't know   57 ☐   2AA

16. Have you ever tried to:-
Lose weight   1. Yes
                  2. No
If 'YES' did you succeed 1. Yes
                          2. No

Cut down or   1. Yes
stop smoking   2. No
If 'YES' did you succeed 1. Yes
                          2. No

Cut down or   1. Yes   58 ☐
stop drinking   2. No
If 'YES' did you succeed 1. Yes   (1)
                          2. No   59 ☐   2AA

17. When you wake up in the morning, do you sometimes:-
    Have a cigarette
        2. Yes   1. No
    Have a drink of alcohol
        2. Yes   1. No   60 ☐ 2AA

18. After taking one or two drinks, can you usually stop drinking:-
        1. Yes   2. No   61 ☐ 2AA

Finally, a few questions on your spending habits.

19. How much money do you spend on cigarettes a week?
        1. None
        2. Up to £2
        3. £2 or more
        4. Don't know   62 ☐

20. How much money do you spend on entertainment per week?
        1. None
        2. Up to £2
        3. £2 or more
        4. Don't know

21. How much money do you spend on alcohol per week?
        1. None
        2. Up to £4
        3. £4-8 (1)
        4. £8 or more (1)
        5. Don't know   63 ☐ 3/4=1

22. If amount of drinking has changed (question 5) did you used to spend
    on alcohol:-

        1. None
        2. Up to £4
        3. £4-8 (1)
        4. £8 or more (1)
        5. Don't know
        6. Not applicable   64 ☐ 3/4=1

(FOR OFFICE USE)

    Points scored   65-66 ☐☐

    Type of Drinker   67 ☐

    Age last Birthday   68-69 ☐☐

II.   THE FAMILY

Patient Index Number   1-4 ☐☐☐☐

The following questions refer to members
    of your family, i.e.:-
        1. Father
        2. Mother
        3. Wife
        4. Husband
        5. Brother
        6. Sister
        7. Son
        8. Daughter
        9. Other relative who has brought you up
        0. Cohabitant

*(If during interview, it emerges that more than 1 member of family is
affected by drink, ask the questions about the spouse, or if no spouse
affected, one member, and make note of the members affected—Section III
No. 2)*

1.   Has any member of your family ever had problems with their *health*
     due to the following:-

     Eating too much
         2. Yes   3. No   4. Don't know
     Smoking too much
         2. Yes   3. No   4. Don't know
     Overworking
         2. Yes   3. No   4. Don't know
     Drinking   (2)
         2. Yes   3. No   4. Don't know   5 ☐

2.   Have there ever been *arguments* in the family
     about some *other* member of the family,
     not yourself, because of the following:-

     Work
         2. Yes   3. No   4. Don't know   6 ☐
     Gambling
         2. Yes   3. No   4. Don't know   7 ☐
     Friends
         2. Yes   3. No   4. Don't know
     In-Laws
         2. Yes   3. No   4. Don't know
     Drinking   (2)
         2. Yes   3. No   4. Don't know   8 ☐

Trouble with Police
  2. Yes   3. No   4. Don't know   9 ☐

If 'YES' has relative been in trouble with
Police:-
        1. Once
        2. Twice
        3. Three times or more.   10 ☐

What were the offences? (Open)

Drunk and disorderly/incapable ⎤
and/or Drunken driving   ⎥ 0 1 2 3 or
and/or offence committed while   ⎰ more times   11 ☐
under influence of drink   ⎦

Other offences   0 1 2 3 or
                          more times   12 ☐

3. Do you think anyone in your family now
    or in the past:-
    Eats too much
        1. Yes   2. No   3. Don't know
    Smokes too much
        1. Yes   2. No   3. Don't know
    Drinks too much   **(1)**
              now
        1. Yes   2. No   3. Don't know   13 ☐
    Drank too much   **(1)**
           in the past
        1. Yes   2. No   3. Don't know   14 ☐

(If no member of family affected by drink, go to Section III)

4. Has any member of your family ever
    had serious *money* problems because of
    the following:-

    Illness
        2. Yes   3. No   4. Don't know
    Unemployment
        2. Yes   3. No   4. Don't know
    Drinking   **(2)**
        2. Yes   3. No   4. Don't know   15 ☐
    Gambling
        2. Yes   3. No   4. Don't know   16 ☐

5. Has any member of you family ever lost
    a job or got into trouble at work, such
    as arriving late, or being off work for
    a few days because of the following:-
    Illness
        2. Yes   1. No   3. Don't know   17 ☐

Disagreement with people at work
    2. Yes   1. No   3. Don't know   18 ☐
Drinking   (2)
    2. Yes   1. No   3. Don't know   19 ☐

Now to finish off, I would like to ask you some questions about
your (   ).

6. Does he/she prefer to drink:-
        1. Alone
        2. In company
        3. Either
        4. Don't know   20 ☐ 1AA

7. Has he/she ever woken up in the morning
    after some drinking the night before and
    found he/she could not remember a part
    of the previous evening, even though he/
    she was not incapable:-

        2. Yes
        3. No
        4. Don't know   21 ☐ 2AA

8. Has he/she ever tried to cut down or
    stop drinking:-

        1. Yes
        2. No
        3. Don't know   22 ☐

    If 'YES' did he/she succeed:-
        1. Yes
        2. No   (1)
        3. Don't know   23 ☐ 2AA

9. When he/she wakes up in the morning,
    does he/she sometimes have a drink
    of alcohol:-

        2. Yes
        3. No
        4. Don't know   24 ☐ 2AA

10. After taking 1/2 drinks, can he/she
    usually stop drinking:-

        1. Yes
        2. No
        3. Don't know   25 ☐ 2AA

END OF INTERVIEW

(FOR OFFICE USE)

      Points scored   26-27 ☐ ☐
      Type of Drinker   28 ☐

III.   QUESTIONS FOR G.P.

1.   About which member of the FAMILY has the informant answered
      questions?

      0. Noone
      1. Full name................ Relationship to
                                  informant   29 ☐

  Who is the doctor 1-7. D.H.H.C. Doctor
                       8. Other Doctor
                       9. Has no Doctor   30 ☐

2.   Are any OTHER members of FAMILY affected by
      drink:-

      1. No
      2. Yes   31 ☐

  If 'YES', who:-
      Full name.................Relationship
                                to informant 32 ☐

      Full name.................Relationship
                                to informant 33 ☐

3.   Do you think informant *is*:-

      1. Social drinker
      2. Heavy drinker
      3. Problem drinker
      4. Alcohol addict   34 ☐
      5. Not applicable
      6. Don't know

4.   Do you think informant *was*:-

      1. Social drinker
      2. Heavy drinker
      3. Problem drinker
      4. Alcohol addict   35 ☐
      5. Not applicable
      6. Don't know

5.   Do you think the *member of family* with drinking
      problem who has been investigated *is*:-

      1. Social drinker
      2. Heavy drinker
      3. Problem drinker
      4. Alcohol addict   36 ☐
      5. Not applicable
      6. Don't know

6. Do you think this affected *member was*:-

    1. Social Drinker
    2. Heavy drinker
    3. Problem drinker
    4. Alcohol addict   37 ☐
    5. Not applicable
    6. Don't know.

7. Has questionnaire already been given to any other member of FAMILY

    1. No
    2. Yes   38 ☐

If 'YES', whom:-
    Full name .... Relationship
                        to informant 39 ☐

    Full name .... Relationship
                        to informant 40 ☐

IV. ALCOHOL AT RISK REGISTER (AARR)

Ring the numbers of any category which informant fits.

01. Physical diseases associated with   (2)
alcoholism.   41-42 ☐☐
    01. Pancreatitis
    02. Cirrhosis of Liver
    03. Peptic Ulcer
    04. Gastritis
    05. Peripheral neuritis
    06. Tuberculosis
    07. Congestive heart failure of
         unknown origin
    08. Epilepsy for first time at 25 years
         or over from no apparent cause
    09. Malnutrition
    10. Obesity (men)
    11. Haematemesis or melaena

02. Mental diseases.   43-44 ☐☐

    01. Anxiety state
    02. Depression
    03. Attempted suicide
    04. Any other—if so, what .... 45 ☐

03. Alcoholic symptoms.   46-47 ☐☐

    01. The shakes
    02. Blackouts
    03. Delirium tremens
    04. Alcoholic epilepsy
    05. Any others—if so, what............ 48 ☐

04. Occupations associated with alcoholism.   49-50

     01. Catering trade
     02. Publicans and others working in a
          pub, or the drink industry
     03. Travelling salesmen
     04. Journalists
     05. Entertainers
     06. Executives
     07. Printing industry
     08. Market porters
     09. Seamen
     10. Miners

05. Work problem   51-52

     01. Three or more jobs in year
          preceding consultation
     02. Three or more spells of absence
          off work in year preceding con-
          sultation for three days or less
     03. Patient requesting certificate for
          absence from work for conditions
          which are possibly not genuine.

06. Accidents   53-54

     01. At work
     02. At home
     03. Road traffic

07. Criminal Offences   55-56

     02. Drunk and disorderly/incapable
          and/or drunken driving, and/or
          offence committed under influence
          of drink
     01. Any other

08. Family problems   57-58

     01. Children suffering from neglect
     02. Family disharmony
     03. Children with mental disturbance
          including nocturnal enuresis

09. Help asked to treat alcoholism by:-   59-60

     02. Patient
     01. Father of suspected alcoholic
     03. Mother of suspected alcoholic
     04. Wife of suspected alcoholic
     05. Husband of suspected alcoholic
     06. Brother of suspected alcoholic

07. Sister of suspected alcoholic
08. Son of suspected alcoholic
09. Daughter of suspected alcoholic
00. Other relative of suspected
    alcoholic
    if so, who......................   61 ☐
11. Member of anciliary staff or
    social agency, if so, which
    category ....

10. Patient smelling of drink at consultation:-   (2)
    01. No   62 ☐
    02. Yes

11. Marital status:-   63 ☐

    01. Single, male, 40 yrs. and over
    02. Married more than once
    03. Divorced
    04. Separated
    05. Other

12. Living in a hostel for destitutes:-   (2)
                                           64 ☐
    01. No
    02. Yes

13. Known alcoholic (confirmed by   (2)
    psychiatrist):-   65 ☐
    01. No
    02. Yes

14. Family history of abnormal drinking:-   66 ☐
    01. No
    02. Yes

15. Informant is interviewed because NHS
    record card has light blue marker:-   67 ☐
    01. No
    02. Yes

16. Informant is interviewed as relative of
    suspected alcoholic because of cate-
    gories 1-9, 11-14   68 ☐

    01. No
    02. Yes

    If 'YES', which category   69-72 ☐☐☐☐

17. Any other reason why informant is
    interviewed:-   73   ☐

      01. No
      02. Yes

    If 'YES' why............................   74   ☐

18. What was *initial* reason for informant
    being interviewed   75-78   ☐☐☐☐

FOR OFFICE USE   79-80   ☐☐

Appendix Two

MODIFICATION OF STAQ 1

The results of the first 98 questionnaires (STAQ 1) administered in the first three weeks of the survey, were examined to determine whether an extra cut-off point could be introduced. This would reduce the size of the questionnaire for some patients and so would be less time-consuming for the doctors administering them. The results were as follows:-

No. of persons admitting *no* heavy drinking and *no* problems	50
No. of persons admitting heavy drinking only; *no* problems	9
No. of persons admitting problems only; *no* heavy drinking	1
No. of persons admitting problems *and* heavy drinking	38
TOTAL number of questionnaires administered	98

There were 38 persons who admitted heavy drinking *and* problems.

All 4 problems (arguments + police considered as one)	9
Arguments + health + money	4
Arguments + health + job	2
Arguments + health	5
Arguments + job	3
Arguments + money	2
Arguments only	10
Health only	2
Money only	1
Job only	0
TOTAL	38
Arguments	35
Health	22
Money	16
Job	14

The patients who admitted to heavy drinking refer to those who admitted to drinking too much either in the present or past. It can be seen that of the 39 problem drinkers, only 1 denied heavy drinking; this patient admitted only to a health problem. Only 1 problem drinker admitted to a money problem only, and no problem drinkers admitted only to a job problem. It was therefore decided to insert a cut-off point *before* the questions on money and job problems. Assuming that the slight change of question order from health—money—arguments—job—heavy drinking to that of health—arguments—heavy drinking—money—job would not affect the response rate, only 1 of the 39 problem drinkers (2.6%) would be missed. This error was considered justifiable in view of the likelihood that the doctors' interview rate would otherwise almost certainly have fallen off.

The opportunity was created by the decision to modify the order of questions to make some further slight alterations.

The types of residential unit were extended to include living with cohabitant, living with dependent children, and living in a Student Hall of Residence.

In STAQ 1 after asking the frequency of the informant's drinking, there followed two questions:

Has the pattern or amount of your drinking changed over the past few years?	1. Yes
	2. No
	3. Don't know.

If yes, do you now drink more or less?	1. More
	2. Less
	3. Not applicable.

In STAQ 2, these two questions were combined into one as follows:

Are you drinking the same, or more, or less, than you used to:-

1. Same
2. More
3. Less
4. Don't know
5. Not applicable.

It was considered that this modification would not significantly alter the responses.

The question in STAQ 1:-
'Have there ever been arguments in your family because of the following' was altered in STAQ 2 by inserting the words 'about yourself' after the word 'family'. It was found on checking the questionnaires that this question was wrongly interpreted by some informants who answered affirmatively—referring to arguments about the drinking of a member of the family and not the informant personally.

Appendix Three

SCORING METHOD

Points were allocated for positive answers to the questions relating to drinking, and for some of the AARR factors. The numbers in brackets refer to the columns used in the coding.

(a) *Informant*

	Points allocated
Drinks every day (34)	1
Change in drinking pattern (35)	1
Problems from drinking (37, 40, 51, 55)	2 each
Drunken offences (43)—1 offence	2
2 offences	3
3 or more offences	4
Informant drinks too much now *or* in the past (45, 46)	1 maximum
Family thinks informant drinks too much now *or* in the past.	1 maximum

(*N.B.* 1 Point was scored for either present *or* past, but if both present and past, only 1 point was scored.)

	Points allocated
Amount spent on drink now—£4 or more (63)	1
Amount spent on drink in past—£4 or more (64)	1
Alcohol addiction questions (AA):-	
Prefers to drink alone (56)	1
Blackout (57)	2
Cut down on drinking and succeeded (59)	1
Cut down on drinking but not succeeded (59)	2
Drinks alcohol in the morning (60)	2
After taking 1 or 2 drinks, cannot stop drinking (61)	2

(b) *Family*

Problems from drinking (5, 8, 15, 19)	2 each
Drunken offences (11)—1 offence	2
2 offences	3
3 offences or more	4
Drinks too much now or in past (13, 14)	1

(*N.B.* 1 point was scored for either present or past, but if both present and past, only 1 point was scored)

	Points allocated
Alcohol addiction questions (AA):-	
Prefers to drink alone (20)	1
Blackout (21)	2
Cut down on drinking and succeeded (23)	1
Cut down on drinking but not succeeded (23)	2
Drinks alcohol in the morning (24)	2
After taking 1 or 2 drinks, cannot stop drinking (25)	2

221

(c) *Alcoholic At Risk Register (AARR)*

Cirrhosis of the liver (41-42)	2
Alcoholic addiction symptoms excluding blackouts (46-47)	2 each
Publican and other workers in drink industry (49-50)	2
Help asked for by informant (59-60)	2
Help asked for by someone else (59-60)	1
Informant smelling of drink (62)	2
Living in hostel for destitutes (64)	2
Known alcoholic (65)	2

(d) *Miscellaneous Rules*

1.   An informant who admitted to a change in drinking habits scored 1 point (35). If he *also* admitted to having tried to cut down or stop drinking (59), he did not score an extra point. Only 1 point could be scored for either question.

2.   Certain AARR factors carried a 2 point score. These points only contributed to the total if the informant had scored a minimum of 2 points from actual responses to the questions.

3.   An informant was classified as a *present* drinker if he admitted that he drinks too much in the present (45), *or* his family thinks he does (47), *or* he spends £4 or more on alcohol per week in the present (63). *Any* of these 3 responses, if they relate to the *present*, took preference over any other response relating to the *past*. For example, if the informant answered that both he and his family thought he only drank too much in the past, but he admits to spending £4 or more in the *present*, then he was classified as a *present* drinker.

Appendix Four

STATISTICAL ANALYSIS

The data analysed comprised the combined results of STAQ 1 and STAQ 2 as no statistical difference was shown between the proportions of the different categories of Informant abnormal drinker identified (Appendix 2). Because of the different cut-off points in the two STAQs, the data for some of the questions was not strictly comparable. Allowance was made for this by including the column 'not applicable' for patients who did not answer certain questions because of an earlier cut-off point.

In those Tables, especially for females, where numbers were small, for the purpose of statistical analysis, the results for social drinkers and heavy drinkers were pooled, and for problem drinkers and alcohol addicts were pooled. The former group considered as 'nonalcoholic' and the latter group as 'alcoholic'.

Omitting of social drinker data from statistical tests

In some of the tables, the social drinker figures were omitted from the statistical tests, because the proportion of 'not applicable' was so high because of an early cut-off point as to make a meaningful interpretation of the social drinkers not possible.

In other tables, the figures for social drinkers were omitted from the statistical tests because they referred to questions which scored 2 points (problems, or symptoms of alcohol addiction). By definition, a social drinker could only score 0-1 point.

Omitting of heavy drinker data from statistical tests

The heavy drinker figures were omitted from the statistical tests for those questions which scored 2 points as, by definition, a heavy drinker could not give a positive response to a 2-point question (*see* above).

Pooling of results for 'no' and 'not applicable'

The results for 'no' and 'not applicable' were pooled in those tables where 'not applicable' could only refer to patients who were teetotal, or the proportion of 'not applicable' results were small.

Footnotes are added to those Tables where any of the modifications mentioned above were adopted.

Statistical Tests employed

The χ^2 test and the exact test (devised by Fisher and others) were used in the comparison of proportions. For calculating probabilities the latter test was used when it was felt that the χ^2 test would not give correct values.

The Kruskall Wallis' one-way analysis of variance by rank was used for comparison of results for 2 or more groups.

The Mann Whitney u-test was used to compare the results based on ranks when only 2 groups were involved.

These tests are described in *Non-parametric Statistics* by S. Siegel, published by McGraw-Hill, New York in 1956.

Appendix Five

COMPARISON OF INFORMANT DRINKERS IDENTIFIED IN STAQ 1 AND STAQ 2

The proportions of the different categories of Informant drinkers identified by STAQ 1 and STAQ 2 were compared.

Table 77   Male informant drinkers (*present and past separately*) identified by *STAQ 1* and *STAQ 2*

Category of male informant drinker	STAQ 1		STAQ 2	
	Present	Past	Present	Past
Social Drinker	50	1	42	1
Heavy Drinker	19	24	10	15
Problem Drinker	18	20	14	13
Alcohol Addict	24	19	15	8
Total	111	64	81	37

Present: $\chi^2 = 1.41$, d.f. $= 3$, $0.80 > p > 0.70$.
Not significant at 5% level.
Past: $\chi^2 = 0.93$, d.f. $= 3$, $0.90 > p > 0.80$.
Not significant at 5% level.

There were no significant differences between STAQ 1 and STAQ 2 in the proportions of the different categories of present and past male informant drinkers identified.

Table 78   Female informant drinkers (*present and past pooled*) identified by *STAQ 1* and *STAQ 2*

Category of female informant drinker	STAQ 1	STAQ 2
	Present + Past	Present + Past
Social Drinker	111	91
Heavy Drinker	19	8
Problem Drinker	12	4
Alcohol Addict	7	1
Total	149	104

$\chi^2 = 7.25$, d.f. $= 3$, $0.10 > p > 0.05$. Not significant at 5% level.

The results for present and past categories of drinker were pooled because of small numbers.

There were *no* significant differences between STAQ 1 and STAQ 2 in the proportions of the different categories of present and past (pooled) female informant drinkers identified.

Statistical tests were not carried out on the family drinkers identified by the two STAQs, as the questionnaires were identical in the family sections.

Conclusion

The results indicate that it is justifiable to combine the results from STAQ 1 and STAQ 2.

Appendix Six

SOCIAL CLASS DISTRIBUTION OF STUDY POPULATION

(according to method adopted for the Practice population: *see* page 63)

SOCIAL CLASS	No.	%
I	4	1
II	33	6
III	169	31
IV	118	21
V	217	39
No information	13	2
Total	554	100

References

1. Wilkins, R. H. (1972). *Dvar Yerushalayim,* Pesach issue, Jerusalem Academy of Jewish Studies.
2. Ministry of Health. (1968). National Health Service: The Treatment of Alcoholism. H.M. **(68)** 37.
3. Department of Health and Social Security. (1973). *Community Services for Alcoholics,* Circular 21/73.
4. Department of Health and Social Security. (1973). *Medical Memorandum on Alcoholism.*
5. Home Office. (1971). *Habitual Drunken Offenders,* Report of the Working Party, H.M.S.O. London.
6. Home Office. (1972). Report of the Departmental Committee on Liquor Licensing, Cmnd. 5154, H.M.S.O. London.
7. Scottish Home and Health Department. (1973). Report of the Departmental Committee on Scottish Licensing Law. Cmnd. 5354. H.M.S.O. London.
8. Keller, M. (1962). in *Society, Culture and Drinking Patterns,* Eds. D. J. Pittman and C. R. Snyder, Wiley, New York.
9. Jellinek, E. M. (1960). *The Disease Concept of Alcoholism,* Hillhouse Press, New Haven, Conn.
10. Bowman, K. M. and Jellinek, E. M. (1941). *Q. Jl. Stud. Alcohol,* **2,** 98.
11. Keller, M. and Efron, V. (1955). *Q. Jl. Stud. Alcohol,* **16,** 619.
12. Keller, M. (1958). *Ann. Am. Acad. Polit. Social Sci.,* **315,** 1.
13. Keller, M. and Seeley, J. R. (1958). *The Alcohol Language,* Brookside Monograph No. 2, University of Toronto Press, Toronto and Buffalo.
14. Marconi, J. T. (1959) *Q. Jl. Stud. Alcohol,* **20,** 216.
15. Jain, S., Paton, A. and Wansbrough-Jones, A. (1973). *Midl. med. Rev.,* **9,** 13.
16. Clark, W. (1966). *Q. Jl. Stud. Alcohol,* **27,** 648.
17. Mendelson, J. H. and Stein, S. (1966). *Int. Psychiat. Clin.,* **3,** 3.
18. Keller, M. and McCormick, M. (1968). *A Dictionary of Words about Alcohol,* Rutgers Centre of Alcohol Studies, New Jersey.
19. Davies, D. L. (1971). *Update,* **3,** 885.
20. Hawker, A., Edwards, G. and Hensman, C. (1967). *Med. Offr.,* **117,** 313.
21. Knupfer, G. (1967). *Am. J. publ. Hlth,* **57,** 973.
22. Edwards, G., Chandler, J., Hensman, C. and Peto, J. (1972). *Q. Jl. Stud. Alcohol,* Suppl. No. 6, 94.
23. World Health Organisation (1951). Tech. Rep. Ser. No. 42.
24. World Health Organisation (1952). Tech. Rep. Ser. No. 48.
25. Gordon, J. E. (1958). *N. Y. St. J. Med.,* **58,** 1911.
26. Seeley, J. R. (1959). *Q. Jl. Stud. Alcohol,* **20,** 245.
27. Popham, R. E. and Schmidt, W. (1962). *A Decade of Alcoholism Research,* Brookside Monograph No. 3, University of Toronto Press, Toronto and Buffalo.
28. Brenner, B. (1959). *Q. Jl. Stud. Alcohol,* **20,** 255.
29. Seeley, J. R. (1960). *Q. Jl. Stud. Alcohol,* **21,** 500.
30. Pittman, D. J. and Snyder, C. R. (1962). *Society, Culture and Drinking Patterns,* Wiley, New York.
31. Office of Health Economics (1970). *Alcohol Abuse,* O.H.E., London.
32. Wlassak, R. (1929). Cited in *The Disease Concept of Alcoholism,* E. M. Jellinek (1962), Hillhouse Press, New Haven, Conn.

33. Edwards, G. (1968). *Br. med. J.,* **4,** 435.
34. Riley, J. W. and Marden, C. F. (1947). *Q. Jl. Stud. Alcohol,* **8,** 265.
35. Blane, H. T., Overton, W. F. and Chafetz, M. E. (1963). *Quart. J. Stud. Alc.,* **24,** 640.
36. Abram, H. S. and McCourt, W. F. (1964). *Q. Jl. Stud. Alcohol,* **25,** 679.
37. Mendelson, J. H., Wexler, D., Kubzansky, P. E., Harrison, R., Leiderman, G., and Solomon, P. (1964). *Arch. gen. Psychiat.,* **11,** 392.
38. Lief, V. F., Brotman, R., Freedman, A. M., Tannenbaum, G. and Ennis, F. (1966). *Int. J. Addict.,* **1,** 42.
39. Cardozo, B. N. (1960). Cited in *The Disease Concept of Alcoholism,* E. M. Jellinek (1960), Hillhouse Press, New Haven, Conn.
40. Rush, B. (1785). Cited in *New Primer on Alcoholism,* M. Mann (1958), Rinehart, New York.
41. Trotter, T. (1788). Cited in *Alcoholism: The Total Treatment Approach,* R. J. Cantazaro (1968), Charles C. Thomas, Illinois.
42. Glatt, M. M. (1958). *Br. J. Addict.* **55,** 51.
43. Ministry of Health (1962). National Health Service: Hospital Treatment of Alcoholism. H.M. **(62)** 43.
44. Rathod, N. H. (1964). *Publ. Hlth, Lond.,* **78,** 181.
45. Walsh, B. M. and Walsh, D. (1968). *J. Irish med. Ass.,* **61,** 115.
46. Glatt, M. M. (1971). in *Progress in Clinical Medicine,* 6th Edn. Eds. R. Daley and H. Miller, Churchill Livingstone, Edinburgh and London.
47. Jellinek, E. M. (1951). World Health Organisation. Tech. Rep. Ser. No. 42, Annexe **2,** 21.
48. Popham, R. E. (1956). *Q. Jl. Stud. Alcohol,* **17,** 559.
49. Lipscomb, W. R. and Sulka, E. (1961). *Q. Jl. Stud. Alcohol,* **22,** 588.
50. Williams, A. F. (1966). *Int. Psychiat. Clin.* **3,** 17.
51. Popham, R. E. (1970). Ed. *Alcohol and Alcoholism,* University of Toronto Press, Toronto and Buffalo.
52. Jellinek, E. M. (1959). *Q. Jl. Stud. Alcohol,* **20,** 261.
53. Registrar General. (1973). Statistical Review of England and Wales for the year 1971. Part I, Tables, Medical, H.M.S.O. London.
54. Registrar General. (1971). Statistical Review of England and Wales for the year 1967. Part III, Commentary, H.M.S.O. London.
55. Duffy, G. J. and Dean, G. (1971). *J. Irish med. Ass.,* **64,** 393.
56. Glatt, M. M. (1972). *The Alcoholic and the Help He Needs,* 2nd Edn., Priory Press, London.
57. Office of Population Censuses and Surveys (1974). Personal communication.
58. Department of Health and Social Security (1974). Personal communication.
59. Department of Health and Social Security. (1969). Psychiatric Hospitals and Units in England and Wales. In-patient statistics from the Mental Health Enquiry for the Years 1964, 1965 and 1966. Statistical Report Series No. 4. H.M.S.O. London.
60. Home Office. (1973). *Offences of Drunkenness, 1972,* Cmnd. 5380, H.M.S.O. London.
61. Home Office. (1973). *Offences Relating to Motor Vehicles, 1972.* Cmnd. 432, H.M.S.O. London.
62. Home Office. (1973). Report of Her Majesty's Chief Inspector of Constabulary for the year 1972. H.M.S.O. London.

63.   Knupfer, G. (1966). *Am. J. publ. Hlth,* **56,** 23.
64.   O'Connor, J. (1973). *Econ. Social Rev.,* **4,** 245.
65.   Ledermann, S. (1956). *Alcool, alcoolisme, alcoolisation; donnes scientifiques de caractère physiologique, économique et social,* Institut National d'Etudes Demographiques, Travaux et Documents, Cahier No. 29, Presses Universitaires, Paris.
66.   De Lindt, J. and Schmidt, W. (1968). *Q. Jl. Stud. Alcohol,* **29,** 968.
67.   Schmidt, W. and de Lindt, J. (1970). *Q. Jl. Stud. Alcohol,* **31,** 957.
68.   De Lindt, J. and Schmidt, W. (1971). *Br. J. Addict.* **66,** 97.
69.   Brewers' Society. (1970). *Problems Behind the Pint of Beer,* Brewers' Society, London.
70.   Britain 1973. (1973). H.M.S.O. London.
71.   Central Statistical Office. (1973). *Annual Abstract of Statistics,* No. 110, H.M.S.O. London.
72.   Nutt, C. J. (1971). *The Grocer,* 13 Nov. p. 58.
73.   Central Statistical Office. (1973). *Social Trends 1973,* No. 4. H.M.S.O. London.
74.   McKenzie, J. C. (1972). *Proc. Nutr. Soc.,* **31,** 99.
75.   Department of Employment. (1973). *Family Expenditure Survey,* Report for 1972. H.M.S.O. London.
76.   Kessel, N. and Shepherd, M. (1962). *J. ment. Sci.,* **108,** 159.
77.   Kellner, R. (1963). *Neurotic Ill-health in a General Practice on Deeside,* D. M. Thesis (unpublished), University of Liverpool.
78.   Herst. E. R. (1965). *An Epidemiological Study of Psychiatric Morbidity in a Suburban General Practice,* M. D. Thesis (unpublished), University of London.
79.   Goldberg, D. P. (1969). The Identification and Assessment of Non-psychotic Psychiatric Illness by Means of a Questionnaire, D. M. Thesis (unpublished), University of Oxford.
80.   Mayer-Gross, W. (1948). *Eugen. Rev.,* **21,** 140.
81.   Primrose, E. J. R. (1962). *Psychological Illness,* Tavistock Publications, London/Charles C. Thomas, USA.
82.   Watts, C. A. H., Cawte, E. C. and Kuenssberg, E. V. (1964). *Br. med. J.,* **2,** 1351.
83.   Shepherd, M., Cooper, B., Brown, A. C., and Kalton, G. W. (1966). *Psychiatric Illness in General Practice,* Oxford University Press, London.
84.   Logan, W. P. D. and Cushion, A. A. (1958). *Studies on Medical and Population Subjects,* No. 14, H.M.S.O. London.
85.   Hughes, J. N. P. (1966). *Med. Offr.,* **115,** 161.
86.   Kearney, N., Lawler, M. P. and Walsh, D. (1969). *J. Irish med. Ass.,* **62,** 1.
87.   Parr, D. (1957). *Br. J. Addict.* **54,** 25.
88.   Grant, A. P. and Boyd, M. W. J. (1962). *Br. J. Addict.* **58,** 39.
89.   College of General Practitioners (1963). Reported in Memorandum of evidence to the Standing Medical Advisory Committee's Special Subcommittee on Alcoholism. Scottish Council of the B.M.A.
90.   Pollak, B. (1971). *Practitioner,* **206,** 531.
91.   Wilkins, R. H. (1974). A Survey of General Practice Prevalence Studies in Great Britain. Paper presented at the 20th International Institute on the Prevention and Treatment of Alcoholism, June, Manchester, England.
92.   Prys-Williams, G. and Glatt, M. M. (1966). *Br. J. Addict.,* **61,** 257.

93. Hawker, A., Edwards, G. and Hensman, C. (1967). *Med. Offr.*, **117,** 313.

94. Moss, M. C. and Beresford Davies, E. (1967). *A Survey of Alcoholism in an English County,* Geigy Scientific Publication, London.

95. Hensman, C., Chandler, J., Edwards, G., Hawker, A. and Williamson, V. (1968). *Med. Offr.*, **120,** 215.

96. Edwards, G., Hawker, A., Hensman, C. Peto, J. and Williamson, V. (1973). *Br. J. Psychiat.*, **123,** 169.

97. Abbott, M. (1970). *J. Alc.*, **5,** 96.

98. Searle-Jordan, V. T. (1970). *The Social Drinking Scene,* London Borough of Hammersmith.

99. Gaind, R. (1971). Personal Communication cited in *Drugs, Alcohol and Tobacco in Great Britain,* Eds. J. Zacune and C. Hensman, Heinemann, London.

100. Roche, M. (1939). Cited in *Lancet* (1968), **ii,** 228, Editorial.

101. Joske, R. A. and Turner, C. N. (1952). *Med. J. Aust.*, **1,** 729.

102. Saint, E. G., Joske, R. A., Mackay, M. A. and Turner, C. N. (1952). *Med. J. Aust.*, **1,** 742.

103. Pearson, W. S. (1962). *N. C. med. J.*, **23,** 6.

104. Nolan, J. P. (1965). *Am. J. med. Sci.*, **249,** 135.

105. Smithurst, B. A. (1965). *Med. J. Aust.*, **1,** 738.

106. Green, J. R. (1965). *Med. J. Aust.*, **1,** 465.

107. Kearney, T. R., Bonime, H. and Cassimatis, G. (1967). *Comm. ment. Hlth J.*, **3,** 373.

108. Barcha, R., Stewart, M. A. and Guze, S. B. (1968). *Am. J. Psychiat.*, **125,** 133.

109. Ewing, J. A. and Rouse, B. A. (1970). Paper presented at the 29th Inst. Congress on Alcohol Dependence, Sydney, Australia.

110. McCusker, J., Cherubin, C. and Zimberg, S. (1971). *N. Y. St. J. Med.*, **71,** 751.

111. Moore, R. A. (1971). *Am. J. Psychiat.*, **128,** 130.

112. Tuason, V. B. and Rhee, Y. W. (1972). *Sth. med. J. Bham. Ala.*, **65,** 408.

113. Patterson, H. R. (1972). *J. Alc.*, **7,** 118.

114. Blaney, R. and Radford, I. S. (1973). *Q. Jl. Stud. Alcohol,* in press.

115. Edwards, G. (1973). *Q. Jl. Stud. Alcohol,* **34,** 28

116. Manis, J. G. and Hunt, C. L. (1957). *Q. Jl. Stud. Alcohol,* **18,** 212.

117. Bailey, M. B., Haberman, P. W. and Alksne, H. (1965). *Q. Jl. Stud. Alcohol,* **26,** 19.

118. Mulford, H. A. and Wilson, R. W. (1966). *Identifying Problem Drinkers in a Household Health Survey,* U.S. Department of Health, Education and Welfare. Public Health Service Publication No. 1000—Series 2, No. 16.

119. Cahalan, D. (1970). *Problem Drinkers: A National Survey,* Jossey-Bass Inc., San Francisco.

120. Nicholas, R. (1970). *Pulse,* 27 June.

121. Kessel, N. and Walton, H. (1965). *Alcoholism,* Penguin Books, England.

122. Medical Council on Alcoholism (1970). 1st Annual Report.

123. Glatt, M. M. (1960). *J. Coll. gen. Practnrs. Res. Newsl.* **3,** 292.

124. Saint, E. G. and Mackay, M.A. (1952). *Med. J. Aust.*, **1,** 742.

125. Block, M. A. (1963). *Med. Times,* **91,** 836.

126. Cooney, J. G. (1963). *J. Irish med. Assoc.*, **53,** 54.

127. Rathod, N. H. (1964). *Curr. Med. Drugs,* **5,** 3.

128. Catanzaro, R. J. (1966). *J. med. Ass. Ga.*, **55,** 49.

129. Pacy, H. (1968). *Med. J. Aust.*, **1**, 712.
130. Bradley, J. J. (1971). *Gen. Practnr., Lond.*, 23 April, p. 8
131. Rathod, N. H. (1971). *Update*, **3**, 501.
132. Steel, R. (1971). *J. Alc.*, **6**, 11.
133. Silversides, J. L. (1967). *Coll. Gen. Pract. Can. J.* 1 Mar.
134. Chegwidden, M. J. (1968). *Med. J. Aust.*, **2**, 148.
135. Williams, L. and Long, R. (1968). *Practitioner*, **200**, 205.
136. Lereboullet (1969). *Med. Offr.*, **122**, 63.
137. Crimm, C. E. (1971). *Virginia med. Mon.*, **98**, 41.
138. Gardiner, T. (1971). *J. R. Coll. gen. Practnr.*, **21**, 379.
139. Kehoe, M. (1971). *J. Irish med. Ass.*, **64**, 243.
140. Owen, J. H. (1971). *J. Alc.*, **6**, 8.
141. Mellor, C. S. (1971). *Update*, **3**, 1145, 1149.
142. Orford, J. (1971). *Update*, **3**, 1005.
143. Wilkins, R. H. (1971). *J. Alc.*, **6**, 44.
144. Wilkins, R. H. (1971). *J. R. Coll. gen. Practnr.*, **21**, 567.
145. Wilkins, R. H. (1973). *Update*, **6**, 1797.
146. Cook, T. (1972). *Update*, **4**, 103.
147. Malherbe, M. (1972). *Update*, **4**, 355.
148. Cooper, J. and Maule, H. G. (1963). *Med. Offr.*, **110**, 331.
149. Edwards, G., Fisher, M. K., Hawker, A. and Hensman, C. (1967). *Br. med. J.*, **4**, 346.
150. Edwards, G., Hensman, C., Hawker, A., and Williamson, V. (1967). *Soc. Psychiat.*, **1**, 195.
151. Hobson, J. A. (1954). *Proc. R. Soc. Med.*, **47**, 333.
152. Williams, L. (1967). *Alcoholism Explained*, Evans, London.
153. Gould, J. (1961). *Med. World, Lond.*, **94**, 514.
154. Shaffer, C. F. (1964). *Med. Times*, **92**, 147.
155. Auerback, A. (1966). *Gen. Practnr.*, **33**, 102.
156. Levy, A. (1964). *Med. Proc. Jhbg.*, **10**, 403.
157. Rathod, N. H. (1967). *Br. J. Addict.*, **62**, 103.
158. Jones, R. W. and Helrich, A. R. (1972). *Q. Jl. Stud. Alcohol*, **33**, 117.
159. Churan, C. A. (1954). *J. Iowa med. Soc.*, **54**, 1.
160. Barnett, J. W. (1965). *General Practice, The Early Years* (unpublished) Copy in Library of Roy. Coll. Gen. Practit.
161. Ford, J. C. (1956). *Linacre Quart.*, **23**, 95.
162. Mathers, G. C. (1970). *Br. med. J.*, **2**, 220.
163. Haggard, H. W. (1945). *Q. Jl. Stud. Alcohol*, **6**, 213.
164. Daniel, R. (1955). *J. Mich. med. Soc.*, **54**, 820.
165. Hayman, M. (1963). *Mind*, **1**, 198.
166. Libby, H. E. (1962). *J. Maine med. Ass.*, **53**, 265.
167. Crimm, C. E. (1968). Proc. of the 28th Int. Congress on Alcohol and Alcoholism.
168. Derivas, C. F. (1969). *Penn. Med.* **72**, 68.
169. Dent, J. Y. (1954). *Med. World, Lond.*, **81**, 245.
170. Livni, S. (1961). *S. Afr. med. J.*, **35**, 1065.
171. Broomberg, A. (1962). *Med. Proc. Jhbg.*, **8**, 369.
172. Solomon, P. (1968). *Am. J. Psychiat.*, **124**, 1116.
173. Parry, R. A. (1970). *J. R. Coll. gen. Practnr.*, **20**, 224.
174. Edwards, G. (1962). *Med. World*, **96**, 102.
175. Pacy, H. (1968). *Med. J. Aust.*, **2**, 335.
176. Glatt, M. M. (1957). *Br. J. Addict.*, **54**, 47.
177. Hes, J. P. (1970). *Fam. Phys. (Israel)*, **1**, 8.

178. Dent, J. Y. (1934). *Br. J. Inebr.*, **32,** 64.
179. Dent, J. Y. (1949). *Br. J. Addict.*, **46,** 15.
180. Dent, J. Y. (1954). *Proc. R. Soc. Med.*, **47,** 331.
181. Moynihan, N. H. (1965). *Practitioner*, **195,** 223.
182. Pollak, B. (1970). *Br. J. Addict.*, **65,** 19.
183. Bastøe, O. (1957). *Tidsskr. norske Laegeforen.*, **77,** 298, Abstracted in *J.A.M.A.* (1957) **164,** 1715.
184. Kessel, W. I. N. (1960). *Br. J. prev. soc. Med.*, **14,** 16.
185. Shepherd, M., Cooper, B., Brown, A. C. and Kalton, G. W. (1966). *Br. med. J.*, **2,** 1359.
186. Brown, A. C. and Fry, J. (1962). *J. psychosom. Res.*, **6,** 185.
187. Hamilton, M., Pond, D. A. and Ryle, A. (1962). *J. psychosom. Res.*, **6,** 157.
188. Ryle, A. and Hamilton, M. (1962). *J. ment. Sci.*, **108,** 265.
189. Rawnsley, K. (1966). *J. psychosom. Res.*, **10,** 84.
190. Jacob, A. (1969). *J. R. Coll. gen. Practnr.*, **17,** 299.
191. Popoff, L. M. (1969). *Clin. Med.*, **76,** 24.
192. Salkind, M. R. (1969). *J. R. Coll. Gen. Practnr.*, **18,** 267.
193. Semmence, A. M. (1969). *J. R. Coll. Gen. Practnr.*, **18,** 344.
194. Sheridan, M. (1962). *Mon. Bull. Min. Hlth and Lab. Service,* **21,** 238.
195. Alberman, E. D. and Goldstein, H. (1970). *Br. J. prev. soc. Med.*, **24,** 129.
196. Glatt, M. M. (1961). *Br. J. clin. Pract.*, **15,** 157.
197. Grundy, L. P. and Day, N. E. (1964). *Maryland St. med. J.*, **13,** 118.
198. World Health Organisation (1967). Tech. Rep. Ser. No. 363.
199. Blane, H. T. (1966). *Int. Psychiat. Clin.*, **3,** 103.
200. Keller, M. (1969). *Med. Offr.*, **122,** 63.
201. Ruprecht, A. L. (1970). *Postgrad. Med.*, **47,** 165.
202. Chafetz, M. E., Blane, H. T. and Hill, M. J. (1970). *Frontiers of Alcoholism,* Science House, New York.
203. Howard, J. M. and Ehrlich, E. W. (1960). *Ann. Surg.*, **52,** 135.
204. Berman, L. G., Dunn, E. and Strachley, C. J. (1961). *Gastroenterology*, **40,** 94.
205. Albo, R., Silen, W. and Goldman, L. (1963). *Arch. Surg.*, **86,** 1032.
206. Cogbill, C. L. and Song, K. T. (1970). *Arch. Surg.*, **100,** 673.
207. Pollock, A. V. (1959). *Br. med. J.*, **1,** 6.
208. Trapnell, J. E. and Anderson, M. C. (1967). *Ann. Surg.*, **165,** 49.
209. Gillespie, W. J. (1973). *Br. J. Surg.*, **60,** 63.
210. Howat, H. T. (1968). *Postgrad. med. J.*, **44,** 733.
211. James, O., Agnew, J. E. and Bauchier, I. A. D. (1974). *Br. med. J.*, **2,** 34.
212. Clark, E. (1942). *Am. J. dig. Dis.*, **9,** 428.
213. Paxton, J. R. and Payne, J. H. (1948). *Surgery Gynec. Obstet.*, **86,** 69.
214. Galambos, J. T. (1969). *Am. J. dig. Dis.*, **14,** 477.
215. Stone, W. D., Islam, N. R. K. and Paton, A. (1968). *Quart. J. Med.*, **37,** 119.
216. Forshaw, J. (1972). *Brit. med. J.*, **4,** 608.
217. Sherlock, S. (1966). *Acta med. scand.* **Suppl. 445,** 426.
218. Sherlock, S. (1968). *Diseases of the Liver and Biliary System*, 4th Edition, Blackwell Scientific Publications, Oxford and Edinburgh.
219. MacDonald, R. A. and Mallory, G. K. (1958). *Amer. J. Med.*, **24,** 334.
220. Rubin, E., Krus, S. and Popper, H. (1962). *Arch. Path.* **73,** 288.
221. Pell, S. and D'Alonzo, C. A. (1968). *Archs envir. Hlth,* **16,** 679.

222. Retterstol, N. and Sund, A. (1962). *J. Neuropsychiat.*, **3**, 345.
223. Barcha, R., Stewart, M. A. and Guze, S. B. (1968). *Amer. J. Psychiat.*, **125**, 681.
224. Haynell, O. and Wretmark, G. (1957). *J. psychosom. Res.*, **2**, 35.
225. Palmer, E. D. (1954). *Medicine, Baltimore*, **33**, 199.
226. Wolff, G. (1970). *Scand, J. Gastroent.*, **5**, 289.
227. Joske, R. A., Finckh, E. S. and Wood, L. J. (1955). *Quart. J. Med.*, **24**, 269.
228. Ferguson, D. (1972). *Brit. J. indust. Med.*, **29**, 420.
229. De Wet Vorster (1964). *Med. Proc. Jhbg.*, **10**, 395.
230. Craddock, D. (1958). *An Introduction to General Practice*, 2nd Edition, H. K. Lewis, London.
231. Wilson, G. C. (1966). *Med. J. Aust.*, **1**, 149.
232. Jolliffe, N. (1942). in *Alcohol Addiction and Chronic Alcoholism*, Ed. E. M. Jellinek, Yale University Press, New Haven, Conn.
233. Judge, C. and Glatt, M. M. (1961). *Med. J. Aust.*, **48**, 586.
234. Fennelly, J., Frank, O., Baker, H. and Leevy, C. M. (1964). *Brit. med. J.*, **2**, 1290.
235. Lewis, J. G. and Chamberlain, D. A. (1963). *Brit. J. Prev. Soc. Med.*, **17**, 149.
236. Pincock, J. A. (1964). *Can. med. Ass. J.*, **91**, 881.
237. Rhodes, R. J., Hames, G. H. and Campbell, M. D. (1969). *Am. Rev. resp. Dis.* **99**, 440.
238. Milne, R. C. (1970). *Med. J. Aust.*, **2**, 955.
239. Foreman, H. M. and Chalke, H. D. (1972). *J. Alc.*, **7**, 12.
240. Saunders, M. G. (1970). *Q. Jl. Stud. Alcohol*, **31**, 324.
241. Brigden, W. (1957). *Lancet*, ii, 1179.
242. Dye, C. L., Rosenbaum, D., Lowe, J. C., Behnke, R. H. and Genovese, P. D. (1963). *Ann. intern. Med.*, **58**, 426.
243. Alexander, C. S. (1966). *Am. J. Med.*, **41**, 213.
244. Härtel, G., Louhija, A. and Konttinen, A. (1969). *Acta med. scand.*, **185**, 507.
245. Pader, E. (1973). *Q. Jl. Stud. Alcohol*, **34**, 774.
246. Priest, R. G., Binns, J. K. and Kitchin, A. H. (1966). *Br. med. J.*, **1**, 1453.
247. Marrinacci, A. A. (1956). in *Alcoholism*, Ed. G. N. Thompson, Charles C. Thomas, Springfield, Illinois.
248. Thompson, G. N. (1956). *Alcoholism*, Charles C. Thomas, Springfield, Illinois.
249. Lees, F. (1967). *Hosp. Med.*, **2**, 264.
250. Glatt, M. M. (1955). *Br. med. J.*, **2**, 738.
251. Danesin, A. (1970). *Electroenceph. clin. Neurophysiol.* **28**, 214.
252. Olsen, A. Y. (1956). in *Alcoholism*, Ed. G. N. Thompson, Charles C. Thomas, Springfield, Illinois.
253. Bates, R. C. (1965). *Appl. Ther.*, **7**, 466.
254. Field, M. (1972). Personal Communication.
255. Bailey, M. B. (1961). *Q. Jl. Stud. Alcohol*, **22**, 81.
256. Whalen, T. (1953). *Q. Jl. Stud. Alcohol*, **14**, 632.
257. Kogan, K. L., Fordyce, W. E. and Jackson, J. K. (1963). *Q. Jl. Stud. Alcohol*, **24**, 227.
258. Kephart, W. M. (1954). *Q. Jl. Stud. Alcohol*, **15**, 63.
259. Lemert, E. M. (1960). *Q. Jl. Stud. Alcohol*, **21**, 679.
260. Flintoff, W. P. (1963). *Br. J. Addict.*, **59**, 81.

261. Moore, M. E. (1937). *New Engl. J. Med.* **214,** 291.
262. Schmidt, E. H., O'Neal, P. and Robins, E. (1954). *J.A.M.A.,* **155,** 549.
263. Palola, E. G., Dorpat, T. L., Larson, W. R. (1962). in *Society, Culture and Drinking Patterns,* Eds. D. J. Pittman and C. R. Snyder, Wiley, New York.
264. Goodwin, D. W. (1973). *Q. Jl. Stud. Alcohol,* **34,** 144.
265. Batchelor, I. R. C. (1954). *J. ment. Sci.,* **100,** 451.
266. Patel, A. R., Roy, M. and Wilson, G. M. (1972). *Lancet,* ii, 1099.
267. Ovenstone, I. M. K. (1973). *Br. J. prev. soc. Med.,* **27,** 27.
268. Kessel, N. (1965). *Br. med. J.,* **2,** 1265.
269. Whitlock, F. A. and Schapira, K. (1967). *Br. J. Psychiat.,* **113,** 423.
270. Smith, J. S. and Davison, K. (1971). *Br. med. J.,* **4,** 412.
271. Seager, C. P. and Flood, R. A. (1965). *Br. J. Psychiat.,* **111,** 919.
272. Jacobson, S. and Jacobson, D. M. (1972). *Br. J. Psychiat.,* **121,** 369.
273. Lemere, F. (1953). *Am. J. Psychiat.,* **109,** 674.
274. Glatt, M. M. (1964). *Lancet,* i, 161.
275. Kessell, N. and Grosman, G. (1961). *Br. med. J.,* **2,** 1671.
276. Smith-Moorhouse, P. M. and Lynn, L. (1969). *Practitioner,* **202,** 410.
277. Ritson, E. B. (1968). *Br. J. med. Psychol.,* **41,** 235.
278. Freed, E. X. (1970). *Q. Jl. Stud. Alcohol,* **31,** 62.
279. Johanson, E. (1958). *Acta psychiat. scand.,* **Suppl. 125,** p. 82.
280. Kay, D. W. K. and Lindelius, R. (1970). *Acta psychiat. scand.,* **Suppl. 216,** p. 60.
281. Walton, H. J., Ritson, E. B. and Kennedy, R. J. (1966). *Br. med. J.,* **2,** 1171.
282. Ritson, B. and Hassall, C. (1970). *Management of Alcoholism,* E. and S. Livingstone, Edinburgh.
283. Mellor, C. S. (1967). *Hosp. Med.,* **2,** 284.
284. Registrar General. (1957). Decennial Supplement, England and Wales 1951, Part 2, H.M.S.O. London.
285. Otterland, A. (1960). Paper read at 26th Int. Congress on Alcohol and Alcoholism, Stockholm.
286. Rose, H. K. and Glatt, M. M. (1961). *J. ment. Sci.,* **107,** 18.
287. Merseyside Council on Alcoholism (1973). 10th Annual Report.
288. Glatt, M. M. (1969). *Lancet,* i, 203.
289. Hughes, J. P. W. (1969). *Trans. Soc. Occup. Med.* **19,** 58.
290. Wessex Council on Alcoholism (1970). 1st Annual Report.
291. Merseyside Council on Alcoholism (1970). 7th Annual Report.
292. Medical Council on Alcoholism (1971). Annual Report.
293. House of Commons Official Report. Parliamentary Debates (1973), 851, Col. 142, H.M.S.O. London.
294. Glatt, M. M. and Hills, D. R. (1965). *Br. J. Addict.,* **61,** 71.
295. Jellinek, E. M. (1947). *Vital Speeches,* **13,** 252.
296. Thorpe, J. J. and Perret, J. T. (1959). *Arch. ind. Hlth,* **19,** 24.
297. Franco, S. C. (1954). *Q. Jl. Stud. Alcohol,* **15,** 453.
298. Williams, L. (1964). *Practitioner,* **193,** 652.
299. Blane, H. T. (1966). *Int. Psychiat. Clin.,* **3,** 103.
300. Storby, A. (1953). Cited in *Publ. Hlth Rep. Wash.,* **81,** 585. H. W. Demone and E. H. Kasey (1966).
301. Brenner, B. (1967). *Q. Jl. Stud. Alcohol,* **28,** 517.
302. Watson, J. P. (1969). *Br. J. Addict.,* **64,** 223.
303. Cavalie, B. (1956). *Arch. Mal. Prof.* **17,** 98.
304. Maxwell, M. A. (1961). *Q. Jl. Stud. Alcohol,* **21,** 655.

305. Wechsler, H., Kasey, E. H., Thum, D. and Demone, H. W. (1969). *Publ. Hlth Rep. Wash.,* **84,** 1043.
306. Kirkpatrick, J. R. and Taubenhaus, L. J. (1967). *Q. Jl. Stud. Alcohol,* **28,** 734.
307. Metropolitan Life Assurance Company (1968). *Illinois med. J.,* **133,** 423.
308. McCarroll, J. R. and Haddon, W. (1962). *J. chron. Dis.,* **15,** 811.
309. Selzer, M. L. and Weiss, S. (1965). *Am. J. Psychiat.,* **122,** 762.
310. Chafetz, M. E. (1971). *Hlth Lab. Sci.,* **8,** 117.
311. Haddon, W., Valien, P., McCarroll, J. R. and Umberger, C. J. (1961). *J. chron. Dis.,* **14,** 655.
312. Jeffcoate, G. O. (1958). *Br. J. Addict.,* **55,** 37.
313. Watson, D. (1961). *Proc. Ass. clin. Biochem.,* **1,** 61.
314. Cassie, A. B. and Allan W. R. (1961). *Br. med. J.,* **2,** 1668.
315. Department of the Environment (1973). Road Accidents in Great Britain, 1971, H.M.S.O. London.
316. Schmidt, W. and Smart, R. G. (1959). *Q. J. Stud. Alcohol,* **20,** 631.
317. Blume, S. B. (1969). *Psychiat. Quart.,* **43,** 734.
318. Clare, A. W. and Cooney, J. G. (1973). *J. Irish Med. Assoc.,* **66,** 281.
319. Glatt, M. M. (1961). *Acta Psychiat. scand.,* **37,** 1, 88.
320. Glatt, M. M. (1965). *Harv. J. Penol. Crime Prev.,* **11,** 274.
321. Gath, D. (1969). in *The Drunkenness Offence,* Eds. T. Cook, D. Gath and C. Hensman, Pergamon, Oxford.
322. Burnett, G. (1971). *World Med.,* 30 June p. 39.
323. Gibbens, T. C. N. and Silberman, M. (1970). *Psychol. Med.,* **1,** 73.
324. Edwards, G., Hensman, C. and Peto, J. (1971). *Psychol. Med.,* **1,** 388.
325. Woodside, M. (1961). *Br. J. Criminol.,* **1,** 221.
326. Joyce, P. (1969). in *The Drunkenness Offence,* Eds. T. Cook, D. Gath and C. Hensman, Pergamon, Oxford.
327. Glatt, M. M. (1958). *Br. J. Addict.,* **55,** 51.
328. Epps, P. (1951). *Br. J. Delinq.,* **1,** 189.
329. Gibbens, T. C. N. and Walker, A. (1956). *Br. J. Delinq.,* **6,** 260.
330. Irwin, C. (1964). *Med. Proc. Jhbg.,* **10,** 398.
331. Batchelor, I. R. and Napier, B. M. (1953). *Br. J. Delinq.,* **4,** 99.
332. Kearney, T. R. and Taylor, C. (1969). *Acta paedopsychiat.,* **36,** 215.
333. Jackson, J. K. (1954). *Q. Jl. Stud. Alcohol,* **15,** 562.
334. Glatt, M. M. (1967). *Br. J. Addict.,,* **62,** 35.
335. Wilkins, R. H. (1972). *J. Alc.,* **7,** 92.
336. Wilkins, R. H. (1973). *Nurs. Times,* **69,** 1071.
337. Horley, F. C. (1960). Compilation of papers, Nat. Conf. on Alcoholism University of N.S.W. 138. Cited in *Med. J. Aust.,* **2,** 523, 1972.
338. Krupinski, J., Stoller, A., Harcourt, A. (1970). *The Deserted Mother in Victoria,* The Victorian Family Council Melbourne. Cited in *Med. J. Aust.,* **2,** 523, 1972.
339. Law Society (1972). Personal Communication.
340. Smith, M. A. E. and Sclare, A. B. (1964). *Scot. med. J.,* **9,** 114.
341. Glatt, M. M. (1967). *Br. J. Addict.,* **62,** 35.
342. Tidmarsh, D. (1970). *Br. J. Addict.,* **64,** 333.
343. Gordon, M. B. (1968). *Med. Times,* **96,** 1169.
344. National Assistance Board (1966). *Homeless Single Persons,* H.M.S.O. London.
345. Edwards, G., Hawker, A., Williamson, V. and Hensman, C. (1966). *Lancet,* i, 249.

346. Priest, R. G (1970). *Proc. R. Soc. Med.*, **63**, 441.

347. Glatt, M. M. and Whiteley, J. G. (1956). *Mschr. Psychiat. Neurol.* **132**, 1.

348. Edwards, G., Williamson, V., Hawker, A., Hensman, C. and Postoyan, S. (1968). *Br. J. Psychiat.*, **114**, 1031.

349. Lodge Patch, I. C. (1971). *Br. J. Psychiat.*, **118**, 313.

350. Mairs, A. (1972). Personal Communication.

351. Walton, H. J. (1971). in *Seventh Symposium on Advanced Medicine*, Ed. I. A. D. Bouchier, Pittman, London.

352. Carney, M. W. P. and Lawes, T. G. C. (1967). *Q. Jl. Stud. Alcohol*, **28**, 59.

353. Harper, J. and Hickson, B. (1951). *Lancet*, ii, 1057.

354. Johnson, L. C., Burdick, J. A., and Smith, J. (1970). *Arch. Gen. Psychiat.*, **22**, 406.

355. Strauss, R. (1952). *Q. Jl. Stud. Alcohol*, **13**, 254.

356. Popham, R. E. (1956). *Q. Jl. Stud. Alcohol*, **17**, 559.

357. Zax, M., Gardiner, E. A. and Hart, W. T. (1961). *Q. Jl. Stud. Alcohol*, **28**, 316.

358. Marconi, J., Varela, A., Rosenblat, E., Solari, G., Marchesse, I., Alvardo, R. and Enriquez, W. (1955). *Q. Jl. Stud. Alcohol*, **16**, 439.

359. Gibbons, R. J. (1954). *Q. Jl. Stud. Alcohol*, **15**, 47.

360. Jellinek, E. M. (1946). *Q. Jl. Stud. Alcohol*, **7**, 1.

361. Cisin, I. H. (1963). *Ann. N.Y. Acad. Sci.*, **107**, 607.

362. Stone, A. R., Neustadt, J. O., Imber, S. D. and Nash, E. H. (1965). *Amer. J. Orthopsychiat.*, **35**, 564.

363. Mulford, H. A. and Miller, D. E. (1960). *Q. Jl. Stud. Alcohol*, **21**, 26.

364. Selzer, M. L. (1971). *Am. J. Psychiat.*, **127**, 1653.

365. Gordon, J. E. (1958). *N.Y. St. J. Med.*, **58**, 1911.

366. Edwards, G., Chandler, J. and Hensman, C. (1972). *Q. Jl. Stud. Alcohol*, **Suppl. No. 6**, 69.

367. Hensman, C. (1972). Personal Communication.

368. Bailey, M. B. (1967). *Am. J. publ. Hlth* **57**, 987.

369. Strauss, R. and Bacon, S. D. (1953). *Drinking in College*, Yale University Press, New Haven, Conn.

370. Bailey, M. B., Haberman, P. W. and Sheinberg, J. (1969). *Millbank Mem. Fund Quart.*, **47**, 235.

371. Bailey, M. B., Haberman, P. W. and Sheinberg, J. (1966). *Q. Jl. Stud. Alcohol*, **27**, 300.

372. World Health Organisation. (1955). Tech. Rep. Ser. No. 94.

373. Connor, R. (1970). *The Drinking and Drug Practices Surveyor*, **1**, 15.

374. Manson, M. P. (1949). *J. clin. Psychol.*, **5**, 77.

375. Hampton, P. J. (1951). *J. Consult. Psychol.*, **15**, 501.

376. Button, A. D. (1956). *Q. Jl. Stud. Alcohol*, **17**, 263.

377. Hoyt, D. P. and Sedlacek, G. M. (1958). *J. clin. Psychol.*, **14**, 69.

378. MacAndrew, C. (1965). *Q. Jl. Stud. Alcohol*, **26**, 238.

379. Rich, C. C. and Davis, H. G. (1969). *J. clin. Psychol.*, **25**, 425.

380. Rosenberg, N. (1972). *J. clin. Psychol.*, **28**, 515.

381. MacAndrew, C. and Geertsma, R. H. (1964). *Q. Jl. Stud. Alcohol*, **25**, 68.

382. Uecker, A. E., Kish, G. B. and Ball, M. E. (1969). *J. clin. Psychol.*, **25**, 287.

383. Vega, A. (1971). *Q. Jl. Stud. Alcohol*, **32**, 791.

384. Manson, M. P. (1949). *Am. J. Psychiat.*, **106**, 199.
385. Selzer, M. L. (1968). *Univ. Mich. med. centre J.*, **34**, 143.
386. Selzer, M. L. (1971). *Am. J. Psychiat.*, **127**, 1653.
387. Pokorny, A. D., Miller, B. A. and Kaplan, H. B. (1972). *Am. J. Psychiat.*, **129**, 342.
388. Bailey, W. C., Horwitz, J., Brown, M., Thompson, D. H., Ziskind, M. M. and Greenberg, H. B. (1973). *Hlth Ser. Rep.*, **88**, 486.
389. General Register Office. (1968). Sample Census, 1966, Great Britain. Economic Activity Tables, Part 1. H.M.S.O. London.
390. Wilkins, R. H. (1972). The Detection of the Abnormal Drinker in General Practice. M.D. Thesis (unpublished), University of Manchester.
391. General Register Office. (1970). Classification of Occupations, H.M.S.O. London.
392. Glass, H. (1972). Personal communication.
393. Glatt, M. M. and Rosin, A. J. (1964). *Lancet*, ii, 472.
394. Hore, B. and Smith, E. (1973). Paper presented at Inst. for Prevention and Treatment of Alcoholism, Belgrade.
395. Coventry and Warwickshire Council of Alcoholism. (1973). Report.
396. Edwards, G., Hensman, C. and Peto, J. (1972). *Q. Jl. Stud. Alcohol*, **Suppl. No. 6**, 120.
397. Bagley, C. and Binitie, A. (1970). *Br. J. Addict.*, **65**, 3.
398. Goodwin, D. W., Crane, J. B. and Guze, S. B. (1969). *J. Psychiat.*, **126**, 191.
399. Rowntree, F. St. D. (1972). An exploratory study into the drinking behaviour of industrial apprentices. M.Sc. Thesis (unpublished), University of Manchester.
400. Davies, D. L. (1962). *Q. Jl. Stud. Alcohol*, **23**, 94.
401. Schmidt, W. (1968). *Addictions*, **15**, 1.
402. Kessler, I. L. and Levin, M. L. (1970). *The Community as an Epidemiological Laboratory*, Johns Hopkins, Baltimore and London.
403. Hore, B. D. and Wilkins, R. H. (1974). A General Practice Study of the Commonest Presenting Symptoms of Alcoholism. To be published.
404. Moser, C. A. (1958). *Survey Methods in Social Investigations*, Heinemann, London.
405. Zigler, E. and Phillips, L. (1961). *J. abnorm. soc. Psychol.*, **63**, 607.
406. Lin, Tsung-Yi, and Standley, C. C. (1962). *The Scope of Epidemiology in Psychiatry*, Geneva W.H.O. Public Health Paper No. 16.
407. Kline, N. S. (1953). *Psychiat. Q.*, **27**, 474.
408. Leighton, A. H., Leighton, D. C. and Danley, R. A. (1966). *Can. Psychol. Ass. J.*, **11**, 167.
409. Shepherd, M. and Cooper, B. (1964). *J. Neurol. Psychiat.*, **27**, 277.
410. Kendell, R. E., Everett, B., Cooper, J. E., Sartorius, N. and David, M. E. (1968). *Soc. Psychiat.*, **3**, 123.
411. Copeland, J. R. M., Cooper, J. E., Kendell, R. E. and Gourlay, A. J. (1971). *Br. J. Psychiat.*, **118**, 629.
412. Beck, A. T., Ward, C. H. Mendelson, M., Mock, J. and Erbaugh, J. (1961). *Arch. Gen. Psychiat.*, **4**, 561.
413. Eastwood, M. R. (1971). *Psychol. Med.*, **1**, 197.
414. Goldberg, D. P., Cooper, B., Eastwood, M. R., Kedward, H. B. and Shepherd, M. (1970). *Br. J. prev. soc. Med.*, **24**, 18.
415. Cronbach, L. J. and Meehl, P. E. (1955). *Psychol. Bull.*, **52**, 281.

416. Dohrenwend, B. P. and Dohrenwend, B. S. (1965). *J. abnorm. Psychol.*, **70**, 52.
417. Bruun, K. (1970). *Drnk. Drug Pract. Surv.*, **1**, 6.
418. Room, R. (1970). *Drnk. Drug Pract. Surv.*, **1**, 4.
419. Flaherty, J. A., McGuire, H. T. and Gatski, R. L. (1955). *Am. J. Psychiat.*, **112**, 460.
420. Hore, B. D. (1974). *Br. J. Addict.*, In press.
421. Cooper, B. (1965). *Br. J. Psychiat.*, **111**, 595.
422. Cahalan, D. and Cisin, I. H. (1968). *Q. Jl. Stud. Alcohol*, **29**, 130.
423. Elinson, J. (1967). *Amer. J. publ. Hlth* **57**, 991.
424. Bailey, M. B., Haberman, P. W. and Sheinberg, J. (1966). *Q. Jl. Stud. Alcohol*, **27**, 300.
425. Summers, T. (1970). *Q. Jl. Stud. Alcohol*, **31**, 972.
426. Guze, S. B. and Goodwin, D. W. (1971). *Q. Jl. Stud. Alcohol*, **32**, 808.
427. Edwards, G., Hensman, C. and Peto, J. (1973). *Q. Jl. Stud. Alcohol*, **34**, 1244.
428. Saint, E. G. and Mackay, M. A. (1952). *Med. J. Aust.*, **1**, 734.
429. Chalke, H. D. and Prys Williams, G. (1971). *Alcohol and the Family*, Christian Economic and Social Research Foundation, Priory Press, Royston, Hertfordshire.
430. Moore, R. A. and Murphy, T. C. (1961). *Q. Jl. Stud. Alcohol*, **22**, 597.
431. Guze, S. B., Tuason, V. B., Stewart, M. A. and Pickers, B. (1963). *Q. Jl. Stud. Alcohol*, **24**, 249.
432. Haberman, P. W. (1963). *J. Hlth Hum. Behav.* **4**, 141.
433. Cartwright, A. (1957). *Appl. Statist.* **6**, 18.
434. Miles, J. (1974). *Patient Care*, **1**, 3.
435. Collins, M. B. and Jeans, P. (1972). Paper presented at the 30th Int. Congress on Alcoholism and Drug Dependence, Amsterdam.
436. Waterston, J. F. C. (1965). *J. Coll. Gen. Practnr*, **10**, 18.
437. Hershon, H. I., Cook, T. and Foldes, P. A. (1974). *Br. J. Psychiat.*, **124**, 327.
438. Department of Health and Social Security (1974). Background to Policy. Paper presented at meeting to discuss Future Planning of Treatment Services for Alcoholics. London, June 1974, unpublished.
439. Office of Population Censuses and Surveys (1974). Morbidity Statistics from General Practice. Second National Study 1970-71. Studies on Medical and Population Subjects No. 26. London, H.M.S.O.
440. Grant, A. P. and Boyd, M. W. J. (1961). *Ulster med. J.*, **30**, 114.
441. Kristinsson, A. (1969). Diagnosis, Natural History and Treatment of Congestive Cardiomyopathy. Ph.D. Thesis (unpublished). University of London.
442. Room, R. (1966). Notes on 'Identifying Problem Drinkers in a Household Health Survey', H. A. Mulford and R. W. Wilson, Paper No. 10, Mental Research Institute, Drinking Practices Study, California.

Index

1594